Eastern
Philosophy

Eastern Philosophy

KEVIN BURNS

Capella

To Andy, Tom, Alex and Alex, who made it possible.
For advice, hard work and encouragement I would like to thank Carla and
Siobhan. I would also like to acknowledge the invaluable help and advice of
Professor Chad Hansen on classical Chinese thought, and that of Macksood
A. Aftab on the Islamic section.

Published by Arcturus Publishing Limited
for Bookmart Limited
Registered Number 2372865
Trading as Bookmart Limited
Blaby Road, Wigston,
Leicester LE18 4SE

This edition published 2004

© Arcturus Publishing Limited
26/27 Bickels Yard, 151-153 Bermondsey Street
London SE1 3HA

ISBN 1-84193-191-8

In Canada published for
Indigo Books
468 King St W,
Suite 500,
Toronto,
Ontario M5V 1L8

Printed and bound in China

Editor: Rebecca Panayiotou
Text design by Chris Smith
Cover design by Alex Ingr

Picture Credits

Hulton Getty Images Ltd
pp17, 28, 31, 33, 71, 72, 73, 76, 78, 79, 80, 81, 82, 89, 92, 96, 99, 113, 115, 121, 123, 135, 137,
138, 139, 145, 160, 161, 169, 174, 175, 177, 178, 179, 181, 182, 185, 186

Mary Evans Picture Library
pp18, 19, 21, 22, 23, 39, 54, 83, 84, 102, 107, 109, 110, 120, 126, 129, 156, 163, 171, 188

Everything should be made as simple as possible, but not simpler.

CONTENTS

Part One

INDIA

INDIAN PHILOSOPHY
INTRODUCTION

*The defining characteristic
of Indian thought,
from whatever tradition,
is its spirituality.*

Brahma, Vishnu and Shiva: the main deities of Hindu tradition. Brahma represents the creator aspect of the divine; Vishnu sustains the creation; and Shiva represents the principle of dissolution, of the destruction of evil, of transcendence.

The oldest literature in human history is that of the Veda, dating from at least as far back as 1200 BCE.[1] For this reason alone, Indian philosophy deserves special attention. There are four Vedas: Rig Veda, Yajur Veda, Sāma Veda, and Atharva Veda. The earliest and most important is the Rig Veda, while the Atharva Veda is thought to

be much the latest. The Vedas were originally collections of hymns (the Mantras). At a later period when formal religion existed the religious precepts of the Brāhmanas were appended. Still later, perhaps 1000–200 BCE, the philosophical discussions of the *Upanishads* were also added. So each Veda now consists of these three sections. The Mantra or Samhitā part of the Vedas is thought to be the product of the Āryans, a tribe living in Central Asia who came to conquer both Iran and India, perhaps being collected when the Āryans met resistance from the indigenous Indian people and wanted to define their culture more strongly. The Vedic hymns of the

---

THE PRINCIPAL NASTIKA
(UNORTHODOX) PHILOSOPHIES

Buddhism
Chārvāka
Jainism

THE SIX ASTIKA
(ORTHODOX) PHILOSOPHIES

Nyāya
Vaisheshika

Sānkhya
Yoga

Mīmāmsā (or Purva-Mīmāmsā)
Vedānta (or Uttara-Mīmāmsā)

Samhitā have many affinities with the Zoroastrian Avesta, perhaps more than they do with the distinctively Indian Brāhmanas and *Upanishads*.

The traditional division in Indian philosophy is between those schools that are astika or orthodox and nastika or unorthodox. This division dates from the time of the principal challenges to the main tradition, around 600–200 BCE. The orthodox schools are those that, nominally at least, accept the Veda as revelatory. However, the question is much more complex than this. Even today it is a commonplace in India that the Vedas are divinely revealed and contain all knowledge, but this does not mean that people actually read them. 'Veda' is not a term used with any great consistency, meaning anything from the actual books of the Veda to a kind of divine and transcendent revelatory power, as expressed by a modern thinker such as Vivekānanda.

The only school that seriously bases itself on the earlier two parts of the Veda is the Pūrva-Mīmāmsā. After that, the Uttara-Mīmāmsā or, as it is more commonly known, the Vedānta is the most orthodox: Veda-anta means 'the end of the Veda', meaning that it bases itself on the *Upanishads*. However, even here there could not be said to be unanimity. The *Upanishads* represent a conscious turning away from the ritualised religion of the Brāhmanas (the second part of the Veda) and, to a lesser extent, from the nature-religion of the early Vedic hymns. So the Vedāntin thinkers, the most prominent in India from the early part of the Christian era onwards, are not really interested in much of the Veda. Of the other four orthodox schools, Sānkhya is atheistic or perhaps agnostic on the subject of God, which makes its orthodoxy very

questionable; Yoga is theistic but builds on the Sānkhya not the Veda; Nyāya is concerned with logic; and Vaisheshika is a realist philosophy dealing with the nature of physical reality. Furthermore, some of the philosophies and religions regarded as unorthodox are closer to certain orthodox systems than they are to each other. Buddhism has remarkable affinities to Vedānta despite their antagonism.

We can see from this that the traditional definition of orthodoxy is unsatisfactory. By the standards of other philosophical traditions, the Indian one is extraordinary for its flexibility and openness. In the *Bhagavad Gītā*, which is the most significant and influential book in Indian culture, Krishna, speaking as an incarnation of God, says, 'however men approach me, even so do I welcome them, for the path men take from every side is mine'. This should be understood not as a meek ecumenism, but as central to the whole Hindu system, in which the divine is regarded as infinitely beyond any human system of understanding, or form of devotion, or way of life. This leads to a broad tolerance and even encouragement of alternative approaches. As K.M. Sen has said, 'Hinduism is a great storehouse of all kinds of religious experiments'. The real issue in early Indian philosophy is not the acceptance of Veda as normative, but the authority of the Brahmin[2] caste. The groups that rejected the Brahmins and the caste system are those that became regarded as unorthodox: notably the materialist Chārvākas, the Jains, the Ajivikas and the Buddhists. From around 1000 CE certain orthodox sects began to work against the caste system, allowing lower-caste Hindus to study and participate fully, but this is a much later development.

Ganesha, one of the most popular Hindu deities.

We have now started to use the word 'Hindu', which is inevitable. In many ways it is an unsatisfactory label. It derives from the name of the river Sind or Indus and was the name given to the people who lived beyond that river by their Western neighbours. 'Hindu' is therefore cognate with 'Indian'. Like many Eastern systems, it is hard to say where philosophy stops and religion begins. There are good reasons to question whether Hinduism is a religion at all: it has no founder, no dogma, no consistent set of beliefs, and there is no tradition of 'conversion' to Hinduism. Buddha may have defined himself against the tradition, but his doctrines (all of which are to be found in the orthodox systems) are far more clear-cut than those he rejected. It would be wrong to regard the Hindu tradition as amorphous, however: it is impossible to formalise because of its rich variety. We should also distinguish between the Hindu religion or religions and the earlier belief-system of 'Brāhmanism' that predominated until about 500 CE.

There seems no good reason to regard the classification of *astika* and *nastika* as final. The traditional narrative of India is that the unorthodox *nastika* systems are rebellions, breaking away from the great tradition. As we have seen, however, the tradition itself is impossible to define either positively or negatively. We speak of Hindu or Jain or Buddhist philosophy, but there is a strong case for grouping them together. India, though huge, is geographically single, being surrounded on three sides by ocean and on the fourth by the world's highest mountain ranges. Its philosophies are also distinctive and have more in common with each other than with those of Greece or China or the Middle East. The defining characteristic of Indian thought, from whatever tradition, is its spirituality. No other culture is so indefatigably concerned with the human spirit and its relation to the universal.

In this part of the book we will consider firstly the *Upanishads*, the most fundamental documents in Indian philosophy. We will then look at the unorthodox schools that emerged in the sixth century BCE, followed by the six orthodox schools. Although most of the six seem to pre-date the unorthodox developments, their clearly-defined forms are in reaction to the challenge of the new philosophies. We then consider the *Bhagavad Gītā*, dated to around the fourth century BCE, followed by a detailed look at the development of the two most important Indian schools in the Christian era, Buddhism and Vedānta.

THE PRINCIPAL UPANISHADS

Various authors, 1000–200 BCE

In considering Indian thinkers, it is essential to look first of all at the *Upanishads*, although their authors are not known. The *Upanishads* are the most fundamental source for all the orthodox Indian systems of philosophy except the Mīmāṃsā, and for many of the unorthodox as well, including Buddhism. 'Later systems of philosophy display an almost pathetic anxiety to accommodate their doctrines to the views of the *Upanishads*, even if they cannot father them all on them.' If the authors of the *Upanishads* had been concerned to identify themselves, they would feature prominently in this book. As it stands, some comments are essential.

The word *Upanishad* is variously derived but probably indicates, 'sitting down near to' a teacher. An *Upanishad* is a philosophical discussion, or a collection of philosophical discussions, often framed in the form of a dialogue between a teacher and a student, or in a more dramatic form such as a contest of sages or a dialogue between a boy and the god of death. One dialogue features a sage whose philosophy is exposed as shallow by the king he attempts to teach. Others are simple expositions without any dramatic context. There are 108 *Upanishads*, of which around ten to sixteen are regarded as essential.

The greatest commentator on the *Upanishads* is undoubtedly **Shankara**. Some, or indeed many, of his commentaries may be by another 'Shankaracharya' or Shankara-Teacher, but regardless of this the Advaita Vedānta philosophy he derived from the *Upanishads*, following **Bādarāyana** and **Gaudapāda**, came to be identified with that of the Upanishadic thinkers. Others within the broader Vedānta tradition such as **Rāmānuja** or **Madhva** advanced their own theories of what the *Upanishads* said. An impartial reading shows that the *Upanishads* cannot be said to 'really' teach any of these alternative views. The attempt to foist a particular consistent philosophy on the *Upanishads* obscures rather than illuminates what they are: a magnificent set of speculations on the most fundamental questions facing humanity. A scientific analogy would be with the theories on the nature of light: scientists have found evidence to support its being particle-like as well as wave-like. Today, science can only say that it seems to be both a particle and a wave depending on one's viewpoint, or that the nature of light is something else that has the qualities of both. Radhakrishnan's comment is telling: the *Upanishads* 'have the consistency of intuition rather than of logic'. Just as scientists must admit that the nature of light is not logical at the present level of understanding, so philosophers must admit that the different metaphysical theories in the *Upanishads*, though not entirely consistent, seem independently and intuitively valid. They are not without their deficiencies, but their greatness is unquestionable.

Historically, the earliest *Upanishads* were written after the earlier parts of the Vedas. The attitude to the Vedic hymns in the early *Upanishads* is, on the whole, respectful; their view of the Brāhmanas, the formalised sacrificial religion of the Vedas, varies from one of respectful distance to one of amused contempt. On the whole the Upanishadic thinkers wished to preserve the culture from which their philosophy grew, without necessarily

Shankara

respecting all of its rigid superstitions.[3] The first six *Upanishads* are written in prose and are generally thought to have been composed between 1000 and 300 BCE. Later *Upanishads* are written in verse and refer to the *Gītā* and to the later philosophies such as Sānkhya and Yoga.

The Vedas already contained the idea of a single reality, a divine fundamental and transcendent principle that corresponds to the Brahman or Absolute of the *Upanishads*. A concept that seems to be original to the *Upanishads* is that of the Ātman or self. The Vedic background already contained the idea of an objective God-essence; the Upanishadic thinkers posited a subjective Man-essence. Their reasoning is as follows: I am not the body, because the body is impermanent and subject to growth and decay; I am not the mind and its thoughts and feelings and dreams, because they too change and pass away; I am not the consciousness in deep sleep, because although there the perception is freed from duality and division, it comes to an end on waking; what I am is the witness of all that persists through all these states[4]. The Ātman is therefore the eternal subject: anything that is perceived is an object, and therefore external; only that which perceives all and is not itself perceived can be the true Self, the Ātman. Although negatively defined, the Ātman is a positive being, enjoying all. It is not to be confused with the ego, or as the Sanskrit has it, *ahankāra*, the artificial sense of individual self.

One of the most important questions in philosophy is that of the relation of man to God, or of the world to the transcendent. The *Upanishads* assert that the Ātman is the Brahman: 'sa Ātman tat tvām asi'; 'That self, you [the Brahman] are that'[5]. If all that we had left of the *Upanishads* was this one idea we would acclaim the culture that produced it as one of the high water marks of human history and long to know more. It is one of the few truly necessary ideas, to be considered and either accepted or rejected, in philosophy.

This being so, the next question is of what relation the Absolute reality bears to the world. The most common modern view follows Shankara in maintaining that the world is an illusion or *maya* superimposed on the fundamental reality of the Brahman. This does not seem to be borne out by the *Upanishads*, which nowhere deny the reality of the cosmos. To say that the final reality is Brahman or Ātman is not to say that the world is unreal. Illusionism or *vivarta* as a doctrine did not exist until the Madhyāmika Buddhism of **Nāgārjuna**, where it is called *shūnyata* (emptiness). From there it was adopted by Vedāntins from Gaudapāda onwards. Illusionism is a possible interpretation of the *Upanishads*, but it could not be said to be essential to them. An alternative view is held by the followers of Rāmānuja, who assert that the Upanishadic view is a qualified non-dualism, Vishishta-advaita: the world has reality, but at a lower level than the Brahman. The Advaitins maintain that the ultimate reality is one and unchanging; the Vishishtadvaitins hold that the world is the expression of the ultimate. A sensible view seems to be that the Upanishadic thought contains both possibilities but sees no contradiction.

A second area of controversy between these two great views of the *Upanishads* is as to the nature of God. To Rāmānuja, the God of the *Upanishads* is the Ishvara, the beloved Lord or Saguna Brahman. To Shankara it is the unqualified Nirguna Brahman, impersonal, absolute, one without a second. Both schools regard the other's ultimate to be a preparatory stage

for theirs. Shankara's approach is lofty, cold and superhuman; Rāmānuja's is warm and devotional. Again, it is not necessary for those without a partial interest to choose: the *Upanishads* do not decide the issue, nor do they see the need to.

This brief examination of the ideas of the *Upanishads* could wrongly suggest that they are dry and intellectual. Nothing could be further from the truth. The *Upanishads* – especially the earlier prose *Upanishads* such as the great Brihadāranyaka – are playful, literary, entertaining and full of the joy of untrammelled philosophy. Many are cast as dialogues, anticipating the Socratic approach or the philosophic atmosphere hinted at in the Analects of **Confucius**. One comes away from them with the exalted sense of an open society of passionate seekers, living in the real world but looking beyond it. The great figures of the *Upanishads* are well aware that the ideas they deal with are audacious and improbable to ordinary awareness, and revel in the humour of the situation. A conference of all the wise is called by the king to find out who is the wisest: a prize of a thousand cows, each with a bag of gold tied to its horns, will be given to the winner. Yājnyawalkya, the great sage of the Brihadāranyaka, asks his disciple to take the cows. There is uproar: how can Yājnyawalkya claim wisdom? 'I bow to the wisest', answers Yājnyawalkya, 'but I wanted the cows'. The interrogation that follows shows Yājnyawalkya to be indeed the wisest, but his refusal to characterise himself as either wise or ignorant typifies the Upanishadic spirit. To claim wisdom is to deny wisdom; to deny wisdom is also to deny wisdom.

CHĀRVĀKA

c. 600 BCE

The name of the materialist philosopher Chārvāka is doubtfully derived from a word meaning 'sweet-tongued', indicating perhaps the importance of pleasure, a key doctrine. Also known as Lokāyata, perhaps best translated as '[the philosophy] of the world' or 'of the people', Chārvāka's philosophy seems to have enjoyed wide popularity up until its disappearance in medieval times. This may have been more due to its convenience as an explanation for pragmatic self-interest than to a genuine interest in its philosophical value, just as Epicureanism was a pretext for hedonism in the West. His doctrines are said to be embodied in the lost Bārhaspatya-Sūtras. Since no work of his and few works of his followers' (known as Chārvākas) are extant, much of what follows is speculative. It is often difficult to surmise what the original teaching of Chārvāka was and what was a

> 'Live well,
> as long as you live.
> Live well even
> by borrowing, for,
> once cremated,
> there is
> no return.'

later addition. The only substantial systematic work of Chārvāka philosophy comes from almost a millennium after Chārvāka himself, the *Tattvopaplavasimha* of Jayarasi, which argues that nothing is real

except the evidence of the senses and that therefore morality is an illusion. Again, this may be a corruption of Chārvāka's original doctrine. The philosophy is best known from its numerous refutations by other schools, both Hindu and Buddhist, who regarded it as the lowest form of philosophy and ethics. One aphorism of Chārvāka became a well-known Hindu proverb and gives a flavour of the school: 'Live well, as long as you live. Live well even by borrowing, for, once cremated, there is no return.'

Chārvāka was unorthodox in that he rejected the authority of the Veda, as well as the existence of God, an afterlife and the self. Of the three pramānas or means of acquiring knowledge accepted by the orthodox schools, he rejects both inference and revelation (or verbal testimony). Chārvāka accepts only sensory perception, which in some ways anticipates the modern Empiricists, notably David Hume. The Chārvāka argument against inference is as follows. The classical Indian example of inference is 'Where there is smoke, there is fire. There is smoke in the mountain. Therefore there is fire in the mountain'. Chārvāka says that unless we have seen all examples of smoke and fire, we cannot know that the initial premise is true. If we had seen all examples then we would have no need to infer the existence of fire in the mountain, because we had seen it. Thus inference is either impossible or unnecessary. This foreshadows Western critiques of inference and inductive reasoning.

Chārvāka's attack on testimony is even stronger: if someone tells me something, I must infer a fact from his or her words, such as 'I have seen fire', that I have not myself

Bathers in the River Ganges during the Kumbha Mela Festival in Varanasi (formerly Benares). The Festival takes place at the confluence of the three sacred rivers (Ganges, Yamuna and the invisible Sarasnati), the holiest of Hindu sites. Bathing here is said to purify the body and the soul and leave one free from the continuous cycle of birth and death.

perceived. However, not only is inference invalid, the words may themselves be a lie. Thus testimony is still more unreliable. This last example illustrates a limitation in the knowledge that can be gained through such a severely positivist outlook: we are prevented from accepting inference and testimony even hypothetically ('let us assume that Kate was telling the truth when she said that the house is on fire'). Jayarasi in his *Tattvopaplavasimha* (delightfully translated as 'The Lion That Devours All Categories') takes this to its extreme. Not only are testimony and inference invalid, even sense perception is not totally reliable. Therefore we cannot conclusively know anything about the world. Only the Chārvāka philosophy is acceptable on this argument, because it makes no assumptions and appeals only to common sense.

A key problem for the Chārvākas is the evident existence of consciousness. Their solution is similar to the theory of a 'primeval soup' from which life emerged, but they use the analogy of making alcoholic liquor. None of the ingredients are alcoholic but through mixing and the fermentation process, alcohol eventually appears. Thus, consciousness (and indeed life) is the result of the right combination of elemental substances. Only matter is real and inference is invalid so we cannot prove the existence of the self, God, afterlife or anything else not perceivable by the senses. We may note the similarity of Chārvāka's views to that of present-day theorists of science, who have the difficulty of building an ethical system on materialist foundations. Chārvāka, of course, has no such problem.

Of all other philosophies, Chārvāka's particular hatred is reserved for the Mīmāmsā[6], which is principally concerned with the Vedic rituals and way of life. The

Vedas enjoined devotees to earn the approval of the gods and ancestors through the performance of rites, and to give gifts to the Brahmin priests. For the Chārvākas this system is designed self-servingly by the Brahmins for their own ends. The Mīmāmsā philosophy was easy meat for the devouring lions of Chārvāka, but the attacks it suffered were to strengthen it in its later, more rational re-emergence, for example in the

Levitating Brahmin, sitting in mid-air, without any apparent support. The Brahmin priests were attacked by Chārvāka and his supporters as self-serving.

work of Kumarila. This is just one example of the useful effect Chārvāka was to have on other philosophies, compelling them to defend and improve their ideas against its ruthless opposition. As Radhakrishnan observes in Indian Philosophy, 'When people begin to reflect with freedom from presuppositions and religious superstition they easily tend to the materialist belief, though deeper reflection takes them away from it'. The materialism of Chārvāka, for all its faults, is a natural and positive step away from rigid ritualism.

Of the four traditional Hindu social values, Chārvāka rejects *dharma* (duty) and *moksha* (liberation) as being not based on the senses. Of the other two, Chārvāka holds that the chief aim of life is *kama* (pleasure) and the chief means to that end is *artha* (wealth). The pleasures to be desired are eating, drinking, song and women. Any means towards these ends are acceptable so long as they are successful. The Chārvāka system does attempt to rein in unfettered pleasure seeking, because this leads rapidly to pains such as illness. As natural supporters of 'might is right', many of the Chārvākas are said to have written Machiavellian handbooks for the education of rulers. An example is the *Artha-Shāstra* ('Handbook of Profit') of Kautilya, written around 300 BCE. As chief minister to the king Chandragupta, the founder of the Mauryan dynasty, Kautilya outlines the steps a king should take to retain and strengthen his power. The *Artha-Shāstra* covers a number of practical topics including taxation, appointment of ministers, warfare and, above all, how to run a secret service. Although Kautilya regards anyone and everyone as corruptible and therefore potentially an enemy, he says – rather self-servingly – that the one person in whom the king should have absolute trust is the minister who runs his kingdom. As with Machiavelli, however, it is easier to feel moral outrage with Kautilya than it is to demonstrate that his advice is not in most cases eminently practical[7].

BUDDHISM IN INDIA

There are three stages in the development of Buddhism in India. The early stage of Buddhism consists of the Buddha's teaching and its formulation by his immediate successors.[8] The second stage is that of the Hīnayāna (or Theravāda), which emphasised the negative aspects of Buddhism. This stage can be identified historically with the reign of King Ashoka, who promoted Buddhism widely in India

hardy ascetics to their goal, it was insufficient for the great mass of humanity. The term Hīnayāna is, of course, a Mahāyāna one: the Hīnayāna Buddhists would call themselves Theravadins for their adherence to the Buddha's original teachings.

Radhakrishnan comments on the Mahāyāna that, 'there is practically nothing to distinguish it from the religion of the *Bhagavad Gītā*'. That is to say, Mahāyāna Buddhism, like the Hinduism of the *Gītā*,

and established a remarkable Buddhist state over a vast area. Gradually, however, a growing number of Buddhists came to feel that the Hīnayāna doctrine lacked emotional appeal. There were a great number of Buddhists who argued for a reform, and the schism resulted in Mahāyāna Buddhism. Mahāyāna means 'Great Vehicle', as opposed to the 'Lesser Vehicle' or Hīnayāna: the Mahāyānists held that while the Hīnayāna would take a few

believes in an ultimate ground of reality, a supreme living god, a multitude of minor deities, and a fundamental self or soul. The reality of all, called in the *Gītā* Brahman, becomes the Dharmakāya; the Lord of All is not Krishna but Buddha; the deities are Hindu gods re-named as Buddhas; and the Ātman or supreme self is the soul, now guaranteed eternal being. This is not a view that most Buddhists will accept, any more than his opinion that the Buddha's teaching is an elaboration of ideas in the *Upanishads*. However, it is a reasonable one. The Mahāyānists followed Buddha in allowing their converts to retain much of their previous practice in becoming Buddhists. Where they went further than the Buddha was in their willingness to allow the faith and superstitions of the converts to influence Buddhism.

The problem with Hīnayāna Buddhism was its rather intellectual, negative and world-denying philosophy. There was very little in it that could inspire people's love and devotion and as a religion it was obviously lacking. Whereof the Buddha was unwilling to speak, Hīnayāna Buddhism was crystal clear. Although it appears to be more faithful to Buddha, the lack of ethical concern and compassion makes Hīnayānism oddly unlike the Buddha we find in the old sūtras of the Theravāda. Mahāyānism, by contrast, developed a pragmatic acceptance of a broad range of religious approaches. Just as Krishna says 'however men approach me, even so do I welcome them, for the path men take from every side is mine', so Mahāyāna Buddhism accepts all comers on their own terms. While Hīnayānism proposed the *arhat* as an ideal – an ascetic who turned away from the world to find the extinction of *Nirvāna* – Mahāyānism has the Bodhisattva, the Buddha-to-be who postpones his own liberation out of compassion for all. Mahāyāna Buddhism has therefore much more of the social concern that inspired the Buddha than the more doctrinally correct Hīnayānism.

The two main branches of Mahāyāna Buddhism are the Madhyāmika or Middle School of Nāgārjuna and the Yogācāra of Vasubandhu. The former is known as the Shūnyavāda, the Doctrine of Emptiness, and the latter as the Vijnānavāda, the Doctrine of Consciousness. Each is considered in detail in the chapters on those figures. However a few comments are worthwhile making here. Although Vasubandhu is thought to be later than Nāgārjuna, his philosophy is regarded as less advanced. Vasubandhu's Doctrine of Consciousness holds that the only reality is consciousness, the mind. *Nirvāna* is the extinguishing of all thoughts, merging with the single consciousness underlying all. That consciousness is undifferentiated and single. Nāgārjuna's Doctrine of Emptiness accepts the contention that the material world is in some sense unreal, empty, but applies the same reasoning to the mind. He treads a 'middle path' between absolutely denying reality and absolutely asserting it. There is a strong case to say that Nāgārjuna's philosophy is the genuine heir of the Buddha's.

In broad geographical terms, Hīnayāna Buddhism spread in South Asia, for example in Sri Lanka and Myanmar, while Mahāyāna Buddhism prospered further north, to Tibet, China, Mongolia, Korea and Japan. Hīnayāna Buddhism uses the Pāli language of the early Buddhist Canon, while Mahāyāna Buddhism in India generally uses Sanskrit, another indication of Hindu influence. Traditional accounts credit figures such as Kumarila Bhatta and Shankara with successfully putting down Buddhism, but the truth is that it lost its vigour and was replaced by a reinvigorated Hindu religion and philosophy. Buddhism gradually died out in India, having made significant contributions to Indian thought and belief. Elsewhere it has continued to flourish down to the present day.

THE BUDDHA (SIDDHĀRTHA GAUTAMA)

c. 563–c. 483 BCE

The Buddha lived in a time of remarkable intellectual ferment. In northeast India, a new branch of Indian civilization was springing up along the Ganges and it found the teachings of the Shramanas or holy wanderers more attractive and accessible than those of the Brahmins. **Vardhamāna**, the founder of the Jain religion, was probably a younger contemporary and was known to the Buddhists. Gosala, the founder of the Ajivikas, a now-extinct sect that lasted some eighteen centuries, was another local figure. In the northwest of India the early Upanishadic literature had been composed by the Brahmins and new *Upanishads* continued to emerge. Across the wider world a remarkable number of great thinkers – including, pre-eminently, **Confucius** in China and Socrates in Greece – flourished independently at about the same time.

The Buddha, which means the Enlightened One or the Awakened One, was born into the wealthy Gautama family and named Siddhārtha. The main aspects of his traditional story are as follows. His mother had a prophetic dream the night before he was born in which a beautiful white elephant entered her side. Experts in dream-interpretation and in the interpretation of marks on a child's body concurred that the baby would grow up either to be a universal ruler or a Buddha. The prophecy stated that he would follow the former course if he stayed at home and the latter if he left home. Fearing that his son would become a wandering ascetic, Gautama's father raised him in great luxury and attempted to shield him from the realities of normal life.

Despite these efforts, at the age of 29 Gautama had the experiences that confirmed his resolve to follow a spiritual path. While out driving in his chariot he saw first an old man, then on the next day a sick man, and on the day after that a dead man. While lost in the contemplation of this revelation of the suffering that characterizes life, Gautama chanced to see a saffron-robed ascetic and was struck by his peaceful appearance in the face of all the evils of life. He then resolved to discover that peace for himself. That night he secretly left the palace

Departure of Buddha – Siddhārtha leaves his father's palace and family after seeing the four signs (old age, death, sickness and a hermit) that were to persuade him to become an ascetic.

and his sleeping wife and newborn son for the life of a mendicant ascetic.

Over the next few years Gautama progressed in his education, studying with learned Brahmins and submitting himself to severe austerities. Eventually he decided that austerities could not give him what he wanted, whereupon his companion monks abandoned him, certain that he had abandoned the spiritual path. Shortly after this, however, Gautama did achieve Awakening while meditating under a bo tree. Now aged 35 and known as the Buddha, he set out to preach his *dharma* or

teaching and established his monastic community or *sangha*. He is said to have died at the age of 80.

What is certain is that the Buddha left a large body of oral teaching, which was written down after his death by a council of his followers. This teaching is known as the Theravāda, as distinct from later additions that were subsequently declared to be orthodox because divinely inspired. Although the Theravāda is in Pāli, here we will generally use the Sanskrit terms for the sake of consistency with the other Indian thinkers and the Mahāyāna Buddhists. There

The sacred Bo Tree at Anuradhapura, grown from a cutting from the tree in northern India beneath which Buddha attained Enlightenment.

are several striking aspects of the Buddha's original doctrine. In his first sermon, delivered to his companions immediately following his awakening, the Buddha taught the 'Four Noble Truths', which are that all existence consists of suffering (*dukha*); that this suffering is caused by desire or thirst (*tanha*); that there is a way to end this suffering; and that the way to end suffering is to follow the Noble Eightfold Path of right views, right intention, right speech, right action, right livelihood, right effort, right mindfulness and right concentration.

Underpinning this apparently simple teaching is a philosophy of remarkable subtlety. Firstly there are his 'Three Characteristics of Being', which state that being is impermanent, has no self, and is made up of suffering. Although nothing is permanent, according to the Buddha, our thirst causes us to imagine the transitory objects we perceive as real and lasting. Chief among these transitory objects is the self: against the orthodoxy of the traditional Vedic religion of the time, the Buddha declared that there was no consistent self or Ātman. This aspect of his doctrine is known

as an-Ātman (no-self). The analogy is with fire, which appears to have a continuing existence but changes from moment to moment. Because of the transitory nature of being, it can never satisfy our thirst and therefore our existence is filled with suffering.

These three characteristics of being, in turn, are derived from the fundamental insight of the Buddha, which is that of dependent origination (*pratitya-samutpada*). Dependent origination states that everything has a cause and in turn is the cause of other things. This doctrine is described by the Buddha as being the middle way between those of the 'Eternalists', such as the orthodox Hindu thinkers, who maintained the eternal existence of being, and those of the 'Annihilationists', who denied not only existence but also causality. The Buddha denies that things really exist, but does not deny causality. This explains how, without a consistent self or God, the illusion of continuity is created through an endless chain of cause and effect. Buddha's successor **Nāgārjuna** was to take up this idea and further develop it, founding in the process the influential school of Madhyāmika (Middle Way).

Using his understanding of causation the Buddha developed the traditional Hindu concept of *karma* (literally, 'action'). According to the Buddha a person was made up of five groups or *skandhas*: body, feelings, perceptions, impulses and consciousness. These five are configured according to past actions in a certain way, and will be reconfigured in a better or worse way in the future depending on the good or bad actions performed in the present. At death, the 'consciousness' *skandha* carries its karmic charge on to its rebirth in a new body. As with the Hindu thinkers, the aim of the Buddha's philosophy is to find a way to get off this cosmic merry-go-round (or perhaps, misery-go-round).

This brings us to what is the best known distinctively Buddhist concept, that of *Nirvāna*, 'extinguishing' – in Pāli, *nibbana*. *Nirvāna* is variously imagined to be either heaven or a form of annihilation, but its literal sense is the extinguishing of the flames of desire, hatred and delusion. The Buddha refused to be drawn on what *Nirvāna* was, or what would happen to an enlightened soul after death, but he did posit an 'unoriginated' realm or substance beyond the illusion of existence, which promised a kind of escape.

There is considerable debate about the Buddha's true belief, centring on the three questions of whether there is an absolute reality, whether there is a permanent self and whether *Nirvāna* is existence or annihilation. The modern Indian philosopher Radhakrishnan says that these questions come to the same thing: did the Buddha believe that there was an ultimate reality? Though refusing to speculate about such questions, is it safe to assume he was an atheist? We noted at the start of the chapter that the Buddha lived in a time of great intellectual ferment. When his doctrines are compared to those of the *Upanishads*, they are seen to share a great commonality. Both aim at liberation, and both move away from the old Vedic tradition. There are many statements in the *Upanishads* that could be attributed to the Buddha. For example, the description of Brahman as 'not this, not that', or the idea of Brahman as silence could, if the word 'Brahman' were replaced with *Nirvāna*,

seem eminently Buddhist. What the Buddha does not do is use positive means of describing reality. The *Upanishads* make use of both negative and positive means of speaking of reality:

> *The wise realise everywhere that which is invisible, ungraspable, without source, without senses, without body,*
> *That which is infinite, multiformed, all pervasive, extremely subtle and undiminishing, and the source of all.*
>
> Mundaka Upanishad 1.i.6.

The Buddha uses only the negative, as when he says 'transient are all compound things . . . sorrowful are all compound things . . . all things are without self' (Dhammapada 278–280).

The debate on this subject continues. A Buddhist scholar such as Walpola Rahula would deny categorically that the Buddha taught anything resembling *Upanishadic* ideas, and would say that that the fundamental assumptions of Buddhism are entirely the opposite to those of the *Upanishads*. On the other side, there are those who maintain that the Buddha's denial of the reality of the self or of an ultimate reality amounts to the same thing as Upanishadic denials of the possibility of saying anything meaningful about ultimate reality. What is certain is that in some later Buddhism, such as the twentieth century Japanese Zen of Nishida, the Upanishadic view predominates:

> As emphasised in basic Buddhist thought, the self and the universe share the same foundation; or rather, they are the same thing.

The view of Walpola Rahula makes sense when Buddhism is treated as an entirely exceptional teaching. Within the context of a survey of Eastern thought such as this, however, it seems much more appropriate to view Buddhist metaphysics as an exceptional expression of a familiar doctrine, rather than as a doctrine contrary to all others.

Walpola Rahula

From this point of view, Buddha's real distinctiveness is as an ethical teacher. Rhys Davids in *Buddhism* sets out an extreme view that is not without justification:

> Gautama was born and brought up and lived and died a Hindu . . . There was not much in the metaphysics and principles of Gautama which cannot be found in one or other of the orthodox systems, and a great deal of his morality could be matched from earlier or later Hindu books. Such originality as Gautama possessed lay in the way in which he adopted, enlarged, ennobled and systematised that which had already been well said by others; in the way in which he carried out to their logical conclusion principles of equity and justice already acknowledged by some of the most prominent Hindu thinkers. The difference between him and the other teachers lay chiefly in his deep earnestness and in his broad public spirit of philanthropy.

The Buddhist *sangha* or monastic community was far more democratic and equitable than that of the early Hindu culture it sought to break with. The Buddha rejects caste entirely, and his treatment of women is broadly equitable. Having said this, the creation of the monastic order, with its surrounding lay community of the faithful, sets up a hierarchy in Buddhist culture that is similar to that which it replaces. Although birth is irrelevant to Buddhism, it is necessary to convert to Buddhism and ultimately to give up worldly life and take up holy orders, which is the highest calling. We have in the reign of King Ashoka, who ruled most of India in 270–230 BCE, an example of an early Buddhist kingdom. It had many remarkably attractive aspects, including what is probably the world's first welfare state, universal tolerance of belief, and a justice system based on Buddhist principles.

As can be seen from the widely varying philosophies of subsequent Buddhists elsewhere in this book, there is almost no doctrine that has not been imputed to the Buddha by his followers. Regardless of this, however, it is possible to distinguish a 'true Buddhism' throughout history, characterised not so much by consistency in doctrine as by universal compassion, equity and justice. The Buddha's ethical teachings are the earliest complete articulations of these ideals and to this day remain one of the greatest Indian contributions to world philosophy.

King Ashoka

VARDHAMĀNA
C. 540 – c. 467 BCE

Along with Hinduism and Buddhism, the third religion present in Indian culture from around the fifth century BCE was Jainism. Its founder, at least for historical purposes, was Vardhamāna, also known as Mahāvīra (the Great Hero), although Jains regard him not as its founder but as the restorer of ancient teaching. He is supposed to have been the 24th Tirthankara or 'ford-builder', but the previous 23 are legendary. He may be the successor of the tradition of Parsvanatha, said to have died in 776 BCE, and of Rishabha, supposedly the first Tirthankara and one of three Jain sages mentioned in the Yajur-Veda. On this evidence the Jain religion in some form is at least 3,500 years

old. Certainly, there are aspects of the faith that seem thoroughly archaic. Alongside these, however, are some highly refined philosophical concepts that are worthy of consideration here, notably Vardhamāna's theory of knowledge.

Vardhamāna lived during a period of considerable fertility for new systems of thought and belief. He is said to have realised a calling at the age of 30 and, like the Buddha, left a life of comfort and a wife and child behind to become an ascetic. He spent time with Gosala, the founder of the Ajivikas, another unorthodox sect that was important in its time although now extinct. He was known to early Buddhists as Nigantha Nataputta and seems to have been a contemporary of the Buddha. The Buddhists' record debates between the two traditions, which coexisted in friendly rivalry. The two traditions have so many similarities that some have speculated that Gautama and Vardhamāna are the same person, but this theory is no longer credible.

Like Buddha, Vardhamāna rejected the revelatory status of the Veda and did not see the need to posit the existence of God. He did, however, believe in the existence of a multiplicity of souls, each tied to a body from which it must strive to liberate itself. There are parallels in this soul-body dualism with Sānkhya-Yoga philosophy but perhaps still more with the Nyāya-Vaisheshika view which sees the soul as active rather than passive and like Vardhamāna holds an atomistic theory of matter. In the Western world there are parallels with pre-Socratic philosophy and with Platonism, another contemporary though unconnected development. At the age of 42 Vardhamāna is said to have achieved Enlightenment, thus becoming a *jina* or 'conqueror', from which his faith takes its name. He lived for about 30 years after this, in which time he built up a considerable following. He finally starved himself to death, an important fact for Jainism.

The Jain ideal is to achieve liberation from bodily attachment through the most severe asceticism. This is depicted in huge Jain statues of naked men, so detached from the physical that vines have begun to climb up their bodies. As with Yoga, the soul is thought of as ascending through the physical body to the highest region of motionlessness, the head. Thus we have the paradox of liberation conceived of as a complete and endless immobility. Ethically, Vardhamāna taught the principle of *āhimsa* (harmlessness), which included strict veganism and was to greatly influence Indian society. Jainism takes this much more seriously than either Buddhism or Hinduism and not only are Jains prohibited from any activity that involves killing animals, such as farming, but they are tolerant of insects and will go to great lengths to avoid accidentally killing one by stepping on or swallowing it. Even vegetables are thought to have souls, which is perhaps linked to the practice of total starvation as death approaches.

The Parasnath Jain Temple in Calcutta.

Paradoxically, this most severe discipline is accompanied by a philosophy both gentle and relativistic. Firstly, there is the idea of *syādvāda*, perhaps best translated as 'maybe-ism'. For Vardhamāna, who must be regarded as the founder of Jain philosophy if not its religion, all viewpoints are partial. The classic story is of a group of blind men who come across an elephant. One grasps its tail and claims that an elephant is like a rope. Another takes it by the trunk and says it is like a snake. A third decides that its leg is like the trunk of a tree, and so forth. The meaning of this is that whatever our worldview, we had better appreciate that it is a partial one and precede our statements about it with a syad: 'maybe, this is how it is . . . '. Jain statements are expressed in seven logical formulae:

> *Maybe it is*
>
> *Maybe it is not*
>
> *Maybe it is and also is not*
>
> *Maybe it is inexpressible*
>
> *Maybe it is, and is also inexpressible*
>
> *Maybe it is not, and is also inexpressible*
>
> *Maybe it is and is not, and is also inexpressible*

Of course, these formulae could function without the 'syad', but its constant presence is a useful reminder of the uncertainty of human understanding. The paradox of tentative relativism and harsh discipline is resolved when we reflect that the Jain logic assumes a fundamental, intractable and objective reality. The blind men may have grasped only part of the elephant, but there is definitely an elephant. The elephant may be grasped

Vardhamāna

fully, as it were, only by the 'knowledge of the free', that understanding possessed by the perfect victor. The Jain ideal is *kevala* (liberation) or *Nirvāna* (deliverance). The Jain view of the latter term is definitely not the extinction professed by some Buddhists, but a positive existence of freedom from the body, a dwelling in peace and blissful rest.

Jainism was for a time a serious rival to Hinduism and Buddhism, but it became a minority faith. There are two traditions in Jainism resulting from a schism in the first century CE, between the Svetāmbaras ('white-robed') and Digambaras ('sky clad'). The latter maintain that a Jain monk should wear no clothing and that a woman cannot reach liberation. The former preserve the Jain canon of written scriptures, while the Digambaras reject it.

Vardhamāna's teaching has, despite this, been tremendously influential. The ideal of *āhimsa* has been absorbed into mainstream Hinduism, most notably in the twentieth century by **Mohandas Gandhi**.

THE SIX ORTHODOX SYSTEMS OF INDIAN PHILOSOPHY

Traditionally there are six main systems of Indian philosophy that acknowledge the authority of the Veda. The word used to describe the systems is *darshana* (view). Already implicit in the idea of a *darshana* is the possibility of a range of alternative

The six darshanas are best seen as a reaction to views that were regarded as beyond the pale: the materialism of the Chārvākas, the Jain viewpoint of Vardhamāna and above all the way of Buddhism.

views. **Buddha** stated on the other hand that he did not propound a view, but a way: an escape route from suffering. But though he declined to offer a view, his followers did not.

The six *darshanas* are best seen as a reaction to views that were regarded as beyond the pale: the materialism of the Chārvākas, the Jain viewpoint of Vardhamāna and above all the way of

Buddhism. The main point about these dissenting systems was that they attacked the traditional structure of Indian society: the caste system, the tradition of the Veda and the authority of the Brahmins. Against these vigorous attacks the Hindu orthodox had to develop their own philosophies, to define and refine the views they instinctively held. All of the *darshanas* share certain terms of reference. All erect a standard of external reality against Buddhist scepticism, called variously *maya*, *prakriti*, atoms or Brahman. All have a theory of the self. All have a cyclical view of cosmic history. All except Mīmāmsā aim at salvation or liberation of the soul.

The six are traditionally grouped in pairs. The usual order, based on a perceived logical progression, is Nyāya-Vaisheshika, Sānkhya-Yoga and Mīmāmsā-Vedānta. There are critics of this system who point out its many inadequacies. It has been followed, however, as useful to someone wishing to get the broad outline of Hindu thought.

NYĀYA-VAISHESHIKA

Nyāya is the philosophy most concerned with logic and epistemology, which examines the basis of knowledge. Vaisheshika is an allied development and is metaphysical, concerned with the nature of reality. Vaisheshika includes an atomic theory of matter. It is thought by some authorities to be much older than Nyāya, which is reasonable given the example of other philosophies in which logic is usually a later development than metaphysics.

SĀNKHYA-YOGA

Sānkhya means 'enumeration': the system recognises 25 categories of existence, with the highest being *purusha* (the spirit). The other 24 are all divisions of *prakriti* (nature). It is the most unorthodox of the six systems as it is often regarded as atheistic and, indeed, some authorities rejected it on this account. The Yoga philosophy is a practical extension of Sānkhya, involving a system of exercises designed to bring the practitioner to a state of knowledge of the difference between the *purusha* and the *prakriti*. Yoga adds a 26th category, namely God.

Sānkhya is considered in the chapter on Kapila and Yoga in the chapter on Patanjali. Both are very important for the *Bhagavad Gītā* and so for the later course of Indian philosophy in general.

MĪMĀMSĀ-VEDĀNTA

The most orthodox of the systems are the Mīmāmsā, or Purva-Mīmāmsā, literally 'Study' of the early part of the Veda, and the Vedānta, or Uttara-Mīmāmsā, the study of the latter part of the Veda, that is of the *Upanishads*. However, the Vedānta maintains an attitude of respectful distance to the Samhitā, or Vedic hymns and is on the whole opposed to the Brāhmanas, so of the three parts of the Veda it is only the *Upanishads* that it regards as revelatory.

Mīmāmsā is examined in the chapter on Jaimini. Vedānta is the most important of the six systems and is represented here by Bādarāyana, its founder, as well as Gaudapāda, Shankara, Rāmānuja, Madhva and Vivekānanda. Gandhi's philosophy is also largely reliant on Vedānta.

A Brahmin performing pujah. *The Hindu orthodox had to defend their philosophy against those who denied the tradition of the Veda and the authority of the Brahmins.*

GAUTAMA
fourth century BCE?

The history of Nyāya ('Right Reasoning' or 'Logic') is very ancient, being mentioned in the *Laws of Manu* and by the philosopher Yājnyawalkya. Here we are concerned with the post-Buddhist Nyāya, founded by Gautama who wrote its first textbook, the *Nyāya Sūtras*. His namesake Gautama, the **Buddha**, and Mahāvīra the founder of the Jain sect, had both mounted attacks on orthodox philosophy some two hundred years before. It is likely that Gautama set out to establish a robust logical system that could defend the Veda from their criticisms. Whereas Mīmāmsā regards the scriptures as the only reliable authority and Sānkhya appeals to a supreme form of Reason, Nyāya makes use of logic and experience, the principal bases of Buddhist and Jain attacks. Many writers have noted the similarity between Nyāya and Aristotle's syllogistic analysis, and some argue that there was direct influence, either from Greece to India or vice versa. There is no conclusive evidence of this, however.

Gautama assumes the Veda to be true and therefore accepts spiritual liberation as a reality. On this basis, he wishes to purge philosophy of false and sentimental arguments, which can only be founded in spurious doctrines. Only when we know what can be known, understand how we can know what we do know, and discover legitimate means of proceeding in our enquiries will philosophy be able to proceed. Logic is not, for Nyāya, merely a process to be tinkered with. Gautama sets out the various forms of debate including discussion aimed at finding the truth, debating to win an argument against an opponent, attacking a position without having a position of one's own, and so on. He emphasises the importance of having the earnest desire to find the truth. Liberation is, according to Nyāya, the self moving beyond the pain and pleasure of existence to pure unconscious being, which is the Ātman.

The main contribution of the Nyāya school to Hindu thought is its logical structure, which is adopted with modifications by all the other schools. Its enumeration of logical fallacies has been useful. The later thinkers were able to refer to Nyāya concepts such as 'the argument in a circle', 'infinite regress', or 'mutual dependence' with no need to elaborate further. There is no space here to consider the finer points of Nyāya logic.

Nyāya and Vaisheshika, though apparently of independent development, subsequently merged to be known as Nyāya-Vaisheshika. Whereas the main concerns of Nyāya are logic and epistemology (the philosophy of knowledge), Vaisheshika develops its thinking into metaphysics.

The modern school of Nyāya was founded in about 1200 CE by Gangesha, who wrote in response to several criticisms of the school by the Vedāntin philosopher Shriharsha. New Nyāya is notable for its hair-splitting tendencies.

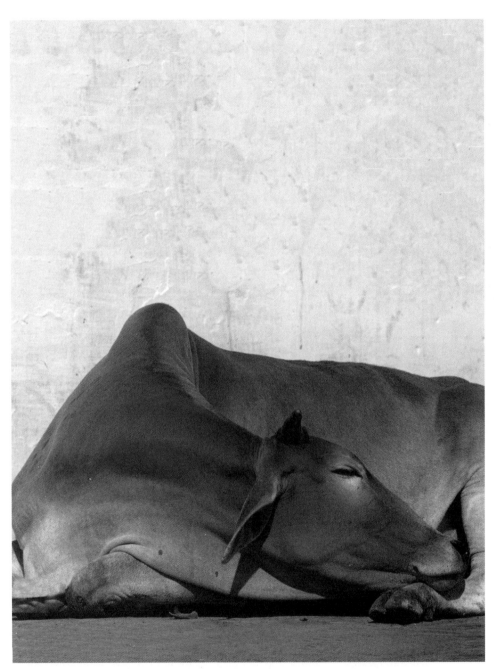

A sacred Brahman cow left to wander freely on the streets of India takes a nap.

WHAT IS A SŪTRA?

'Sūtra' is a word used to describe learned writings in both the Hindu and Buddhist traditions. However, they do not mean the same thing for both. The word literally means a 'thread' in Sanskrit. 'Pithy, unambiguous, laying out all the essential aspects of each topic, and dealing with all aspects of the question, free of repetitiveness and flaw – those learned in the sūtras say that such is a sūtra', is the account of the Padma Purāna.

In the Hindu tradition, the sūtra format was one of the earliest literary forms. A Hindu sūtra is the model of brevity, consisting of a series of short phrases or verses, often with no apparent connection or argument. This is misleading, because the sūtra was never intended to be studied alone, but to act as an aide-memoire or a series of headings on which the guru *(sage) or* acharya *(teacher) would expound. Reading the key texts of Hinduism can be rather like reading the chapter headings of a book. The sūtra is the 'thread' on which the gems of the teacher's learning are hung. It also often provides a subject for meditation: having heard and understood an exposition on a sūtra, the student can reflect on its words. The sūtra thus comes to represent the understanding of the subject arising out of oral discussion between teacher and student, rather than being itself a full discussion. There are numerous references in the* Upanishads *to the warm bond between teacher and student, as in the prayer, 'May He protect us both together. May He nourish us both together. May we both acquire strength together. Let our study be brilliant. May we not cavil at each other.'*

The key texts of the Hindu philosophies are contained in sūtras, for example the Yoga Sūtras of **Patanjali**, *the Brahma Sūtras or Vedānta Sūtras of* **Bādarāyana** *and the Sānkhya Sūtras of* **Kapila**. *The form was widely used for all forms of knowledge, ranging from Pānini who wrote the world's first grammar around 500 BCE in sūtra form to the most famous of all sūtras, the sex-manual* Kama Sūtra *(The Sūtra of Desire).*

The Buddhist sūtra (in Pāli, a sutta), on the other hand, normally refers to words attributed to the Buddha. Thus, the Fire Sūtra, the Love Sūtra and the Sūtra of Advice to Sigala are examples of the recorded utterances of the Buddha. Later, Mahāyāna Buddhism accepted a much wider definition of sūtra. Works of great wisdom produced by later Buddhists were accepted as the revealed teaching of the Buddha. They normally followed the format of a sermon or sūtra given by the Buddha, for example the Diamond Sūtra sometimes attributed to Nāgārjuna or the Garland Sūtra that inspired Huayen Buddhism in China. Most Buddhist traditions base themselves on a particular sūtra, with the notable exception of Chan or Zen Buddhism, which repudiates the sūtra tradition, relying instead on direct oral transmission of teaching.

KANĀDA
third century BCE?

Kanāda, whose name means 'atom-eater', founded the Vaisheshika school of philosophy. His real name may have been Kāshyapa. His philosophy is very close to that of Nyāya, and the two complementary schools came to be regarded as one, called Nyāya-Vaisheshika, from the eleventh century onwards. Nyāya deals with problems of logic and epistemology, while Vaisheshika is concerned with metaphysics. Vaisheshika is a realist school and regards the objects of knowledge as having a real existence independently of the knower and of the process of knowing, a view that has some affinities with the Buddhism of the time.

Accordingly, Kanāda explores the nature of matter in great detail. Because the senses perceive real objects, each sense corresponds to an element. Thus smell corresponds to earth, taste to water, sight to fire, touch to air and hearing to the fifth element ether or space. The inference of the fifth element is typical of Indian metaphysics. All of the elements, except for ether, are made up of indivisible, indestructible and eternal atoms. According to Kanāda atoms have no dimension, which

is problematic because he has no explanation for the way in which a number of atoms come to add up to a quantity. Two atoms make a dyad and three dyads make a triad, which is the smallest thing visible to the human eye.

Vaisheshika is a pluralist philosophy, which means that it regards things as being many. Each individual (Ātman) has according to Vaisheshika a separate existence; matter is made of vast numbers of tiny atoms; time and space also are real and indestructible; even God (in later Vaisheshika) is simply the Param-Ātman or Supreme Self. The mind, or Manas, is physical and atomic and has no dimension. It can apprehend more than one thing at a time because it has no size and so can move at infinite speed between two or more objects of thought. Thus even the mind is in a sense physical. Although Vaisheshika is proto-scientific in many ways, the mysterious force *adrishta* ('unseen') is there to explain everything that is not explained by the known objects of existence. Magnetism, the rising of fire and the journey of the soul after death are some of the many topics covered by *adrishta*.

It is doubtful whether Kanāda's scheme includes God, but later Vaisheshikas felt the need to include a divine power. God is the efficient cause of the universe in that he ordains its creation, but not its material cause, as the objects of the universe are eternally present. God's role is to organise the universe such that it provides a moral space in which the Ātmans or individuals may play out their destinies. It is assumed that the individuals already have an accumulation of good and bad action (*karma*) from before the beginning of a cycle of creation, which gives form and structure to the universe.

KAPILA
seventh century BCE?

Author of the lost Sānkhya-Pravacana Sūtras, Kapila is generally acknowledged to be the founder of the Sānkhya philosophy. Sānkhya literally means 'counting up' or 'number', perhaps due to its fondness for categorization. Other authorities point to early uses of the word to indicate 'philosophical reflection'. Of the six orthodox Hindu philosophies, perhaps only Mīmāmsā is as old, or older than Sānkhya. Nevertheless, it is more advanced than the Nyāya-Vaisheshika system and was the most influential and important system apart from the Vedānta.

We know of Kapila's ideas only indirectly through the work of his successor Ishvarakrishna (c. fourth century CE), who wrote what is supposed to be a commentary on Kapila's work, the *Sānkhya-Karika*. So although it is difficult to be certain about what Kapila wrote, Sānkhya is generally identified with Ishvarakrishna's philosophy, which is spiritual but atheistic. Kapila apparently says

that God cannot be proved to exist, and that the assumption of God's existence is unnecessary to Sānkhya. The argument as to whether Sānkhya is essentially atheistic continues. Its earliest roots are found in the Vedic hymns, but it seems reasonable to accept its claim to be based on ideas in the *Upanishads*. The later *Upanishads*, the law-manual *Manu*, the *Mahābhārata* and the *Bhagavad Gītā* all show knowledge of Sānkhya as a philosophical system, but in most cases God seems to be part of the equation. Radhakrishnan speculates that Ishvarakrishna's predecessors in the early Buddhist era may have attempted to argue on purely rational grounds against the Buddhists and come to the conclusion that God could not be proved. His view is that Sānkhya was probably originally theistic. Certainly it later became so: the influential sixteenth century Sānkhya writer Vijnānabhiksu also accepts the existence of God, as does the Yoga philosophy that develops from Sānkhya. The influence of the *Gītā* alone would tend to make later Sānkhya thought accept God. Nevertheless, the fact remains that Sānkhya in its pure classical phase does seem to have been atheistic. Of all the orthodox Hindu philosophies Sānkhya is undoubtedly the closest to unorthodoxy – in many ways its ideas resemble those of Jainism. The unorthodox systems argue not against Sānkhya, for the most part, but against Mīmāmsā.

Sānkhya enumerates 25 categories of existence, of which the first is the *purusha* or spirit and the other 24 aspects of *prakriti* or nature. These are too complex to enter into here, but Sānkhya is a dualistic philosophy, the division between *purusha* and *prakriti* being much more fundamental than any of the other subdivisions. *Purusha* is the root word for the English 'person' but it also carries a masculine connotation, whereas *prakriti* is generally thought of as female, as in Mother Nature. One important Sānkhya allegory is of *prakriti* as a dancing-girl who displays herself to those who are interested and withdraws from those who are not. When *purusha* comes into contact with *prakriti* the insentient nature of the latter is animated and given shape, and the cycle of life begins. Liberation is effected through the analytical realization of the difference between these two – between what is conscious and what is inanimate. It is our ignorance that binds us, while knowledge is the route to freedom. An unusual characteristic of the Sānkhya system is that the *purushas* are at once the eternal self and multiple entities. While multiple individual souls (normally called the *jiva* in India) are easy to conceive of, a universe with millions of eternal *purushas* is more problematic.

An important point to understand here is that in Sānkhya, as in much of Hindu thought thereafter, the intellect or *buddhi* is counted not as *purusha* but as *prakriti*. A key error, according to Sānkhya, is to confuse the self or *purusha* with *buddhi*. Because the insentient *Prakriti* is responsible for the creation of the entire psychophysical organism, Sānkhya views all individuals as identical mechanisms. The apparatus of mind is animated by consciousness, but is not that consciousness itself. Thus the fundamental division is not between mind and matter, which is a quintessentially Western concern, but between the conscious and the mechanical. Another way of looking at Sānkhya philosophy is to regard it as an exploration of subject-object dualism. The subject is conscious, the object unconscious. It is not subjectivism such as we find in the Consciousness-Only School of Buddhism[9], because the reality of the object is not denied. One of the problems facing any system based

upon the subjective is its tendency towards egotism. Sānkhya distinguishes between the conscious divine *purusha* (the true self) and the inanimate *ahankāra* or 'self-sense', which holds together the sense of identity of all the elements of *prakriti*. The *ahankāra* leads the *purusha* to identify with the *prakriti* and its actions.

The second important concept of Sānkhya, that is very influential in Hindu thought, is its analysis of *prakriti* as composed of three qualities or *gunas*. These are *sattva* (light), *rajas* (energy) and *tamas* (darkness). Each plays its part in every aspect of human life: thought under the influence of *sattva* is clear, measured and enlightened; *rajasic* thought is impassioned, agitated and imbalanced; *tamasic* thought is dull, heavy and ignorant. Again, the qualities need to be appreciated for what they are, an aspect of *prakriti*. The conscious *purusha* is beyond the qualities and can observe their interplay dispassionately. The *Bhagavad Gītā* has an extended section on the *gunas* and they are part of the Indian conception of the universe, even to the present day. Each of the *gunas* corresponds to a different type of moral individual: *tamasic* man is slothful and ignorant; *rajasic* man is fiery and impulsive; and *sattwic* man is enlightened and peaceful.

It is an interesting point that whereas in the West our habits of thought tend towards dualism – good/evil, mind/body, reason/emotion – the Indian mindset is, in general terms, triformal, seeking in any dualism a third point from which the duality is seen to be unreal. So although we speak of Sānkhya as a dualistic system its legacy is more complex and subtle than this might suggest. The *gunas* were hugely influential and even today are a commonplace idea in Indian society.

PATANJALI
second century BCE?

The name Patanjali is a pseudonym and may belong to several individuals who contributed to the literature on Yoga and other subjects. Patanjali is credited with two great works, the Yoga-sūtras and the Mahabhashya ('great commentary'), which is a defence of the grammarian Pānini against his critic Kātyāyana. It is probable that these two works are by different authors. Even the Yoga-sūtras, which we will consider here, are regarded as being the product of several hands, with the earliest being composed in the second century BCE and the latest around the fifth century CE.

As author of the Yoga-sūtras, Patanjali is the greatest figure in the Yoga system, which is related to and traditionally twinned with Kapila's Sānkhya philosophy. Yoga is less theoretical, however, and to Kapila's conception of knowledge as a means to liberation adds physical and mental disciplines. Patanjali also assumes the existence of a personal, all-powerful and all-knowing God and gives four traditional Yogic proofs for God's existence. Liberation, as with Sānkhya, is effected by disentangling the self from its identification with the psychophysical organism and understanding the separate natures of *purusha* or conscious self and *prakriti* or unconscious nature. The process is very different, however, and involves not only reasoning but also the disciplining of the attention so that an intuitive realization is arrived at.

Patanjali's introduction of God to the atheistic or agnostic Sānkhya system is intriguing. God is not necessary to Yoga, but Patanjali rather generously says that by devotion to and meditation on the eternal, infinite deity an individual may achieve liberation by an easier route than the arduous exercises and disciplines of Yoga.

According to both Sānkhya and Yoga, the first step in the downward evolution of man is *buddhi* (sometimes also called *chitta*) or intellect or reason. Everything else within man (the senses, the body, etc.) is a modification of reason, which should be understood not as a purely logical function but as Plato used it, with certain emotional, physical and even mystical aspects. Thus, because Yoga gives the practitioner mastery over the reason – which is the foundation of the mental and physical world – the Yogi can develop apparently supernatural powers. Patanjali describes these but cautions against them as a distraction.

Although the popular conception of Yoga is as a system of exercises, its purpose is to refine attention. Patanjali's eight steps towards completely focussed attention include bodily postures and breathing exercises as the third and fourth steps, but also include self-restraint, good conduct and various stages of meditation. The final deliverance of the Eightfold Path is the complete cessation of the activity of the intellect. Even the eighth stage, Samadhi, in which the identification of the mind with the object of attention is total, needs to be transcended as here the mind is still taken with the object.

The influence of Yoga, like Sānkhya, is very broad. In the wider sense of the term, 'Yoga' can be used to describe a 'way', as in the *Bhagavad Gītā* where, for example, Jnāna-Yoga is 'the way of knowledge' and Karma-Yoga is 'the way of action'. Even in the restricted sense of a system of exercise or meditation it is found in both Hindu and Buddhist traditions.

Yoga Meditation

JAIMINI
c. 400 BCE

Perhaps the earliest recognizable Hindu philosophy is Pūrva-Mīmāmsā (literally 'Study of the Earlier [part of the Veda]'), which is thought to have developed in its early form between 1500 and 500 BCE. Whether or not it did pre-date the other schools is a matter of debate, but it makes logical sense to regard the Pūrva-Mīmāmsā as the earliest because the subject of its study is the older parts of the Veda[10]. The Vedānta philosophy is sometimes known as Uttara-Mīmāmsā ('Study of the Later [part of the Veda]'). For simplicity, however, 'Mīmāmsā' will refer here to the Pūrva-Mīmāmsā, while 'Vedānta' refers to Uttara-Mīmāmsā.

Mīmāmsā is an Activist philosophy, which means that it regards action as the primary reality of the universe. Accordingly, it is concerned mainly with *dharma* – duty or right action – as opposed to contemplation. Only through continual observation of *dharma* and correct performance of ritual can man reach heaven. This associates the Mīmāmsā with the Brahmins, because the sacrifices and rituals can only be carried out under their auspices. Although Jaimini, who lived around 400 BCE, inherited perhaps a millennium of philosophical speculation, he is generally regarded as the father of Mīmāmsā. He codified and developed its ideas in his Pūrva-Mīmāmsā Sūtra. Jaimini attacked the view of an earlier Mīmāmsā scholar, Bādari, who held that the injunctions of the Veda were to be carried out regardless of their results. His view, and that of Mīmāmsā after him, was that the Vedic rituals were designed specifically to allow their performer to reach heaven. The Vedas propound a life of action and ritual. Statements in the Vedas that contain injunctions to act are therefore treated by Mīmāmsā analysis as primary, and those that do not are secondary. The lowest class of *shudras*, as well as those outside the caste system, are barred from the sacrifices[11].

All of this may sound very much like a particularly ritualistic and hidebound form of religion, but the philosophical aspect of Mīmāmsā is fascinating. Of the various means of discovering knowledge, Jaimini accepts only scripture (that is, the Veda) as authoritative on the subject of *dharma*. Interestingly, although Jaimini claims that the Veda is not written by a human author, he does not claim that it is the word of God. His view is that 'the relation of the word to its meaning is eternal'. The scriptures, articulated in the pure Vedic Sanskrit, are perfect and unassailable truth. The sound of the words and their meanings and the effect of hearing them are inextricably linked forever. Any word carries its meaning within it; if we do not know the word and understand it on first hearing, this is due to our own deficiency. Even apparently inarticulate sounds – noises – are said to be letters, each with its own Vedic meaning. The theme of the relationship between the fabric of the universe and *shabda* (which means 'sound' and also the 'testimony' of others or of the Veda) is one that will recur throughout Hindu thought down to the present day.

From the Mīmāmsāka emphasis on ritual develops an intriguing Activist theory of linguistics: the verb is the main part of the sentence, and the primary form of the verb is the optative form commanding one to undertake an action, such as a ritual or sacrifice. Closely related to Mīmāmsā in this respect, although more extreme, is the Nairukta or Lexiconist philosophy that regarded the Ātman, the only reality, as a kind of eternal activity: the Great Verb in the sentence or book of the universe.

Jaimini wrote at a time when opposition to his culture was growing … the Brahmin monopoly of religion was unacceptable to those who had spiritual leanings but were debarred from taking part in Brahmin ritual.

Mīmāmsā is the most orthodox of the Hindu philosophies and it is mainly against the ideas of Jaimini's predecessors that the unorthodox schools such as the Buddhists, Jains and Chārvākas directed their early attacks. It is easy to see why: the Brahmin monopoly of religion was unacceptable to those who had spiritual leanings but were debarred from taking part in Brahmin ritual. The *Upanishads* – the earliest of which, at least, pre-date Jaimini – are similarly unimpressed by the ritualised culture of the Veda and attempt to supersede it. Jaimini wrote at a time when opposition to his culture was growing, from both within and without. His work can therefore be seen as an attempt to clearly define the practices of the old Vedic culture and to defend it from

opposition. All of these factions developed arguments in opposition to Mīmāmsā, and the friction probably contributed much; not only to their development but also to Mīmāmsā itself and to subsequent Hindu philosophies.

The relationship of Mīmāmsā to Vedānta is interesting, for while the former regards action as the means to liberation, Vedānta tends to favour contemplation. The analogy with Christian debates about faith versus good works is a tempting one. With respect to action, Vedānta agrees with Jaimini's *bête noir*, Bādari that it should be carried out without regard for results. The first Vedāntin text, that of the Brahma Sūtras, was written by **Bādarāyana**, regarded by some scholars as a near contemporary of Jaimini. Whereas Jaimini is concerned with right action and Ātman (the individual soul who will receive the heavenly reward for its sacrifices), Bādarāyana's main concern is the nature of Brahman or ultimate reality, the universal form of God. Mīmāmsā does not regard Vedānta as a philosophical enemy such as Buddhism, however. Vedānta is cited by the Mīmāmsākas as useful for understanding the Ātman.

Jaimini's successors are Sabara, who wrote a commentary on Jaimini's work in about 400 CE, and Kumarila Bhatta and Prabhakara, two philosophers from around 800 CE who commented on both Jaimini and Sabara, each thus founding a different school of Mīmāmsā philosophy. Prabhakara also supports Bādari, but his was to be a less popular branch of Mīmāmsā than was that of Kumarila. Kumarila is traditionally said to have been instrumental in the final defeat of Buddhism in medieval India, but this neat end to the struggle between Mīmāmsā and unorthodoxy seems to be an invention.

BĀDARĀYANA
first century CE?

An indication of the prestige of Bādarāyana, sometimes known as Vyāsa, is that he is traditionally conflated with the mythical sage Vyāsa who compiled the Vedas, the Mahābhārata, the Purāna and other sacred texts. However, as the name Vyāsa means simply 'compiler' this may be the source of the confusion. The historical Bādarāyana lived possibly in the first century CE[12] and was the author of the Brahma Sūtras, or Aphorisms on Brahman. Of his life almost nothing is known but he seems, unusually, to have been a layperson rather than a Brahmin.

Although the Brahma Sūtras are sometimes spoken of as one of the three great pillars of Hinduism, together with the *Upanishads* and the *Bhagavad Gītā*, they are better seen as the founding work of Vedānta philosophy. The Brahma Sūtras are also known as the Vedānta Sūtras because they principally comment on the *Upanishads*, which are the 'Veda-anta' or that which comes at the end of the Vedas. There is a possible reference to the Brahma Sūtras in the *Bhagavad Gītā* (XIII, 4), but most scholars believe that the *Gītā* pre-dates Bādarāyana.

Like the Vedas, the Brahma Sūtras are better known in India by their reputation than through reading them for themselves. A sūtra is a concise aphorism, written in unbelievably dense and economical language. One result of this brevity is that it is almost impossible to understand the Brahma Sūtras without a commentary. Bādarāyana assumes the reader (or perhaps listener) to have an intimate knowledge of the Vedas and the *Upanishads* as well as contemporary philosophical discussions, and it may be that the intention is for them to remain mysterious to anyone without a well-versed Brahmin teacher to instruct them. The entire work is only 555 sūtras long and could be printed in just a few pages, but commentaries can be vast. The English translation of **Shankara's** commentary is some 900 pages long. Bādarāyana quarries a coherent philosophy out of the bedrock of the Hindu tradition, while simultaneously attacking rival views from other contemporary and traditional schools. But whereas Shankara's commentaries are appended to a particular text, Bādarāyana considers the entire scriptural and philosophical tradition. Generally, in keeping with the obsessively economical sūtra form, he neglects to say even what part of the tradition he is speaking of.

The first two of the four sections of the Brahma Sūtras are a consideration of the scriptural references to Brahman, showing the Vedic tradition to be non-contradictory and consistent. According to commentators, he expounds his view of Brahman as the first and material cause of the universe and attacks at length the opposing Sānkhya philosophy, with more cursory arguments against, among others, the Vaisesika, Buddhist and Jaina viewpoints. Having established this, he goes on to consider all of the ways in which Brahman is spoken of in the tradition: the blissful one, the being inside, space, *prana*, light, the eater, the internal ruler, the one that is unseen, the infinite and so on. Other sections concerned with more ritualistic aspects are of less interest here.

THE FIRST FIVE BRAHMA SŪTRAS

Athato Brahmajijnasa
Janmadyasya yatah
Sastrayonitvat
Tattu Samanvayat
Ikshaternasabdam

Translation
Now, therefore, the enquiry into Brahman
From which is the origin of this [world],
The scripture being the source [of knowledge]
Indeed, that is its purpose
As perception is not based on scripture.

This translation by the author is as close as possible to the actual Sanskrit. Certainly there seems to be a message about the primacy of scripture over direct perception but more than that is difficult to follow. According to commentators, the opening lines are an attack on the Sānkhya philosophy. I think that the reader can get a sense from this that although much of Hindu philosophy is pleasingly accessible, the Brahma Sutras are not for beginners.

If the *Bhagavad Gītā* is a work of poetry of a devotional and inspirational nature and the *Upanishads* have a mystical turn, the Brahma Sūtras are more purely philosophical in the Western sense. This is why they are known as the Nyāya-Prasthana or logical aspect of the Hindu canon. Bādarāyana was *astika* (orthodox) in that he accepted the absolute authority of the Vedic hymns, the *Upanishads*, the *Bhagavad Gītā* and so on. Taking this as his starting point, Bādarāyana seeks to explain what it is that the scriptures are really saying. In doing so he sets the pattern for the great commentators of the medieval period, but because of the gnomic style of the Sūtras, he himself became the subject of commentary. The earliest known commentary is by Shankara who found in Bādarāyana's great work the ideas of Advaita Vedānta. Subsequent commentaries, often in response, were written by **Rāmānuja**, **Madhva**, Nimbarka, Vallabha and others, all of whom were able to fashion from the Brahma Sūtras a confirmation of their own interpretation of the Vedānta tradition. There are more than a dozen major commentators on Bādarāyana's Brahma Sūtras. Sivānanda, a modern commentator, indicates the prestige of the work when he says that 'if any [teacher] wishes to establish his own cult or sect or school of thought he will have to write a commentary of his own on the Brahma Sūtras. Then only it will be recognised'.

Sivānanda, a modern commentator on Bādarāyana's Brahma Sutras.

THE BHAGAVAD GĪTĀ

Author unknown, some time between fifth and second century BCE

Lord Krishna imparting the message of the Bhagavad Gītā *to Arjuna.*

The vast epic Mahābhārata tells the story of the war between two branches of the Bhārata family, the Kauravas and the Pāndavas. It is easily the longest work of epic literature in any culture, being, for example, seven times longer than Homer's *Iliad* and *Odyssey*, and three times longer than the Bible. It is a repository of all aspects of Indian culture, history and thought. Far and away its most important section, however, is the *Bhagavad Gītā* or 'Song of the Lord'. It is

not known whether the *Gītā* is an integral part of the Mahābhārata or an interpolation. The *Gītā* is a discussion on the battlefield between Arjuna, the greatest warrior of the Pāndavas, and his charioteer, Krishna. Arjuna sees his friends, cousins and teachers in the enemy lines and protests that he cannot fight against them. It would be better to die than to kill these men. Krishna's advice to him amounts, in its eighteen short chapters, to a complete philosophy.

This is not the place for a detailed account of the philosophy of the *Gītā* and so our main purpose here is to indicate its position in the history of ideas. The *Gītā's* thought is derived from the classical *Upanishads* but different in its emphasis. The principal difference is that it is a more religious work. The new element in the *Gītā* is the ideal of devotion or Bhakti to the Supreme Lord, Ishvara, who turns out to be incarnated as the charioteer Krishna. The traditional view of the relation between the two is that 'the *Upanishads* are the cows, Krishna is the milker, Arjuna the calf, and the nectar-like *Gītā* is the excellent milk'. Some verses in the *Upanishads* are also found in the *Gītā*, in particular those of the *Katha Upanishad*, suggesting that the *Gītā* may pre-date that and other of the principal *Upanishads*.

Strictly speaking the *Gītā* is not classed by Hinduism with the great *Upanishads* as *shruti* (heard) or divinely revealed teaching, but as *smriti* (remembered), a lower class of important scripture. Its philosophy is perhaps not quite comparable to the *Upanishads* for richness and speculative daring, being more dogmatic. Despite this, no Indian philosopher or religious thinker can ignore the *Gītā*. The *Bhagavad Gītā* is the most influential book in Indian history. T.S. Eliot ranks it, together with Dante's *Divine Comedy*, as one of the two greatest poems ever written, by which he means that they both combine literary greatness with a consistent and systematic philosophy. Leaving aside their relative literary qualities, there is no doubt as to which is the more important as philosophy. The *Divine Comedy* is a product of medieval Christianity, but the *Bhagavad Gītā* has lost none of its power to surprise and stimulate, shock and console.

Among the orthodox philosophies, the most important for the *Gītā* are the closely allied pair of Sānkhya and Yoga. Kapila is mentioned in the *Gītā* and many important Sānkhya concepts including the *gunas* ('qualities'), *purusha* and *prakriti*, *buddhi*, *ahankāra* and so forth are used. An important early declaration of Krishna's is:

> *In this world there is a two-fold basis [of devotion]*
> *Taught since ancient times by Me,*
> *O Arjuna:*
> *That of knowledge – the yoga of the followers of Sānkhya*
> *And that of action – the yoga of the yogins .*[13]
>
> III, 3.

According to Radhakrishnan this should not be taken too literally as an endorsement of the twinned philosophies of Sānkhya-Yoga. 'Sānkhya' can mean simply 'knowledge' or 'enumeration' and 'Yoga' is used in many different ways throughout the *Gītā*. He would translate

this verse less literally than does Winthrop Sargeant here. Certainly there are significant differences between the Sānkhya-Yoga philosophy and that of the *Gītā*. We will not enter into these here, except to indicate that the Sānkhya is an atheistic philosophy[14], while the *Gītā* is the exact opposite.

The other four orthodox philosophies are less significant for the *Gītā*. The Mīmāmsā in its preoccupation with ritualism is rejected:

> *The Vedas are such that their scope is confined to the three qualities*[15];
> *Be free from those three qualities;*
>
> II, 45.

'Veda' here means the early part of the Veda – the Vedic hymns and the ritualistic Brāhmanas – and not the Vedānta or *Upanishads*. It is not clear whether the founder of Vedānta philosophy, **Bādarāyana**, is earlier or later than the *Gītā*, but of all the six it is the philosophy closest in spirit to that expressed here, simply because, as we have seen, the *Gītā* also draws on Upanishadic thinking.

There are a great many later commentaries on the *Gītā*. The commentary by **Shankara** is now regarded as being probably the work of a later follower, but even so the Advaita Vedānta philosophy is one of the important interpretations of the *Bhagavad Gītā's* meaning. Its main rival, if we disregard the explicitly religious interpretations as being too extreme, is the Vishishta-Advaita of **Ramanuja**. A crux occurs in chapter XII, when Arjuna asks about the relationship between those who worship Krishna as Ishvara or Lord and those who worship Him as Akshara or eternal and unmanifest. This question is vitally important later, because the Advaita view is that Jnāna-Yoga or the 'Way of Knowledge' is the greatest; while the Vishishta-Advaita view is that Bhakti-Yoga or the 'Way of Devotion' is better. Krishna's answer is a model of diplomacy: the devotees are the 'most devoted' and have the easier path,

Krishna

> *But those who honour the*
> *imperishable,*
> *The indefinable, the unmanifest,*
> *The all-pervading and unthinkable,*
> *The unchanging, the immovable,*
> *the eternal,*
>
> *Controlling all the senses,*
> *Even-minded on all sides,*
> *Rejoicing in the welfare of all*
> *creatures,*
> *They also attain Me.*
>
> XII, 3–4.

The most fundamental message of the *Bhagavad Gītā* is not its support for one or other *darshana* or 'view', but the figure of Krishna Himself, who embodies better than any other figure in Indian culture the spirit of universal tolerance: 'however men approach me, even so do I welcome them, for the path men take from every side is mine' (IV, 11).

Thus, even someone who worships another god worships Krishna, and even someone who has lived an evil life can reach the Supreme. Of the ways advocated by Krishna, commentators have distinguished three as the most important. These are the way of *karma*, performing action while renouncing the results of the action; the way of *jnāna*, that of knowledge; and the way of *bhakti*, that of devotion.

NĀGĀRJUNA
c. 150–250 CE

The dates of Nāgārjuna's life are hard to determine, but most scholars place him between 50 and 280 CE. The earliest biography is that by the Chinese translator Kumarajiva in 401 CE. His works are known in Chinese, Tibetan and Sanskrit and although many are undoubtedly the work of others, the historical Nāgārjuna certainly wrote two highly important texts, the *Fundamental Middle Way Verses* (Mula-Madhyamaka-Karika) and *Refutation of the Objections* (Vigrahavyavartani). As such, he is the first major figure of Mahāyāna (Greater Vehicle) Buddhism. Mahāyāna was a reinterpretation that set itself apart from the earlier Buddhism of the Theravāda, which is also known as the Hīnayāna, or Lesser Vehicle. These names signify the view that the Mahāyānists held that their tradition would be able to carry a far wider

populace into the Buddhist community. Within Mahāyāna, Nāgārjuna is the founder of the important Middle Way (Madhyāmika) school. This school takes its name from the idea, central to its teaching, that the **Buddha** treads a middle path between total affirmation and total denial of certain things. Although Nāgārjuna seems to have been earlier than **Vasubandhu**, the central figure in Yogācāra, the other main branch of Mahāyāna Buddhism, philosophically his ideas would seem to be an advance. It may be that Vasubandhu formulated ideas that had been around for many centuries, and that the two systems developed side by side.

Nāgārjuna was influenced by the early Mahāyāna tradition expressed in the Perfection of Wisdom writing, where the idea of *shūnyata* or emptiness is explored. He took the idea much further than anyone had before, however, in making it the whole basis of his philosophy.

The *Mulamadhyamakakarika* is a remarkable document, composed in verse couplets, setting out a philosophy that is both austere and highly fruitful. Its key concept is *shūnyata* or 'emptiness' – Nāgārjuna's philosophy is also known as the Shūnyavāda. Shūnyata is a famously difficult concept but worth spending time to understand. It is variously misunderstood as a denial of the experience of life, or a metaphysical void, or some kind of mystical state. It is none of these, but a technical term used to deny the Hindu philosophical concept of *svabhava* ('self-being' or 'self-existence'). The quality of self-existence is, according to most orthodox Indian philosophers, possessed by the Brahman and by the Ātman or inner self. Some, such as the dualist Sānkhya philosophers (see **Kapila**) hold that nature has a similarly self-existent quality, while the followers of **Chārvāka** seem to have believed that matter alone possessed self-existence. Generally self-existence implies permanence.

Against this, the Buddha claimed that the Brahman, the self and nature were not self-existent but *shūnyata* (empty). Beneath the web of 'dependent origination'[16], of cause and effect, there is emptiness. Nāgārjuna's verses are aimed at bringing the reader to an understanding of the nature of shūnyata:

> *For him to whom emptiness is clear,*
> *Everything becomes clear.*
> *For him to whom emptiness is not*
> *clear,*
> *Nothing becomes clear.*[17]

To this end, Nāgārjuna uses emptiness to undermine everything, not just worldly things or (as he would see it) Hindu misconceptions, but *dharma*, *sangha* (the Buddhist monastic community) and even the Buddha himself and his teaching. All are said to be empty. Thus, on the authority of the Buddha's teaching, the teaching itself is rendered empty and without a lasting basis. 'There is not the slightest difference between cyclic existence [*samsāra*] and *Nirvāna*', he writes.

Having shown *shūnyata* to be the nature of everything, thereby dismantling the Buddhist teaching, Nāgārjuna rebuilds it with his concept that the Buddha taught 'two truths: a truth of worldly convention, and an ultimate truth'. The conventional truth was created by the Buddha out of compassion to help those on the path towards the ultimate truth, but on realization of the ultimate truth the conventional was rendered meaningless. This idea perhaps conflicts with the Buddha's assertion that he had no esoteric teaching, that there was nothing in the 'closed fist of the teacher'. On the other hand Nāgārjuna could argue that the esoteric truth was already present within the exoteric. Although Nāgārjuna's tradition may indeed have influenced **Shankara** in his own use of a 'two truths' theory, it was already explicitly stated in the *Upanishads*[18]. In any case, the two-truths view allows Nāgārjuna to show that although the principle of emptiness does indeed undermine everything, it provides a meaningful way of looking at concepts such as *Nirvāna*. In order to understand the unconditioned reality that *Nirvāna* represents, the concept of *Nirvāna* itself must be shown to be empty, like all other concepts. Only by understanding emptiness as it really is – the Buddha's higher truth – can the Buddhist come to enlightenment.

The subtlety of Nāgārjuna's application of *shūnyata* lies in his adherence to the Buddha's principle of *madhyāmika* – maintaining a middle course between denial and affirmation. Nāgārjuna's 'position' is to take no position. *Shūnyata* should not be seen therefore as a negative principle; it neither completely denies nor completely affirms anything. Its denial is of the lower truth only; its affirmation is of the higher truth only, and cannot be applied in the context of lower truth. Its use is analogous to modern mathematicians' use of irrational numbers such as the square root of -1. Though it is impossible to conceive of *shūnyata*, it proves to be a practical tool for certain otherwise impossible problems.

Nāgārjuna's system is superior in many ways to that of Vasubandhu. While Vasubandhu maintains that the material world is illusory and that consciousness is the fundamental reality, Nāgārjuna calls into question the mind as well. Vasubandhu says that because the physical world is unintelligible, it is unreal. Nāgārjuna says that the mind is itself unintelligible, in the sense that we have no way of knowing it, and therefore it is unreal, empty. Paradoxically, it is the very emptiness of everything that makes things possible. Nāgārjuna argues that in a perfect, real and eternal universe there would be no possibility of change. All of the Hindu systems and the Yogācāra system deal with this by the introduction of an extra element, usually *avidya* (ignorance). In the Sānkhya system, it is the stored-up potentiality of the past actions of the eternal souls that restarts the creation and the play of the *prakriti* (nature)[19]. This extra residue, like a grain of sand in the oyster, causes the evolution of the universe. Nāgārjuna has no need of such an extra element. The universe is empty of self-existence and has only a conditional reality. This is why it is able to change.

The development of Buddhism has been compared to that of British rationalism, moving from the naive realism of Locke, which accepts a common-sense view that the senses give us real information of real things, to the sceptical idealism of Hume, who destroys all certainty. Russell notes that according to Hume's philosophy, if I believe myself to be a poached egg, all that could be said of this view is that it is a minority one. Nāgārjuna's philosophy is open to the same charge. In consistency and rigour it is second to none, but for practicality and as a system to inspire people to Buddhist compassion, it has serious drawbacks.

Nāgārjuna's *shūnyata* is a way of conceiving of the absolute truth or *Paramartha* of which the Buddha spoke, without reducing the absolute to human terms. To all intents and purposes *shūnyata* is the Brahman of the *Upanishads*, the ultimate reality that surpasses understanding. As Radhakrishnan says, 'From our point of view the absolute is nothing. We call it *shūnyam*, since no category used in relation to the conditions of the world is adequate to it.' He also quotes Duns Scotus, 'God is not improperly called nothing.' If *shūnyata* is God, then what has happened to the atheism of the Buddha? By defining the ultimate reality as shūnyata in its essence and *Nirvāna* in its experience, Buddhism creates a conception of God to which no ideas lower than the reality of an absolute, transcendent God will stick. Nāgārjuna's philosophy may be mind-bendingly difficult, but it is faithful to the Buddha's mistrust of metaphysical speculation, unlike the more florid Yogācāra and later elaborations such as the Chinese Huayen. It has affinities in later Buddhism to Zen, but it is much closer to Advaita Vedānta as developed by **Gaudapāda** and Shankara, stripped of its dependence on the Hindu scripture. This is not, of course, a comparison that either the Madhyāmika Buddhists or the Advaita Vedāntins would have enjoyed. Of all the Indians, perhaps only Shankara is of greater importance as a philosopher than Nāgārjuna.

VASUBANDHU
fourth or fifth century CE

Mahāyāna, or Great Vehicle, Buddhism, the most widespread and important branch of the religion, is itself divided into two main sub-branches. These are the Madhyāmika, the central figure of which is **Nāgārjuna**, and the Yogācāra of Vasubandhu. The Madhyāmika is characterized by its basic doctrine of *shūnyata* or emptiness. Yogācāra Buddhism, on the other hand, is monistic (meaning that it believes reality to be one) and idealistic (meaning that it believes the one reality to be the mind).

Vasubandhu is a controversial figure because there is some doubt as to whether the historical account refers to a different Vasubandhu than the one that is important to Buddhism. The traditional account given by Paramartha (499–569 CE), which has been questioned but not

disproved, is that he was the younger brother of a Mahāyānist called Asanga. Asanga perceived his brother's great abilities and feared that he would use them to attack the Mahāyāna. He pretended to be ill and when Vasubandhu returned home to visit him he used the opportunity to convert him to Mahāyānism. Asanga was himself an important thinker, making them one of the very few examples of brother-philosophers[20]. Vasubandhu went on to write commentaries on the Mahāyāna scriptures (he was already credited with a famous commentary on the Hīnayāna text, the *Abhidharma*), including the Perfection of Wisdom verses[21], the Garland Sūtra[22], the *Nirvāna* and the Vimalakirti. He also wrote a number of important texts expounding his Yogācārin ideas.

As has already been said, Yogācāra Buddhism is based on the assumption that the mind is the only true reality. It is thought to have developed out of a criticism of the theories of the two main Hīnayāna (Lesser Vehicle) schools. The first point of view is that the world we perceive is straightforwardly real, which is called naive realism. That is to say, if I see a tree, what I see is a real thing called a tree. The second school believes that the world we perceive is real, but that we have no direct connection with it through perception. That is to say, there is really a tree, which I infer from my visual impression of a tree, but what I see is a mental image, not the tree itself. Vasubandhu's philosophy is an extension of the second Hīnayānist point of view. It is not a great leap from the idea that our perceptions merely relate to external reality, to the view that there is no external reality. Both Hīnānyanist views

Vasubandhu with his brother Asanga.

are dualistic in that they believe in the reality of both the mind and of the world. Vasubandhu argues on the other hand for a monistic view in which the only reality is the mind. This is close to the idealism of Berkeley. I may have a perception of an apparent tree, or imagine a tree, or dream of a tree, but there is no tree. Another name for Yogācāra is Vijnāna-vāda, the Consciousness-ism. A simple formulation of its philosophy is that 'the world is entirely intellectual'.

Vasubandhu argues that we may wake up from ordinary waking consciousness and see that the material world is seen to be illusory.

Vasubandhu, like any idealist[23], has the problem of how to account for the apparent consistency and independence of the material world. The comparison is made between the dream and waking state: when we wake up the dreams are seen to have been illusory. Vasubandhu argues that we may wake up from ordinary waking consciousness and see that the material world is seen to be illusory. One of the great critics of Buddhism, **Shankara**, points out that when we wake up from a dream we know that it is illusory because we experience the greater reality of the physical waking world. The question that faces Vasubandhu is this: if we wake up from the ordinary world, what is the greater reality that allows us to see that we had previously only dreamt? One solution would be that there is a higher level of consciousness that is ultimately and eternally real, and which reveals the lower levels as merely conditional realities. This is the solution of the Hindu Vedānta philosophy[24]. However, the **Buddha** declared that everything changes, that permanence does not exist. As an alternative, Vasubandhu proposes a complex structure of the mind, as follows.

Vasubandhu distinguishes eight types of consciousness, the most fundamental of which is the great 'storehouse of consciousness', the alaya-Vijnāna. The *alaya* corresponds to the unconscious of Freudian psychology. In our unenlightened state we are aware of only a tiny proportion of the storehouse; the rest is unconscious. Within its storehouse all knowledge exists, but beyond the reach of ordinary awareness. It serves to explain the operation of *karma*: the consequences of our mental actions are stored in the *alaya*, waiting the right time to re-emerge. Underlying the *alaya* is the ultimate reality of *tathata*, the true nature. The *alaya* is the tathata with the addition of *avidya* or ignorance.

The *tathata* is rather like the idea in the *Mandukya Upanishad* of *prajna*, the undifferentiated consciousness of deep, dreamless sleep. There is mere consciousness without duality, 'one without a second'. The experience of the *tathata* is what falsifies the lower consciousness of illusion, the skandha-Vijnāna. The practice of Yoga is advocated to cleanse the consciousness of its defilement by the *skandhas* or elements of illusory existence. When the consciousness rises out of its preoccupation with the material world and rests in mere consciousness without subject or object, then the world of ordinary consciousness with all of its troubles and suffering is transcended. The seeds of past actions within the *alaya* are then allowed to play themselves out and are not replaced with new ones, liberating the soul from rebirth. *Nirvāna* is the state of dwelling in reality and is defined negatively as the cessation of ignorance and false perception.

Siddhārtha Gautama

It is a good question as to whether this theory really provides an alternative to the Vedāntin metaphysics, or merely conceals the same old answer. Just as the Aristotelian cosmology adopted by the Muslim thinkers seeks to finesse the problem of how God creates by proposing a hierarchy of divine agents[25], Vasubandhu's philosophy seems to be based on a non-Buddhist Brahman or ground of reality, with which the self or Ātman can be united. As Radhakrishnan writes, 'The philosophical impulse led the Yogācārins to the *Upanishad* theory, while the Buddhist presuppositions made them halting in their acceptance of it.' It is only fair to comment that the Buddha's own teaching does not rule out Yogācārin metaphysics. He refused to speculate on metaphysical matters, but hinted at one point at an 'unoriginated' ground of existence, a realm to which *Nirvāna* promised escape. If we understand the Buddhist critique of self, God and absolute reality to be an attack on our psychological understanding of such concepts, then they are not denied. It is not that there is no self, but that being the self is radically different from thinking about it. Such an interpretation could not be described as orthodox Buddhism, but as discussed in the chapter on Buddha, it seems the only philosophically reasonable view.

Ironically for a system that is aimed at bringing us to a state of pure consciousness of nothing at all, the Yogācāra philosophy of Vasubandhu has an elaborate complexity that is only hinted at in the foregoing sketch. It foreshadows the still greater complexity of the Chinese Huayen system[26] and is in many ways an admirable psychological picture that foreshadows developments over a thousand years later in the West. But as Vasubandhu says, the very idea that 'all this is perception only' is itself an idea. The final deliverance of Yogācāra is to move beyond the ideas presented by its philosophy to the experience of reality.

GAUDAPĀDA
d. c. 700 CE

The first of the major commentaries on the *Upanishads* is the *Karika*, or Verses, of Gaudapāda on the *Mandukya Upanishad*. **Shankara** speaks of Gaudapāda as his teacher Govindapada's teacher, but he may have died almost two hundred years before Shankara. Not much is known about Gaudapāda the man, although it is conjectured that he may at one time have been a Buddhist. Certainly, his thought and language owe much to Buddhist works, although as we will see he adapted them to the Advaita (non-dual) Vedānta philosophy.

Gaudapāda was the pioneering example for Shankara's method of evolving philosophy by commentating on the scriptures. Indeed, Shankara wrote a commentary on the *Karika* itself, including it as part of his commentary on the *Mandukya*. The *Karika*, which is written in the Shloka verse-form consisting of sixteen-syllable couplets that is also found in works such as the *Bhagavad Gītā*, is the first clear statement of Advaita Vedānta.

One important teaching in Gaudapāda's philosophy is *ajata* (non-becoming). Gaudapāda denies the idea of creation: the universe is not a play, or the will of Brahman, or a divine illusion, but simply the unchanging nature of Brahman: 'what desire can one have whose desire is always fulfilled?' He is also a proponent of *vivarta* (illusionism). The universe is an illusion born out of ignorance, so vast and entrancing that even the Brahman is, apparently, taken in. Gaudapāda says, 'This is the Maya [illusion] of that God by which He Himself is deluded'. This surprising statement is one which Gaudapāda is compelled to make as a consequence of his radical non-dualism: because there is only one unchanging reality, the person that is suffering from the delusion is, in some sense, the Brahman. Most thinkers after Gaudapāda have regarded this as too extreme. Radhakrishnan in *Indian Philosophy* sums up this criticism of Gaudapāda when he says:

> *The theory which has nothing better to say than that an unreal soul is trying to escape from an unreal bondage in an unreal world to accomplish an unreal supreme good, may itself be unreality.*

Shankara's explanation is that the delusion of the Brahman is only an apparent one: the most important illusion is not the *maya*, but the illusion that He is in fact fooled by it. In this he departs from the view of Gaudapāda.

It is interesting that Gaudapāda should have chosen the *Mandukya Upanishad* as the basis of his commentary. Among all the classical *Upanishads* the *Mandukya* is the most purely abstract, its twelve short verses encapsulating a philosophy of static, eternal majesty in which the entire universe is the primal sound AUM, which is Brahman. By contemplating this single word the aspirant may attain enlightenment. 'Mandukya' is generally translated as 'the teaching of Manduk', but a more poetic translation is 'the frog', because with three jumps a frog can go from the parching heat of the day (representing the illusion of life) to the cool deeps of the water (representing the peace and joy of knowledge). These three jumps are the three letters of AUM, representing respectively the states of waking, dreaming (or thinking) and deep sleep. Understanding any one of these brings great benefits; understanding the Primal Word in full brings liberation, which corresponds to a fourth state known as *Turiya*. The *Upanishad* represents a kind of auditory equivalent to Plato's great vision of the universe from beyond time in the Timaeus. It is worth noting that we do not find in the Eastern tradition such a preponderance of visual metaphors for knowledge as in the West. The *Mandukya Upanishad* is one of the key texts expounding the Hindu idea of God not as light (*jyotir*), but as sound (*shabda*).

The short Upanishadic text is the basis for Gaudapāda's *Karika*, which, though concise and pithy, is almost twenty times as long. In fact, only the first chapter is a direct commentary, the remainder being a remarkably clear and readable exposition of early Advaita Vedānta. The fourth and longest chapter, consisting of 100 shloka-verses, is entitled Alatashantiprakarana, which means, 'Quenching the Firebrand'. This is a common Buddhist illustration: just as a firebrand moving in the dark appears as an arc, so consciousness appears to vibrate between subject and object. When realisation of the truth occurs, all objects disappear and the consciousness shines by itself, illuminating nothing as there is nothing other than itself to illuminate. Arriving at this state, the individual should pretend to be yet ignorant, but will naturally live modestly and with restraint. Gaudapāda argues throughout the *Karika* that the waking and dreaming states are equally illusory: when we are awake we see

things that we cease to see on sleeping, and vice versa. Because Gaudapāda holds reality to be permanent and unchanging, this demonstrates their illusory nature.

In the closing *karikas* Gaudapāda makes repeated use of the word 'buddha', meaning, 'awakened', finally stating:

> *The knowledge of the awakened man [a 'buddha'], who is all-pervasive, does not extend to objects; neither do individual souls reach out to objects. This view was not expressed by the Buddha.*

Gaudapāda has throughout the *Karika* made use of Buddhist terminology and arguments. Here, in the penultimate verse, Gaudapāda protests that his philosophy is not Buddhism. Just as the **Buddha** questioned Hindu terminology (for example, he compared a 'true Brahmin' who showed fine qualities to one who was merely born in a Brahmin family), Gaudapāda contrasts a true buddha or 'awakened one' with the historical Buddha whose knowledge, he implies, was incomplete. In Gaudapāda's view the knowledge of one who is awakened is of the self, the subject, as opposed to objects. The emptiness expounded by Buddhists such as **Nāgārjuna** finds its parallel in Gaudapāda's negation of objective reality. But whereas the Buddha declined to discuss the nature of *Nirvāna*, Gaudapāda states that it consists in a consciousness that corresponds to reality, that is, an awareness that no longer reaches out to illusory objects but rests in the contemplation of itself: in his words 'a knowledge that is comparable to infinite space'.

SHANKARA

c. 700–750 CE

to write commentaries on Vedantic literature, most notably on some of the *Upanishads* and the Brahma Sūtra of **Bādarāyana**. Other than this, his oeuvre is extremely doubtful: a vast literature is credited to Shankara, but modern scholarship based on linguistic research regards much of it as being the later work of others. His successors at four monasteries in India over the past 1200 years are known as 'Shankaracharyas' (Shankara-teachers) which, added to the relative disregard in India for historical dates and persons, perhaps explains the

'Brahman is truth, the world is untruth, the individual self is not different from the Brahman.'

Shankara was born, according to tradition, in the south Indian region of Kerala. One tradition dates his birth to 788 CE, but some experts now believe he was born almost a century earlier. As a teenager he is said to have resolved, despite his mother's opposition, to become a Sannyasin monk. He travelled to Badrinath, where he became the disciple of a sage called Govindapada. Not much is known of Govindapada, but he was a follower in the tradition of **Gaudapāda**, who wrote the first known Upanishadic commentary, his *Karika*, on the *Mandukya Upanishad*. Following the example of Gaudapāda, Shankara went on

great bulk of Shankarist works. Among the questionable texts are his commentary on the *Bhagavad Gītā*, his Vivekacudamani (Crest-Jewel of Wisdom) and many devotional hymns. Despite this, Shankara's philosophy is one of remarkable clarity and consistency.

Shankara lived in a time of flux for Indian culture. Of the unorthodox systems, Jainism seems to have been at its height, while Buddhism, as reported by a Chinese visitor of the time, was in obvious decline. Of the orthodox systems, Mīmāmsā with its emphasis on ritual failed to satisfy either emotionally or intellectually. Brahmanism, the old religion based upon the Veda, was beginning to give way to Hinduism as we know it today, with the rise of Saivism (worship of Siva), Vaishnavism (worship of Vishnu), Shaktaism (Goddess worship), and of a

Siva the destroyer, the most powerful god of the Hindu pantheon and one of the godheads in the Hindu Trinity.

thriving culture of temple-worship. Shankara's aim was to revive the study of the Vedānta or *Upanishads*, founded by Bādarāyana and continued by Gaudapāda,

and to steer Indian culture away from the influence of the later works such as the Purānas. At the same time it would be totally wrong to regard Shankara as an opponent of tradition. His view of the Indian orthodox religion of the earlier part of the Veda is the same as that expressed in the *Upanishads*: profound respect, mingled with a far greater respect for pure philosophy.

Shankara's philosophy purports to be no more than a transmission of that of the *Upanishads*, the Vedānta. This is, in one sense, perfectly true. Radhakrishnan in *Indian Philosophy* quotes Jacob, 'It may be admitted that if the impossible task of reconciling the contradictions of the *Upanishads* and reducing them to a harmonious and consistent whole is to be attempted at all, Shankara's system is about the only one that could do it.' It is not that Advaita Vedānta is the philosophy of the *Upanishads*, but that it is the most consistent philosophy that could be derived from them. The only serious rival to this claim is the view of Rāmānuja, whose Vishishta-Advaita or 'Qualified Non-Dualism' emphasises the devotional and theistic elements in the *Upanishads*. Most scholars regard Rāmānuja's view, examined in the next chapter, to be a valid extrapolation of the *Upanishads*, but closer still to that of the *Bhagavad Gītā*. Although Shankara's philosophy owes something to the Madhyāmika Buddhism of Nāgārjuna, his debt is far less than that of Gaudapāda. The charge that Advaita philosophy is 'purified Buddhism' or 'secret Buddhism' is not justified in Shankara's case. Both Buddhism and Advaita bear strong resemblances to the *Upanishads*, but Shankara's link to the wider Hindu culture is strong and genuine.

The central tenet of Shankara's system, Advaita, means literally not-two or non-duality. 'Advaita Vedānta', the name of his philosophy, therefore means the non-dualistic interpretation of the Vedantic tradition. Advaita Vedānta has been hugely influential down to the present day and has in the past two centuries assumed a pre-eminent position in India, partly due to its adoption by Western thinkers. This fact tends to obscure the existence of alternative forms of Vedānta and of the other Indian philosophies. The power and appeal of Advaita Vedānta principally arises from the clarity of its essential doctrine. It depends on a handful of pithy statements, all of which are taken from the *Upanishads*. The positive aspect is 'sa Ātman tat tvam asi' ('you [Brahman] are that self') or 'aham Brahmasmi' ('I am the Brahman'); the negative is 'neti, neti' ('not this, not that'), meaning that nothing that is experienced is the Brahman. Shankara's genius was to apply these ideas rigorously. His doctrine can be summarised in the sentence 'Brahma satyam, pagan mithyā, jīvo Brahmaiva nāparah' ('Brahman is truth, the world is untruth, the individual self is not different from the Brahman.'). A story told of Shankara as a boy communicates something of the attractive drama of Advaita Vedānta. Some boys were arguing over how many seeds were in a melon. Shankara said that the number of seeds in this melon was equal to the number of gods that created the universe. When the melon was cut open, it was found to contain only one seed.

From Gaudapāda Shankara took the idea of *vivarta* or illusionism, the idea that all of apparent existence is an illusion (*Maya*) or dream founded on ignorance. He also made use of Gaudapāda's concept of a higher and a lower level of truth or knowledge. Shankara develops this scheme, however, distinguishing three levels: lowest of all is the world of illusion, as when we mistake a coil of rope for a snake; next is the world of everyday appearance, as when we recognise the rope for what it really is; and finally there is the ultimate reality of the Brahman. Shankara's view is that with the recognition of a higher level of truth the lower level is totally cancelled out, or sublated (*bādha*). This means not only that an error has been corrected, but also that the reality of the previous, lower truth is utterly rejected in favour of the latter, new truth. The dramatic shift between each of the three levels of reality is altogether more radical than is found in, for example, Plato's four-level reality in *The Republic*. Whereas for Plato a physical body's shadow or reflection tells us something of the appearance of that body, and the body in turn is a 'shadow' of its 'form' or 'idea', for Shankara there is no such relationship. A lower level may indeed lead on to a higher, but when the higher is manifest, the lower is discarded. The classic example of a rope that is mistaken for a snake is useful in illustrating this. When the rope is seen as it is, the fear and ideas associated with a snake are of no further use. In just this way, we are to understand the realization of the non-dual nature of the Brahman and the *jiva* or individual soul. Following the recognition of the reality, there is no reference back to the knowledge of the apparent duality that preceded and led up to it.

The evidence that Shankara's work includes a number of interpolations by other Shankara-Teachers serves to clarify certain issues. The details of this controversy are beyond the scope of this introduction, but just to give an example, in the commentary on the *Isa Upanishad* 'Shankara' imports an additional negative 'a-' into verse 14, blandly remarking that this meaning fits better with his interpretation. A subsequent commentator from a rival tradition remarks sarcastically, and with some justice, on his 'unprecedented skill in grammar'. The general view of Shankara's scholarship is that it is generally careful and accurate, as well as being characterised by a vision and subtlety unrivalled in Indian thought. Shankara's commentaries are an impressive achievement, and were a benchmark against which subsequent Vedānta thinkers tested their mettle.

Shankara is also said to have travelled extensively in India. He seems to have focussed his initial efforts on rural areas as the cities were strongholds of rival philosophies. His commentaries reflect this, being punctuated with semi-dramatised debates between Shankara and an objector, and there are many stories of Shankara taking on and defeating local pundits, who by tradition were then bound to become his disciples. This custom gave Shankara, who was a supreme debater, the opportunity to spread his doctrines across India. His most famous victory in debate won him his greatest disciple and interpreter, Sureshvara, who was then appointed as the head of a monastery or *ashram* he founded at Sringeri. Shankara's work in founding monasteries was socially important because it satisfied the need of those Hindus wishing to retreat from the

Shankara and his disciples.

world. Again, many people with this bent would previously have been drawn towards Buddhism. He went on to found similar monasteries at Puri, Dvaraka and Joshimath. These four centres still exist

By rooting his philosophy in the Vedic tradition Shankara was able to exert a much broader and deeper influence, emotionally, intellectually and politically than would otherwise have been possible.

today, led by sages known as Shankaracaryas (Shankara himself is sometimes known as Adi Shankara, the first Shankara) who are acclaimed as Jagadgurus, or 'World Teachers'.

It is worth mentioning here Shankara's contemporary Bhāskara, who was concerned to re-establish the importance of the traditional Brahminical *dharma* or rule of life against the potentially corrosive effect of otherworldly Advaita. Bhāskara was the greatest proponent of the philosophy known as Bhedābheda: the view that God is both divided in manifestation in the world, and non-divided. The analogy is with the waves of the ocean, which are real, although part of a greater reality, i.e. the ocean. If the world is an aspect of God rather than an illusion founded on ignorance, then our

behaviour in it is highly significant. Shankara was able to defeat this doctrine on both logical and theological grounds, but it is an interesting precursor to the challenge of **Rāmānuja** some three centuries later. Advaita Vedānta is, as outlined by Shankara, essentially concerned with *Jnāna* or knowledge. Although Shankara's achievements included the restoration of Hindu culture and religion to a central place in India, his doctrines are intellectually based. Those for whom the two alternative paths of *Karma* or especially *Bhakti* (respectively, action and devotion) held greater attractions would never be fully satisfied by Shankara's philosophy.

It is possible to make the criticism of Shankara that his philosophy has no need of its reliance on scripture. If there is only one Self, identical with Brahman, it seems absurd to regard knowledge of the *Upanishads* as essential to its self-realization. The self is not a historical concept. It is likely, however, that the importance Shankara places on scripture was part of his overall aim to absorb and build on tradition rather than to emphasise his own importance. In any case, its effect was to inspire a revival of Indian thought through genuine study of its key texts. By rooting his philosophy in the Vedic tradition Shankara was able to exert a much broader and deeper influence, emotionally, intellectually and politically than would otherwise have been possible.

This may be behind the legend of Shankara as we find him within the Shankarist tradition, as a kind of Hindu Renaissance man. More religious than the devotee, more intellectual than the scholar and more heroic than the greatest Hindu generals, Shankara's symbolic significance belies the traditional 32 years of his life. Radhakrishnan's comment that 'in a few years Shankara practised several careers, each enough to satisfy an ordinary

'Love is greater than the law.'

man' has to be taken in the context of later studies that have revealed the extent of confusion about whether a particular 'Shankaracharya' is Adi ('the first') Shankara or not. The Shankarist tradition became synonymous with the re-establishment of Hinduism as the central faith and philosophy of India that took place in succeeding centuries. Thus Shankara, as its figurehead, is supposed to have been a military leader when necessary, defeating enemies who could not be won over by reason. There are many legends surrounding Shankara, including a number of miracles associated with him from boyhood onwards, indicating his dual significance, both as philosopher and as religious figure. Although it is difficult to know what truth there is in such stories, some do seem to provide a useful indication of his significance to India. The most common traditional story told about Shankara has the ring of authenticity. Although a Sannyasin and therefore bound to observe the principle of non-attachment to other beings, Shankara returned to his mother's house in the last days of her life and, after her death, built and lit her funeral fire. This again was a violation of Sannyasin

code, which forbade the kindling of fire. One of Shankara's twentieth century successors, Shāntānanda Saraswatī, related that when challenged by the local orthodox pundits Shankara replied simply, 'Love is greater than law'. In another story Shankara met with a Chandala or Untouchable in the street, from whom he drew back. The Chandala accused him of failure to adhere to his own principles of non-duality, whereupon Shankara composed a hymn with the refrain, 'He who has learnt to look on phenomena in the light of Advaita is my true Guru, be he a Chandala or be he a Brahmin.' Advaita Vedānta does not in itself have a socially radical import, but the idea of there being one Self that is also Brahman is clearly erosive of rigid caste boundaries. This was certainly a legacy of **Rāmānuja** and **Madhva**, each of whom developed versions of Vedānta with more explicit ethical concern.

The tradition of Shankarism has added much over the centuries to what is certainly there in Shankara himself. It is difficult to trace a historical development of Shankarism, but it today includes a substantial ethical element as well as a devotionalism akin to that of **Rāmānuja**. It would be wrong to suppose, however, that Adi Shankara, the first Shankara, has been entirely hidden by the hagiographers and the later Shankaracharyas. His essential doctrine of Advaita, shorn of its religious trappings, has in the past two centuries established itself both as the principal philosophy within India, and as India's main philosophical export. Its influence on the West has been particularly marked.

RĀMĀNUJA
c. 1017–1137 CE

Rāmānuja took **Shankara's** Advaita Vedānta or non-dualism in a theistic direction. In this he was influenced by his upbringing in the Tamil tradition of devotional hymns to the god Vishnu, in particular those of the Alvar Saints. Rāmānuja's life is known to us only through his hagiographers, but legend has it that he was born in a pious Brahmana family and studied with Yādvaprakāsha, a Shankarist teacher. His brilliance was evident early on and showed itself in several instances where he challenged his teacher's interpretations, to the point where he eventually broke with him. Rāmānuja's questioning was, however, based on a deeply felt love for Vishnu, of whom he subsequently had a vision.

Rāmānuja became a temple priest at Kancipuram and was summoned by the great Vaishnavite teacher Yamuna, then on his deathbed, to be his successor at Srirangam. Rāmānuja is also said to have made a 20-year pilgrimage around India in which he displayed his matchless skill in debating with opponents. He converted King Bittideva at Mysore to Vaishnavism (worship of Vishnu), which increased his influence manifold. On his return he continued his work, establishing 74 monastic centres before dying, according to tradition, at the age of 120.

Rāmānuja succeeded in founding a new and powerful form of Vedānta philosophy, Vishista-Advaita, which built on Advaita's strength while making room for a warmer and more devotional approach. The main problem of philosophy for Rāmānuja is not ignorance, as with the more intellectual schools, but unbelief. He disputed with the logical tradition of the Nyāya philosophers (see **Gautama**), for whom the divine is reached through reasoning. Wishing to strengthen faith, Rāmānuja systematically attacked arguments attempting to prove the existence of God. By demolishing such proofs Rāmānuja established his view that Brahman transcends all human reasoning. The parallels with Christian belief are evident, although Rāmānuja's arguments intriguingly foreshadow modern Western rationalist philosophy.

His greatest influence, and also in some ways his greatest adversary, is Shankara. Rāmānuja wanted to establish a philosophy that centred not on knowledge, as in Shankara, but on devotion. According to Rāmānuja's view, the paths of Karma Yoga (the 'way of action') and Jnāna Yoga (the 'way of knowledge') are merely preparations for Bhakti Yoga (the 'way of devotion'). This may seem like a scholastic quibble, but its implications are important and fascinating and will be considered in more detail below. The intellectual underpinning that Rāmānuja lent to Bhakti has been very influential in Indian philosophy. The key to this is his conception of God, not as the infinite transcendent Nirguna ('without qualities') Brahman, but as the manifest Saguna ('with qualities') Brahman. The qualities of Brahman are principally knowledge, consciousness and bliss, and

it is identified in Rāmānuja with the personal God, specifically Vishnu, the sustainer, whose *avatars* include Rama and Krishna. Vishnu and Siva are the two personifications of God that have traditionally attracted the most worshippers in India.

Vishishtadvaita means literally 'qualified non-duality'. Rāmānuja holds that there are three orders of existence: God, soul and matter. This idea he adapted from Bhartriprapanca, a philosopher older than Shankara. Rāmānuja holds that at the level of God, everything is God and there is no

Rama, the seventh incarnation of Lord Vishnu, said to have taken birth on earth to annihilate the evil forces of the age.

other, but at the lower orders the substance of God is 'qualified'. The analogy is with the soul and the body: the body is said to be the servant of the soul, and to have no reality separately from it, and yet it retains its own character as a body. Another important aspect of Vishishtadvaita is that it attributes reality to the world. In this he follows Bhāskara, a younger contemporary of Shankara, who promulgated the view that God was both divided and non-divided (*bhedābheda*), just as the waves of the ocean are real, although part of a greater reality, i.e. the ocean. Shankara had attacked *bhedābheda* on logical grounds, pointing out that it imagined mutually contradictory attributes for the same thing. Rāmānuja resolved this and other problems with *bhedābheda* by arguing that reality does not necessitate independence. The souls are real, but their existence is dependent on God; they are its body. Similarly, the material universe is also real, though dependent. It is important to recognise that there is no duality (as in the Sānkhya philosophy of Kapila) or multiplicity (as in the Vedānta of Madhva) in Rāmānuja's teaching. He must make room for a kind of subject-object relationship to satisfy the need for worship, but his theories adapt non-dualism rather than shatter it. Rāmānuja allows for the possibility of release through unity as described by Advaita, but gives it a secondary position to the pure joy of adoring God in heaven, which is true *moksha* or liberation.

Rāmānuja developed his philosophy by commenting on and re-interpreting the traditional texts of Vedānta including the *Upanishads*, the Brahma Sūtras and, late in life, the *Bhagavad Gītā*. The 'Vedārthasangraha' established Rāmānuja's philosophy with its closely argued examination of apparently contradictory statements in the *Upanishads*. Rāmānuja argued that only Vishishtadvaita could make sense of these contradictions. The most important of Rāmānuja's commentaries is, however, that on the *Bhagavad Gītā*. Despite the difficulty of dating Hindu works, it is certain that the *Gītā* adds something new to what is already present in either the ritual religion of the Veda or the philosophy of the *Upanishads*. That new element is *Bhakti* or devotion. If it was Shankara's genius to perceive the importance of non-dualism for the *Upanishads*, it was Rāmānuja's to expand on the devotionalism of the *Gītā*.

Rāmānuja's interpretation of the *Gītā* is that it puts forward a vision of devotion to the Lord (in this case, Krishna) that is a higher ideal than the self-realisation ('*atma-jnāna*') of pure Shankarism. Brahman is not the Supreme Lord, but is the *atmatattva*, the 'soul-stuff' which is the true nature of a human being. When a human soul realises its identity with the Brahman it becomes purified of its association with lower things such as the body and the individual ego. This stage, which is the highest ideal for Advaita, is merely preparatory for Vishishtadvaita. The soul then becomes fit for the divine vision of the Lord, with whom it has a 'supreme likeness' in the words of the *Mundaka Upanishad*. The love of the soul for God and of God for the soul becomes a self-perpetuating and blissful union, which is the highest heaven. Indeed, Rāmānuja regards self-realisation as a slightly dangerous aim for the average person, who he advises 'to engage in actions without regard for their fruits: let him forget about self-realisation if he would reach his goal[27]'.

Rāmānuja's analysis of the *Gītā* is a powerful

and persuasive one, and is regarded by many scholars as the closest to the intention of its unknown author. It relates self-realisation to the Sānkhya and Yoga philosophies (see chapters on **Kapila** and **Patanjali** respectively), in which the aim is to separate the conscious element in man from the unconscious or natural part, as well as to Vedānta. Rāmānuja was able to demonstrate that devotion to Saguna or manifested Brahman was not of lesser importance, as Shankara had argued, but the final aim of philosophy and religion. His philosophy incorporated that of his predecessors and overlaid it with the devotionalism of his Tamil homeland.

Rāmānuja is generally thought to be the most credible opponent of Shankara. His system is analogous to the mysticism of the Sufis, which like his is devotional and religious in direction[28]. There is some justification for regarding it as the counterpart of Advaita Vedānta: while Shankara eliminates from his system all that is not Brahman absolute, Rāmānuja builds towards a conception of Ishvara through appreciation of his divine qualities. Both approaches are validated by different aspects of the tradition including the *Upanishads*.

Rāmānuja's influence is most clearly seen today in India not in philosophy but in religion. Sri Vaishnavism (Devotees of Lord Vishnu), inspired by him, is still the largest Hindu sect. It derives much of its popularity from Rāmānuja's assertion that anyone, regardless of caste, could reach Vishnu. This alone represents a significant contribution by Rāmānuja, as traditionally the lowest *shudra* caste was barred from many religious activities. The two main centres of Sri Vaishnavism are in Srirangam in the South and Tirupati in the North.

Lord Vishnu

MADHVA
1197–1276 CE

Another branch of Vedānta, increasingly the most prominent of the philosophical systems, was created by Madhva in the thirteenth century. His position is in many ways opposed and antithetical to **Shankara's**, so instead of Advaita Vedānta we have the doctrine popularly known as Dvaita Vedānta, the doctrine of duality. Madhva, who is also known as Ānanda-Tirtha, was acclaimed even while alive as a divine incarnation sent to combat the evil incarnated in Shankara and his allegedly deceptive teaching. Madhva's life story, as traditionally narrated, also contains many parallels with that of Jesus, including miracles such as walking on water and feeding a multitude with loaves and fishes. This is probably due to Christian influences in South India, as we will see.

The *Upanishads* contain several key statements generally thought to confirm non-duality. Madhva held the *Upanishads* to be revealed truth, and yet espoused an opposite view. To do this, he had to interpret the *Upanishads* in a new, and very unorthodox, way. We saw in the chapter on Shankara how he did not scruple to propose alterations to the *Upanishads* to support his own view. Madhva, perhaps following his adversary's example, used similar techniques to reverse the meaning of the key statements of the *Upanishads*. For example 'Sa Ātman tat tvam asi', 'You [the Brahman] are that self', becomes 'You are not that self'. Madhva claims that a negative prefix 'a-' is hidden in the statement, which is indeed not grammatically impossible. The argument is just about feasible, but not widely accepted.

However, from a philosophical point of view the question of correct interpretation is perhaps less important than the reasons behind Madhva's approach. His system is more complex than mere duality and the term Dvaita Vedānta is, though convenient, somewhat misleading. Madhva's followers today prefer the term Tattva-vāda, which means, more or less, Reality-ism, but a more precise term is Bheda-vāda, or Difference-ism. Madhva's essential doctrine of differences is that God (identified with Vishnu), the self and matter are real, separate and different. In addition, there are multitudes of selves and multitudes of material objects, all different and separate. Only Vishnu is independently real, however, while all other things depend for their existence on him. Much of Madhva's thinking is drawn from the Sānkhya philosophy of **Kapila**: Vishnu is the efficient cause of the world, but its

Lakshmi, Vishnu's consort and the goddess of wealth and prosperity, both material and spiritual.

material cause is nature or *Prakriti*, identified with Vishnu's consort Lakshmi. Vishnu's contact with Lakshmi animates the world and sets into motion the three *gunas* or qualities.

Another influence on Madhva is thought to be Christianity. It is generally acknowledged that the apostle St Thomas travelled to India and founded a mission that was still influential in South India in Madhva's time. Because of the tolerance of doctrinal heterodoxy in Indian culture, Christianity could co-exist with and influence Hinduism over hundreds of years, although conversion has never been a large-scale phenomenon. Western readers will easily recognise in Madhva's cosmology – millions of souls, fashioned of common matter but superintended by a transcendent God – echoes of Christianity, even if it has its beginnings in Sānkhya. Intriguingly Madhva also posits a version of predestation that is similar to that developed by John Calvin in sixteenth century Europe, although for different reasons. It is part of the Sānkhya system that at the beginning of a cycle of creation souls start with a certain karmic disposition. The creation is set in motion by the Lord as a mechanism for the playing-out of these dispositions. Madhva's view of souls as particular individuals causes him to imagine their several fates. Some are fated to find liberation from the cycle of *karma* through union with Vishnu in heaven. Others will continue to follow the path of birth, death and rebirth, which is his version of purgatory. Still others – and here we must find Western influence, as he differs from all other Indian thinkers – are bound for eternal suffering and damnation. This vision of the universe is highly mechanistic and has parallels to Western philosophies that emerged with the rise of science. Some commentators have noted that it paradoxically weakens the power of God, who is reduced to a superintendent-like role by the requirement of *karma* to play itself out in individual souls. Like **Rāmānuja**, Madhva argued that devotion and the scriptures was the only true route to God, but he was less antagonistic to logic and provided several proofs for his existence.

VIVEKĀNANDA

1863–1902

In the last 250 years, Indian thought has for the first time been widely available to the West. The most immediately attractive forms were the most sophisticated: Buddhism and Advaita Vedānta. This book is not the place to review the impact of the translations of Indian texts in the late eighteenth and nineteenth centuries on European culture. Suffice to say that practically every major figure in philosophy and the arts active between 1790 and 1850 was an enthusiastic reader of the *Upanishads*, the Buddhist canon, or of Sanskrit literature in translation. The philosopher Schopenhauer's work, to take one example, has been described as a popular version of Buddhism. This trend continued into the twentieth century with figures like the poets T.S. Eliot and W.B. Yeats. What could be regarded as the first wave of Indian influence has considerably abated: modern philosophers, novelists and poets do not these days quote the *Upanishads*. The second wave, which has spread its influence more widely through society, was the arrival in the West of a number of authentic teachers from the Indian traditions. The first, and perhaps most dramatic of these, was Swami Vivekānanda.

The scene for Vivekānanda's appearance was the World's Parliament of Religions in Chicago in 1893. At the age of 30 Vivekānanda took the stage as the Hindu representative and electrified his audience with his account of Advaita Vedānta. A newspaper account of the day called him 'an orator by divine right and undoubtedly the greatest figure at the Parliament.' Vivekānanda had only uttered the words 'Sisters and Brothers of America' when he was drowned out by a two-minute ovation, a reception not given to previous speakers from the Greek Orthodox, Confucian, Buddhist and reformist Hindu Brahmo Samaj speakers. He continued:

> *It fills my heart with joy unspeakable to rise in response to the warm and cordial welcome which you have given us. I thank you in the name of the most ancient order of monks in the world. I thank you in the name of the mother of religions, and I thank you in the name of millions and millions of Hindu people of all classes and sects.*

Vivekānanda's message was not just about the greatness of his own tradition, however:

The present convention, which is one of the most august assemblies ever held, is in itself a vindication, a declaration to the world of the wonderful doctrine preached in the Gītā: 'Whosoever comes to Me, through whatsoever form, I reach them; all are struggling through paths which in the end lead to Me.'

Vivekānanda's message that 'all religions are true' seemed to encapsulate what the conference was about. His powerful oratory and spiritual depth had a power far beyond watery ecumenism. Vivekānanda's personality and thought entranced America. On the one hand, he was a highly educated and talented individual, versed in Western and Eastern thought, acclaimed by a British professor as the most brilliant student he had ever encountered. On the other, he was the favourite disciple of the extraordinary Hindu saint, Ramakrishna, who died in 1886. These two aspects are reflected in the name chosen for Narendranath Datta – his real name – before leaving for America. Vivekānanda means 'the bliss of viveka (reason)'. The combination of intellect and genuine spiritual experience enabled Vivekānanda to deliver a message that resonated widely: 'only the man who has actually perceived God is religious … religion is not in books and temples. It is in actual perception'. After the Parliament he agreed to conduct a lecture tour of the United States, taking to the same gruelling round of lectures in cities and one-horse towns that entertained figures such as Dickens and Wilde. Having travelled widely in the West he returned to a hero's welcome in India. His health was undermined by exhaustion, however, and except for one brief visit to America to open some centres devoted to the study of Vedānta and Ramakrishna, he remained in India, returning to the austere life of the ascetic renunciate monk. The Ramakrishna and Vedānta societies he founded still thrive today, complemented by literally hundreds of other organizations dedicated to understanding and studying Advaita.

We will not consider here the Advaita Vedānta philosophy promoted so successfully by Vivekānanda, which is covered more fully in other chapters. However, it is worth noting the particular emphasis he gave to Advaita, reinterpreting it for the modern era. According to Vivekānanda there are two sources of knowledge: science and the Veda. Science is the knowledge arrived at through the senses, while the Veda is 'that which is known through the subtle, supersensuous power of Yoga'. The Veda is normally regarded as the collection of hymns, rituals and Upanishadic philosophy on which Indian thought is founded[29]. Here Vivekānanda posits a higher, transcendent Veda, analogous to Islamic notions of the Quran and to the Word or logos of Greek philosophy. This transcendent Veda is reflected above all in the Vedānta or *Upanishads*. This is Sanatana Dharma or Eternal Religion. Thus Vivekānanda succeeds in articulating a vision of Hinduism that is both loyal to its own spirit and answerable to the need for a global spiritual faith.

MOHANDAS GANDHI
1869–1948

Gandhi was born in Porbandar, Gujarat, into a political family with deep religious convictions, both Hindu and Jain. His father was prime minister at Porbandar. He was married at 13 and at 19 was sent to England to complete his education and to train as a barrister. He returned after three years in 1891 but was unable to find work in India and in 1893 accepted a one-year post in Natal, South Africa at an Indian law practice. Gandhi's experience there of racial oppression inspired him to political activity and the development of his technique of non-violent protest called *satyagraha*, literally 'holding on to truth'. Gandhi distinguished *satyagraha* from passive resistance, as practised by activists such as the English suffragettes, because unlike them he rejected all violence. He

stayed until 1913, when he returned to India. At that time India was under the Raj, the rule of Britain. The injustice of a piece of British legislation moved Gandhi to take to the political stage once again. He was to dedicate the rest of his life to political struggle and to the cause of Indian independence, called *swaraj* or self-rule. The movement was finally successful, but Gandhi himself fell victim to the deep divisions in India between Hindu and Muslim when he was assassinated by a Hindu fundamentalist.

Members of Gandhi's ashram *gather around his body shortly after his assassination.*

Gandhi's work as a political activist was deeply infused with religion and philosophy. As has already been indicated, there were both Hindu and Jain influences in his upbringing. His Hinduism was essentially that of Advaita Vedānta, the non-dualist philosophy perfected by **Shankara** and which came to be the predominant form of Indian thought. Gandhi's Advaita emphasised truth (*satya*) as opposed to Brahman, perhaps because it carried less sectarian associations. His Truth carries essentially the same meaning: 'Truth alone is eternal, everything else is momentary'. The motto

A crowd watching Gandhi's funeral procession.

adopted by India after Independence shows this influence: 'Satyam eva jāyate na anritam' (Truth alone wins, not untruth)[30]. Gandhi added Jain ethics to the Advaitin philosophy, in particular the principle of *āhimsa*, meaning 'harmlessness' or 'non-violence' or (as he sometimes translated it) 'Love'. Gandhi taught that Love, Truth and God are interchangeable terms. Based upon this, he developed techniques to resist oppression that involved arousing compassion in the oppressor by the acceptance of suffering. Gandhi's assumption was that love, being more fundamental than injustice, would eventually win through.

Essential to Gandhi's work was his personal asceticism, which included the practice of poverty, chastity and spiritual endeavour to cleanse the individual of impurities associated with egotism. Gandhi believed that the best way to promote a philosophy was to be a living example. The lofty ideals of Gandhian philosophy would be impossible if its practitioners, the *satyagrahi*, were subject to fear and personal concern. Imprisonment, abuse and physical suffering could hold no terror to one who had conquered himself.

Another highly important principle for Gandhi was *sarvodaya*, meaning 'the good of all'. Like **Vivekānanda**, Gandhi was aware of, and rejected, the Western nineteenth century philosophy of utilitarianism. Utilitarianism is based on the assumption that to do good to one involves the deprivation of another. Its highest ideal is the happiness of the greatest number, defined materially. For Gandhi, this is an impoverished and 'heartless' philosophy because 'in order to achieve the supposed good of fifty-one percent, the interest of forty-nine percent . . . should be sacrificed'. *Sarvodaya* demands a more creative and compassionate form of accounting for happiness. It includes material prosperity,

Gandhi sitting.

but is primarily concerned with personal self-realization. Gandhi founded several *ashrams* or spiritual centres to pursue the ideals of *sarvodaya*. Politically, it inspired Gandhi 'to wipe every tear from every eye'. It led him to oppose discrimination of all kinds, whether based on race, sex, religion or caste. So, for example, although Gandhi upheld traditional gender roles, he believed that women should be accorded equal honour and respect. Again, Gandhi fought for the rights of the low-caste and the untouchable, who he called the Harijan, 'Children of God'. Again, *sarvodaya* draws on a wide range of Indian ethical traditions, including the universal compassion of Buddhism.

Gandhi's politics and economics were inspired by his philosophy. He rejected the welfare state as an assault on the dignity of every individual's ability to be responsible for themselves. For Gandhi, the state should intervene very little in the lives of the people, but should create conditions for local self-government. The symbol he adopted to represent his ideal of village life was that of the spinning wheel. He opposed rapid industrialization because he saw its ideal of endless economic growth to be inhuman and destructive. Gandhian 'small is beautiful' economics may have seemed backward at one time, but today seem relevant and prophetic.

Gandhi is not an original thinker as such; nor is his religious and philosophical synthesis entirely consistent. But to judge Gandhi on such criteria would be to deny the remarkable achievements of one of the twentieth century's towering figures. He taught leaders like Martin Luther King and Nelson Mandela to oppose and defeat injustice. Even to mention the leading figures of the Communist struggle such as Stalin and **Mao** is to show how important Gandhi was as an alternative: a practical philosophy of life built not on hatred, conflict and division but on love, truth and the good of all.

Part Two

THE
MIDDLE EAST

ISLAM AND
ZOROASTRIANISM

ISLAMIC PHILOSOPHY
INTRODUCTION

*Seeking knowledge
is an ordinance
obligatory upon every Muslim.*

*A man praying and reading the Koran in
Iran.*

The term 'Islamic Philosophy' has a
strange sound to non-Islamic ears. Even
before the recent rise in 'Fundamentalism'
fuelled fresh prejudices against Islam, it
was commonplace in the West to
disregard its contribution to philosophy.
The perception was that its importance
was only as the transmitter of Greek
philosophy onwards to Medieval Europe.
Bertrand Russell's summary in his *History
of Western Philosophy* that 'Arabic
philosophy is not important as original
thought' is typical of an attitude that
existed until recent times. This neglects
the importance of Islamic contributions to
rational philosophy as founded by the
Greeks and – more importantly – the ideas
that were original to Islamic thinkers.

Having said this, the Western ignorance of
Islamic philosophy does reflect a certain
suspicion within the tradition itself.
Muslim philosophers have often had to
argue for the validity of speculative
thought.

The principal flowering of philosophy in
the Arab–Muslim world took place in the
700 years following the death of the
Prophet Muhammad in 632 CE, the period
we examine in this book. There were
three main aspects to Islamic enquiry:
kalam, literally the 'word' of God and, by
extension, theological work based on this;
falsafah, or philosophy; and mysticism, or
Sufism. This tripartite division is a useful
one to bear in mind, even though the line
between *kalam* and *falsafah* is not as
simple as it might seem: *kalam* includes
philosophical aspects, while *falsafah* has
much that Western readers would regard
as theological. For the purposes of this
book, we will regard all three aspects as
fertile sources of new thinking.

A major topic of discussion in the Islamic
world is as to the extent and nature of
knowledge that is necessary to a Muslim.
Advocates of both philosophy and
theology could quote the Quran: 'Seeking
knowledge is an ordinance obligatory
upon every Muslim.'[31] Muhammad in many
places speaks of high regard for

knowledge, but others could counter that the Prophet had also said, 'we seek refuge in Allah from useless knowledge.'[32] The debate as to what knowledge the Prophet regarded, or would have regarded had it come to his attention, as valid and necessary continues to this day. In the early years of Islam much intellectual effort centred on the text of the Quran and, later, on the traditions of reports of the life of the Prophet (the *Hadith)* and the customary practices of Muhammad and his followers. Speculative thought was not encouraged and belief was regarded as more important to a good Muslim. Comparisons with other traditions show that the important founder-figures often focus on ethical matters and discourage speculation. The examples of **Confucius** and the **Buddha** elsewhere in this book show that this is no bar to their successors undertaking such activity.

Indeed, after a time it became obvious to the Muslims that some questions were not dealt with specifically in the traditional sources, and that in its collision with other faiths and systems of thought Islam needed to become more sharply defined. This brought about the development of *kalam* and, later, of the *falsafah* or philosophy that came from the Greeks, whose sophisticated cosmology, metaphysics and logic dominated thought in the Mediterranean region of the time. Greek philosophy, transformed into *falsafah*, gave Islam a structure that allowed it to deal with the challenges of rival thought-systems. The undoubted forefather of Islamic philosophy is Aristotle, but the influence of Plato and the Neoplatonists is also important. In time, some Islamic thinkers would come to regard *falsafah* as equal to or, in some

cases, more important than the scholasticism of *kalam*. This did not mean that the Quran ceased to be the reference point, however. It would be true to say that rational philosophy as such is generally a subsidiary pursuit in Islam, a means to the truth rather than an end in itself. Islamic philosophy set the tone for the Christian Middle Ages and the world of a thinker such as St Thomas Aquinas. Its theology and mysticism, though less directly influential, have much in common with that period in the Western tradition.

Sufism is the third important strand. It seems that there were Sufis already at the time of Muhammad, wool-robed ascetics who made pilgrimage to Mecca and walked around the Ka'ba. Certainly this is the view of the important Muslim historian of the middle ages, **Ibn Khaldūn**. Whether or not this is so, by the time of the main flowering of Sufism it had become a branch of Islam, albeit a highly exceptional one. There are three main schools of thought on the origin of Sufism, insofar as it is not just a natural effusion of spirituality such as is found in many cultures. The traditional Islamic view is that it represents the esoteric or mystical teaching of Muhammad. There is not much evidence for Muhammad as a mystic and, on the face of it, his prophesy was principally concerned with ethical and social issues: how to be a good Muslim and a good person. Also, as we have seen, there is some evidence that Sufis predated Muhammad. However, this view is the one held by most Sufis and there is no decisive evidence against it. The second school of thought holds that Sufism is a development of either Indian or Persian origin as a reaction against Judaeo-Christian religion. Certainly the Indian

Depiction of Muhammed fleeing from Mecca to Medina, where he built his model theocratic state and converted much of Arabia. The Islamic calendar begins with this flight (hegira).

Vedantic philosophy[33] seems to have influenced the later development of Sufism, but it cannot be proved to have been its source. Equally, the Persian theory is unprovable although Zoroastrian elements influenced the Middle-Eastern world in general. Thirdly and finally, there is the view that Sufism sprang from Neoplatonism. This is historically plausible, given the extent of Neoplatonic thought known to the Arab world. Gibbon, in *Decline and Fall of the Roman Empire,* records that seven Neoplatonist philosophers were forced to flee the emperor Justinian to the Persian court in 532 CE.

Whatever its source, Sufism became an integral part of orthodox Islam, especially after the time of **al-Ghazālī**, who was both a Sufi and the greatest Islamic theologian. His views are generally regarded as normative by most subsequent thinkers and his support for

Devout Muslims praying at a mosque in Cairo.

kalam and Sufism was equalled by his attacks on some of the *falsafyah* that preceded him. Al-Ghazālī's great skill and authority succeeded in finding an accommodation between orthodoxy and Sufism, despite certain heterodox elements within the mystic tradition. Sufism has intermittently conflicted with the orthodox throughout history, and this is true to this day with the rise of 'fundamentalist' Wahabism that particularly disapproves of Sufism[34]. Although like *falsafah*, Sufism was persecuted periodically for perceived or actual unorthodox beliefs or practices, it is best seen as an integral part of Islamic history, which makes less sense without its mystic core.

Islam could be seen as a relative latecomer by comparison with its rival religious and philosophical traditions. The Prophet died in 632 CE, between six and eleven centuries after the key figures in most other cultures. But while most of Europe was plunged into its dark age, Islam flourished, founding universities and theological colleges, translating the Greeks and developing its arts and sciences. From a Western point of view, therefore, the importance of Islamic *falsafah* has primarily been the preservation and transmission onwards of the Hellenistic tradition of Plato, Aristotle and the Neoplatonists, principally Plotinus. Although some vestiges of the old Classical civilization persisted in the monasteries on the edge of the Atlantic, it owes much of its survival to the work of Islamic scholars. The rediscovery by the West of the Greek tradition was to have a decisive effect on the development of medieval Christianity in the thirteenth century, and on the proto-science following that period.

The Western perspective emphasises the scholarly translators and Aristotelians and tends to obscure others. The most important Islamic name for the medieval

Scholastic thinkers was **Averroës** (ibn Rushd) for his translation and commentary of Aristotle. **Avicenna** (ibn Sīnā), though also a philosopher, was better known for medical works in the tradition of Galen. Islamic thinkers had influence on a number of other areas, in particular medicine and mathematics. Al-Khwarazmi translated a Sanskrit text in around 830 CE that, translated in Latin in the twelfth century as *Algoritmi de numero Indorum* gave us both the mathematical term 'algorithm' and the 'Arabic' number system, although of course the system is Indian. The Western tradition did not value the thought of the Islamic world for itself and so names such as **al-Ghazālī** and **Ibn Khaldūn** were not westernised. The originality of their ideas has only recently been recognized.

This is not the place for a discussion of Islam as a religion, but a few comments are worthwhile and necessary. Firstly, it should be said that the modern Western perception of Islam as a warlike and intolerant culture is mistaken. It is true that war was an important part of early Islam and inspired the growth of an Empire almost the equal of Rome; but it is wrong to imagine that 'Holy War' was part of the Prophet's message. Rather, it grew out of an Arab culture older than Muhammad in which raiding other tribes was a way of survival. After Muhammad achieved the unification of the Arabs, war on wealthier neighbours was primarily a political and economic rather than a religious aim – a culture that was based on raiding one's neighbours was transferred to a wider stage. It is true that the early Muslim conquests had a religiously inspired ethic of liberation, and indeed that most of the conquered peoples

regarded their new overlords as a better lot than those they had replaced. But conversion was not an important priority, and Muhammad's attitude to the other religions he knew of was of mutual tolerance and respect: 'our God and your God is one and the same, and it is unto Him that we [all] surrender ourselves.'[35] Even within Islam, heterodox beliefs were always less of a problem than heteropraxy, behaviour thought to be un-Islamic. To take another example, his treatment of women seems to have been thoroughly even-handed: the universal veil and the subjugation of women in modern Islam is

Muezin calling

a later arrival. Indeed, even after his time we have a woman such as **Rābi'ah al'Adawiyah** (717–801 CE), the first of the great Sufis. The unfavourable image of Islam developed in the West is partly a legacy of Christian propaganda beginning in the First Crusade, and partly a consequence of the increasingly anguished and defensive positions taken up in the Islamic world in the past century. Having said this, it is important to acknowledge that, as with Christianity, the world of Islam could, and can, be brutal and intolerant, whatever the qualities of its founder. Islam has traditionally been more accepting of the heterodox views and beliefs of non-Muslims than those of its own people, and the brutal execution of the Sufi **al-Hallāj** in 922 CE was an example of what could happen if orthodoxy was pushed too far.

taken by his contemporary al-Razi (865–925 CE) who, as a Platonist, was naturally more inclined to assign the primary importance to reason. Al-Razi believed in God, but not in religion, and attacked the whole principle of prophesy as flawed: he argued that every human being has access to reason and demonstrated that the prophets

The Badshahi Mosque in Lahore, Pakistan.

Finally, a few comments about the general patterns of Islamic thought. The Hellenic influence was almost that of another religion, together with Judaism and Christianity. Just as both the Old and the New Testament were accepted as revelatory, so Aristotle and Plato came to be seen as another tributary of Islam. Muhammad's concerns were primarily social, ethical and theological; the relative lack of speculative thought in his work left a void in which it could flourish, with an early thinker such as **al-Ash'ari** (?874–?935 CE) arguing that although *falsafah* was not found in the Quran, there were also many other good things not found there. A stronger line still was

contradict each other. In this he was, of course, beyond the pale of Islam. The opposite argument was most strongly put by al-Ghazālī (1058–1111 CE), author of *The Incoherence of the Philosophers*. Faith is seen to be weakened and not strengthened by the support of reason, and explanations such as that of Avicenna (980–1037 CE) as to the nature of a prophet came close to reducing the miraculous to psychology. Al-Ghazālī's critique of *falsafah* is a powerful one, anticipating some of the arguments of Hume. After al-Ghazālī most Islamic philosophy moved to the West, notably Averroës (1126–1198 CE) who made a powerful defence of the discipline and stated that philosophers are higher than theologians for their ability to use scientific reasoning. In this he shows the Aristotelian influence.

The third aspect of Islam was, as we have seen, Sufism. From the beginning, it was seen as a second source of revelation, with apocryphal tales pitting the young girl **Rābi'ah** in debate against the aged and sombre Hasan (an early theologian), and always coming off better. The martyrdoms of al-Hallāj and 'Ayn al-Qudat (1098–?1121 CE) were warnings that 'drunken' Sufism, in which the mystic is lost in the contemplation of God and liable to make controversial statements such as 'I am the Truth', was a dangerous game, at least when spoken openly to the populace. This point was reputedly made by al-Hallāj's master al-Junayd, founder of 'sober' Sufism, when he repudiated him not for heresy but for proclaiming openly a secret doctrine. Al-Ghazālī, who had spent time as a Sufi mystic, did much to influence the development of 'sober' Sufism, which requires reflection and consideration, as it were the morning after, before the Sufi declares what she or he has seen in a state of mystical transport.

While the Hindu tradition, for example is accretional and positively welcoming to new unorthodoxy, the Islamic tradition frequently yearns for a return to a pure unadulterated Islam. This is naturally identified with the period of the Prophet's life and immediately afterwards. Philosophically it generally means a clear-out of alien concepts, mainly those of Greece. Often this has had a revivifying effect on Islamic thought, clearing out the dead wood of intellectual constructs, as in the example of al-Ash'ari and Ibn Khaldūn,

but at other times the result was stifling. The attack of al-Ghazālī in *The Incoherence of the Philosophers* was perhaps a combination of both. Its attack on Greek-influenced philosophy

A Muslim raises his hands in prayer at Mecca, the holy shrine of Islam in Saudi Arabia. The city of pilgrims' tents at the foot of Mount Ararat can be seen in the background.

effectively crushed it, at least in the Eastern end of the Muslim world, while the philosophy he proposes in its place has proved fruitful in its own right. Sufism too has suffered from this, being accused of setting up its mystics as rivals to the Quran's unique status as well as for the idolatry of its reverence for saints and their tombs.

ZOROASTER (ZARATHUSTRA)

Lived some time between 1700 and 1000 BCE?

The traditional date for Zoroaster is derived from a Greek source and places him '258 years before Alexander'. This indicates, together with other evidence, that Zoroaster was probably born in around 628 BCE. However, there are problems with this dating. In particular, the language of the Zoroastrian *Avesta* and the *gathas* or hymns attributed to Zoroaster, has been found to be very close to the Sanskrit of the Veda. This, together with many common gods and concepts, suggests that the two are closely linked. The Rig Veda is thought to have been composed no later than 1200 BCE,

possibly much earlier. Another theory suggests that Zoroaster might have been writing in a formal sacred language preserved, as Sanskrit or Latin is today, many thousands of years after its formation. This seems far-fetched. A much safer assumption is that the *gathas* are what they seem to be, effusions of an oral tradition much like Homeric Greek or the hymns of the Rig Veda. The later dating seems to have arisen out of confusion over King Vishtaspa, who was converted by Zoroaster, and a much later king of the same name.

In the prehistory of Central Asia, a tribe known as the Āryans migrated southwards. Some of the Āryans conquered northwest India, worshipped a group of gods called the *devas,* and wrote the Vedas, founding the Indian culture. The second, who migrated to Persia, worshipped the *ahuras,* literally 'lords'. Their holy book is called the *Avesta.* Zarathustra was their prophet and his writings, hymns known as *gathas,* form part of the *Avesta.* His name was later translated into Greek as Zoroaster, the most common name used today. Zoroaster converted King Vishtaspa by healing his horse and enjoyed the hospitality of his court, where he seems to have composed and recited the *gathas.*

Zoroaster seems to have been heir to a folk-religion underlying both the *Avesta* and the Veda. His role in the formation of the Zoroastrian tradition was that of a Prophet. He was not a Prophet in the sense that Muhammad was, a lightning conductor of God, but an inspired poet and a philosophical thinker. He selected and worshipped one of the Avestan gods, Mazda Ahura, above all the others. Mazda

Ahura is the embodiment of good; his enemy is Angra Mainyu, the head of the *devas* and evil personified. It appears that Zoroaster viewed the *devas* as symbolic of the pillaging warriors that worshipped them, representing destruction, falsehood and violence. The *ahuras* were, on the

created by Mazda Ahura for the protection of the Ox and the Ox-keeper from the violence of 'the followers of the Lie'. It is not clear whether the divide in Āryan society between peaceful and righteous herds and warlike cattle-thieves really was as Zoroaster portrays it. At one point he

Baptism by fire, practised by the Parsees of Bombay State, India, followers of Zoroaster to whom fire is sacred.

other hand, the gods of a peaceful pastoral existence. In the Veda relics of *ahura*-worship exist, with the gods Varuna and Mitra being classified among them, but elsewhere in the Veda the *asuras* (as they are in Vedic Sanskrit) are a class of demons. Zoroaster is characterized in the *gathas* as being

speaks of himself as a refugee, crying, 'To what land shall I go to flee, whither to flee?'

A major question concerning Zoroastrianism is whether it is monotheistic or dualistic. The description given above, characterising the religion as an opposition of good and evil, brings out the latter tendency. The former is emphasised in the portrayal of Mazda Ahura as the one God of all. At one point in the *gathas* Zoroaster speaks of the 'two primeval spirits, who reveal themselves as Twins, ... the Better and the Bad'. Spenta Mainyu (the Holy Spirit) is the good twin to Angra Mainyu's Evil Spirit. Mankind is given the free choice between the two, but it is suggested that Mazda Ahura is perhaps the creator of both, and that the twins have each chosen for themselves between good and evil. Another version that developed in the early centuries of the Christian era, but which is not based on the *Avesta*, is that both Mazda Ahura and Angra Mainyu are the children of a greater spirit called Zurvan. The debate continues, but a sensible approach seems to be one that regards the Zoroastrian tradition as somewhere between extreme dualism and a qualified monotheism. The former might be represented by Manicheanism, a Persian sect from the third century CE that was influenced by Zoroastrianism and saw life as a continuing struggle between opposing good and evil forces, and the latter by Christianity, in which the Devil is real but is part of God's creation.

To the picture of Mazda Ahura and his opponent are added six spirits, the *amesha spenta* or beneficent immortals, who are created by Mazda: Asha Vahishta (Justice, Truth), Vohu Manah (Righteous Thinking), Spenta Armaiti, (Devotion), Khshathra Vairya (Desirable Dominion), Haurvatat (Wholeness), and Ameretat (Immortality). These spirits can be seen either as entities or as eternal qualities.

Depending on this emphasis Zoroastrianism seems either more or less polytheistic.

Zoroastrianism as a religion had its high point as the official religion of the Persian empire of third to seventh century CE. It was then supplanted by Islam when the Arabs conquered the Persians, and was persecuted. In around the tenth century a community of Zoroastrians gathered in India, particularly in Bombay, where they were tolerated and known as Parsis (Persians). Today there are an estimated 200,000 Zoroastrians. The original thought of Zoroaster is hard to make out, but as a religion it is tolerant and peace loving, upholding ideals of freedom, service, community life, courage and a sensuous and responsible feeling for nature.

Despite its dwindling numbers, the influence of Zoroastrianism has been very great. The Christian and Islamic belief in the Resurrection of the Body was originally a Zoroastrian doctrine. In the eighteenth century the discovery of the *Avesta* inspired a European elite hungry for the revelations of the Orient. Zoroaster presented a tantalising glimpse to European freethinkers beginning to question the Church of a monotheistic, peaceful and ethically centred culture long before Christ. Perhaps because of the ambiguity of the *Avesta*, he became something of a talisman. Zoroaster was transformed by Mozart into the Sarastro of *The Magic Flute* and by Nietzsche into the prophet in his philosophical fable *Thus Spake Zarathustra* – neither representation owing much to the original figure.

RĀBI'AH AL'ADAWIYAH

717–801 CE

A Prayer of Rābi'ah

O God, if I worship You for fear
of Hell, burn me in Hell,
And if I worship You in hope of Paradise,
Exclude me from Paradise.
But if I worship You for Your Own sake,
Grudge me not Your everlasting Beauty.

The first major mystic of Sufism and Islamic saint was a woman, Rābi'ah al'Adawiyah. She is best known through the compilations of her sayings by later biographers, notably Farid Ud-Din 'Attar (d. c. 1230 CE). She was born to a poor family in Basra, Iraq, and sold into slavery as a girl. She was reputedly freed by her master when he witnessed her maintain night-long vigils after a long day at work.

Sufism is analogous to the Christian mysticism of the middle ages. Its practitioners, named Sufis after the woollen robes they wear as a sign of solidarity with the poor (*tasawwuf*, 'to dress in wool'), are doctrinally part of the Sunni tradition of Islam. Their main emphasis, however, is a devotional form of mysticism that takes them beyond the Islam of the ordinary practitioner or scholar of the day. There is evidence that Sufism was present as a form of worship associated with the Ka'ba in Mecca before Muhammad. The revelations of Sufi saints are regarded as authoritative, while the stories of their lives are accorded a respect and importance similar to the sayings of Muhammad, the *Hadith*. For this reason Sufism has often been regarded with some suspicion by the non-mystical Muslim. It does seem to have drawn inspiration from Neoplatonic philosophy and early Christian mysticism. Its striking quality, however, is an overwhelming emphasis on the love of God. The accounts of Muhammad's own mystical transports have helped to validate the Sufi experience, but their emphasis is much more emotional and devotional. The favourite Sufi text from the Quran is 'the people whom He loves and who love Him'[36].

The Two Loves

I love You with two loves-a selfish love
And a Love that You are worthy of.
As for the selfish love,
it is that I think of You,
To the exclusion of everything else.
And as for the Love that
You are worthy of,
Ah! That I no longer see any creature, but I
see only You!
There is no praise for me in either of these
loves,
But the praise in both is for You.

In this context, Rābi'ah was an important early exemplar of Sufism. She is popularly portrayed as the opponent of Hasan al-Basri (642–728 CE) in lively theological discussion about Islam, although these stories have more symbolic significance than historical accuracy. Hasan was an acquaintance of some of the companions of the Prophet and a rather severe early theologian. He is credited by some with the foundation of *kalam*, scholastic reflection on the Quran. He seems to have been a rather gloomy thinker, much occupied with thoughts of hell. Rābi'ah, on the other hand, argued that the fear of hell is not a reason for worshipping God. Neither should the hope of heaven be a selfish motivation, but only the love of God. There are according to Rābi'ah two aspects to this: the personal joy felt in the presence of God, and love given without hope of reward. In the stories of the verbal duels between the two, it is Rābi'ah, the uneducated former slave girl, who invariably comes out best. Rābi'ah's devotionalism added to the otherworldly asceticism of Hasan could be said to set the pattern for future Sufism.

Several principles important to Sufism are illustrated in Rābi'ah's life story. The pure love for God to the exclusion of all others is called by Rābi'ah *sidq*, or sincerity. Rābi'ah was apparently asked by someone if she loved Muhammad and she replied that with the deepest respect to him, she had only one beloved. In this we see the beginnings of the Sufi tendency towards statements that could be wrongly interpreted by the unreflective faithful. *Tawakkul* is the principle of total trust in God, even to the point of not providing for oneself, akin to Christ's injunction 'take no thought for the morrow'. This leads to *rida,* a positive and active acceptance of the will of God. In her tales of verbal jousts with Hasan the concept of *ma'rifah* or gnosis is implicit: the mystical

experiences of the untaught girl giving her access to a knowledge greater than that of the leading theologian. Perhaps the most important Sufi concept is that of *fanā'*, the extinction of the individual ego, or *nafs,* in union with God. As with Buddhist

Rābi'ah was ... asked by someone if she loved Muhammad and she replied that with the deepest respect to him, she had only one beloved.

shūnyata or emptiness, *fanā'* indicates a realm of existence beyond thought and ordinary experience. It is in the attempt to communicate something about *fanā'* that Sufism has developed its love of paradox.

In all of this it should not be forgotten that the real Rābi'ah was an uneducated woman. It is impossible at this remove to say how many of the stories about her have any basis in truth, and how many of her sayings are authentic. Nevertheless, as in the example of Dame Julian of Norwich, her lack of formal education should not lead to the assumption that she therefore lacked the ability to use deep and radical concepts in her explication of mystical experience. Her symbolic significance for later Islam was considerable.

AL-KINDĪ
801–873 CE

Al-Kindī was the first true Islamic philosopher, although he is sometimes regarded as more of a theologian. He was learned in Greek and Arabic languages and translated a number of works, including those of Aristotle and Plotinus. He was unfortunately responsible for mistakenly publishing the *Enneads* of the latter as *The Theology of Aristotle*, which caused much confusion in Islamic philosophy. He was descended from a man said to have been one of the companions of the Prophet and his father was governor of Kufah, with Basra then one of the two main centres of Islamic learning. His upbringing was privileged and in adult life he lived in famous luxury, possessing an enormous library. He seems to have incited jealousy in others and at one point was beaten and exiled, with his library being confiscated.[37] He reputedly wrote

some 270 works on a wide range of subjects, most of which are lost, and some of which were translated in Europe, spreading his fame. Al-Kindī was acclaimed by the Italian mathematician Cardano as one of the twelve greatest minds. His reputation and importance was nevertheless even greater in the Islamic world.

His view of philosophy was that it consisted of three parts: physics, mathematics and theology, in ascending order of importance. By making theology a part of philosophy, albeit the highest part, al-Kindī naturally ran into opposition from theologians, the most extreme of whom went so far as to claim that the acquisition of knowledge was atheism. Nevertheless, it was his view that religion and philosophy were in harmony with each other. His philosophical work did not include a system of logic, which was introduced by **al-Fārābī**. In *First Philosophy* al-Kindī defines philosophy as:

> *The knowledge of the true nature of things in so far as this is possible for man. The aim of the philosopher is, as regards his knowledge, to attain to the truth, and as regards his action, to act truthfully.*

This definition–true knowledge and true action was to be influential on all subsequent Islamic philosophy, because it connects philosophy to the central issue in Islam, how a Muslim should behave. He distinguishes 'divine science', i.e. prophesy, from 'human science' including philosophy. Al-Kindī gives examples of philosophical problems that are resolved by the Quran, arguing that philosophy would not of itself have been able to arrive at such a solution.

The effect of this was to make the Quran for the first time a subject of philosophical examination. This is the nature of the harmony he established between philosophy and religion, thus paving the way for **al-Fārābī**, **Avicenna** and **Averroës**.

The 'first philosophy' or the highest part of philosophy is, according to al-Kindī, as to the nature of God, and he had found in the Greek thinkers a conception of God that was similar in some respects to that of Islam. The Aristotelians asserted that God was uncompound, immutable and the unmoved mover of all. According to the Quran God was one, created the world from nothing and was the support of all creatures. Unlike later philosophers, al-Kindī was orthodox in maintaining that the world was not eternal. He argued against the existence of infinity in space, time, or in a chain of causality. This is a proof of God's existence (normally called the cosmological argument), because there must be a first cause that is not an effect. His other main proof is the argument from design or teleological argument, in which he says that the order and harmony of the universe is evidence of a creator. Both these proofs were later refuted by **al-Ghazālī**.

Al-Kindī's main originality is not so much in his ideas, many of which are drawn from Hellenistic sources, but his success in examining Islam through a philosophical lens. This was important for the development of Islamic thought, because the Quran is much more concerned with conduct than with speculation. By his synthesis of Aristotle and Islam al-Kindī showed the way for the philosophers that followed him. And to those orthodox that would condemn philosophy he showed that even they would have to acquire it: one cannot reasonably condemn that of which one is ignorant.

Muhammed and his followers. Al-Kindī is reputedly descended from one of Muhammed's companions.

AL-HALLĀJ
c. 858–922 CE

The development of early Sufism, beginning with its first saint **Rābi'ah,** finds its apotheosis in Al-Hallāj, its first martyr. A highly controversial figure, he was prone to utterances that the orthodox found unacceptable. A clash was inevitable given the tensions that existed between the dualistic worship of God essential to Islam and al-Hallāj's tendency towards monism, the doctrine of the identity of the self with the divine. This may have been accentuated by Indian influences in early Sufism: al-Bistami (d. 874 CE), who was the chief proponent of a kind of monism, was taught by a master from Sind and may have been initiated in yogic practices. Al-Bistami's descriptions of his mystical experiences led to his being described as a 'drunken' Sufi, and with al-

Hallāj this mystical ecstasy in which anything, it seemed, might be said, became threatening to the authorities. Like **Rābi'ah**, al-Hallāj was not, strictly speaking, a philosopher. However his *ma'rifah* or mystical insight led him to say things with profound philosophical and religious implications.

Al-Hallāj (also known as Mansur) was born in Iran and his father may have been a wool-carder. In his early youth, having learned the Quran by heart, al-Hallāj took up with a number of the leading Sufis of the time, completing his studies under the highly respected 'sober' Sufi al-Junayd in Baghdad. He completed three pilgrimages to Mecca before returning to Baghdad in around 908 CE. He had also led the first Islamic mission to India and Turkistan and gained a number of followers. Arriving in

> *His most grievous error, according to the authorities, was to say, 'Anā al-Haqq', which means, 'I am the Real' or 'I am the Truth'.*

Baghdad, al-Hallāj attracted the suspicions of the civil authorities and was suspected of having had a part in instigating a rebellion of black slaves. His attempts to preach moral and political reform in Baghdad led to his being arrested for rabble-rousing.

SOME SAYINGS ATTRIBUTED TO AL-HALLĀJ

I find it strange that the divine whole can be borne by my little human part,
Yet due to my little part's burden, the earth cannot sustain me.
(Akhbar al-Hallāj, 11)

I have seen my Lord with the eye of my heart, and I said: 'Who are You?' He
said: 'You.'
(Diwan al-Hallāj, M. 10)

I do not cease swimming in the seas of love, rising with the wave, then
descending; now the wave sustains me, and then I sink beneath it; love bears
me away where there is no longer any shore.
(Diwan al-Hallāj, M. 34)

(MEDIEVAL INTERNET SOURCE BOOK, © PAUL HALSALL)
http://www.fordham.edu/halsall/source/all-hallaj-quotations.html

Al-Hallāj spent eight years in jail, in which time his case was closely debated. Although his political activities may have been the principal reason for his imprisonment, the charge of heresy was more significant. Al-Hallāj loved to take up paradoxical positions, speaking of his admiration for the devil and rejecting Allah's injunction to bow down to Adam. His most grievous error, according to the authorities, was to say, 'Anā al-Haqq', which means, 'I am the Real' or 'I am the Truth'. Al-Haqq is one of the qualities attributed to Allah and this led to the allegation that Al-Hallāj had claimed to be God. Having upset the political leaders of his day as well as the religious orthodoxy, and even alienated Sufis like al-Junayd by putting aside the Sufi robe to preach to the masses, it is hardly surprising that in the end al-Hallāj was put to death. His execution was a thoroughly brutal affair involving public torture, mutilation, crucifixion, decapitation and burning. Al-Hallāj is said to have borne all of this stoically, forgiving his tormentors. In many ways his life parallels that of Jesus, for whom he expressed admiration.

His subsequent influence has been powerful. Al-Hallāj's life recalls not only Jesus but also the Islamic model of the true teacher who is killed by the worldly, as with the early Imams. He also contributed to Sufism its tradition of paradoxical statements designed to unsettle the intellect and bring the devotee closer to a true understanding. However, al-Hallāj was a warning beacon rather than a rallying point for Sufis. The Sufi poet Hafiz said of al-Hallāj that his death was a punishment for his having revealed the 'secret teaching'. Although many of the things al-Hallāj said would have been acceptable within the esoteric circle, it was untenable for Sufism to continue along a separate track to traditional Islam. There was a need for a synthesis between the two, which was not to be effected until the time of **al–Ghazālī** (1058–1111 CE).

Al-Ghazālī's solution, probably under the influence of the tradition of al-Junayd, was to say that it was wrong for Sufis to be held responsible for their mystical experiences, but that they should reflect on their validity before giving them utterance. The standard position of Sufism is not the absolute monism expressed by al-Hallāj, but a qualified monism in which the individual soul adores Allah while acknowledging its whole existence is entirely dependent on Him. This position is very close to that of the later Indian philosopher **Rāmānuja**, whose thought explores all of its implications. Rāmānuja's conclusion that absolute monism is merely a step on the way to the love of God is very close to that of the Sufis. In this light the 'secret teaching' of Hafiz is perhaps not meant to be understood as the ultimate teaching. The empirical experience of singularity of the soul is a secret because it seems at first to contradict Islam and could mislead the faithful. It is however only a step on the way to the experience of devotional union with Allah, which is unity without identity. The Sufi has no experience of his or her self as separate from the divine, but as a lover of the divine still has another who is the beloved.

Young Egyptian boys with wooden boards on which are painted the words of the Koran. The boys sing the words to learn them.

The Harmonization of the Opinions of Plato and Aristotle, was that it was entirely unified. Thus, Plato and Aristotle propounded the same philosophy, as did the Stoics, Epicureans, Neoplatonists and so on. Any divergence or disagreement is not due to the philosophers, but to partisanship

> *So let it be clear to you that, in what [Plato and Aristotle] presented, their purpose is the same, and that they intended to offer one and the same philosophy.*
>
> The Philosophy of Plato and Aristotle, p. 50

AL-FĀRĀBĪ
c. 870–950 CE

Abu Nasr al-Fārābī lived until the age of 50 in a village near Fārābī in Turkey. He then moved to Baghdad to further his studies, where he remained for twenty years before, in his old age, moving to the court at Aleppo. His works are all thought to have been written in the last thirty years of his life, making al-Fārābī a remarkable example of late blooming. He became famous in Muslim philosophy as the 'Second Master' (Aristotle being the first). His funeral at Aleppo was attended by the Amir.

Although very learned, it does not seem that al-Fārābī understood Greek. His understanding of Greek philosophy was however good, and he was also talented at explaining it to an Islamic audience. His view of philosophy, set out in, for example,

by their followers. By the same token, Islam and philosophy are also at one, though externally different. In this he goes further than the Neoplatonist Porphyry who reconciled Aristotle and Plato, and sets the example for **Avicenna** and **Averroës**. Al-Fārābī was not the first of what might be called the 'perennial' philosophers, arguing that there is only one true philosophy, but he was the most comprehensive. He is similar in this enterprise to the Renaissance Christian Humanist, Marsilio Ficino, although Ficino had an easier task in bringing together the already Platonised Christianity with Platonic philosophy.

Naturally, al-Fārābī had to work hard to harmonise such a wide spread of thought and belief. The main issue at stake was the widespread belief that Aristotle had held several opinions that went against both Platonic thought and Islamic teaching. Al-Fārābī was helped in arguing against this by **al-Kindī's** mistaken publication of the *Enneads* of Plotinus as *The Theology of*

Aristotle, a misunderstanding that lasted for centuries. The question as to whether al-Fārābī was really taken in, or was being disingenuous, is open to question. In a lesser-known work, *The Philosophy of Plato and Aristotle*, he makes no mention of *The Theology of Aristotle* in his exploration of Aristotle's ideas, and shows himself perfectly aware of the two philosophers' different theories (while indicating that he still

> *In al-Fārābī's Emanationism the intellect can rise up through the spheres to become united to the primary intellect through reasoning and contemplation.*

regards them as reconcilable). Neither did **al-Ghazālī** in his later attack on al-Fārābī regard the latter's perennialist philosophy in his widely published *Harmonization* as worthy of serious debate. It may be, therefore, that al-Fārābī held one set of opinions privately and another publicly. In any case, his synthesis of systems of thought did not start from ignorance of their differences.

Al-Fārābī's predecessor al-Kindī was the first Islamic philosopher but, despite his prodigious work, he did not put forward a system of logic. This was a major addition of al-Fārābī's to the tradition. Part of this was his division of reasoning into five categories: the demonstrative, the dialectical, the rhetorical, the sophistical and the poetical. Only the demonstrative leads to certainty, and this is the province of the philosophers and scholars. The next best is the dialectic of the theologians such as his contemporary **al-Ash'ari**, while the rhetorical is merely persuasive; the sophistical is misleading; and poetical reasoning produces pleasant or unpleasant feelings. In al-Fārābī's view it is a mistake to address the common people with demonstrative reasoning. That is the function of religion, whereas philosophy should disguise itself in the clothes of mystification. This may seem elitist, but he was wiser than some of his successors who suffered persecution at the hands of the ignorant.

Al-Fārābī's cosmology attempts to explain how the One, God, creates multiplicity through 'emanation'. It also tries to show how the immutable may create without changing itself. The concept of creation through emanation from God is taken from Plotinus, but the synthesis with Aristotle is al-Fārābī's own. Intelligence, souls and matter (this triad he takes from Aristotle) are emanated from the first intelligence, God, who rules the first sphere, with the earth being presided over by the 'Active Intellect', identified with the Angel Gabriel, ruler of the tenth, sublunary, sphere. In al-Fārābī's Emanationism the intellect can rise up through the spheres to become united to the primary intellect through reasoning and contemplation. This completes the Aristotelian picture, with earth at the centre and with the cosmos rotating around it in crystalline spheres.

A criticism of the ten intelligences theory is that it does not really help with either the issue of how One becomes many, or of how the unchanging may create. The divine

Now these things are philosophy when they are in the soul of the legislator. They are religion when they are in the souls of the multitude. For when the legislator knows these things, they are evident to him by sure insight, whereas what is established in the souls of the multitude is through an image and a persuasive argument. Although it is the legislator who presents these things through images, neither the images nor the persuasive arguments are intended for himself. As far as he is concerned, they are certain. He is the one who invents the images and the persuasive arguments, but not for the sake of establishing these things in his own soul as a religion for himself. No, the images and the persuasive arguments are intended for others, whereas, so far as he is concerned, these things are certain. They are a religion for others, whereas, so far as he is concerned, they are philosophy. Such, then, is true philosophy and the true philosopher.

The Philosophy of Plato and Aristotle, p. 47

hierarchy could be regarded as a smoke-and-mirrors trick, disguising the problem of a logical gap with tiny steps. The problem is of course merely academic today, but modern commentators would side with al-Ghazālī in regarding it as logically fallacious. Nevertheless, al-Fārābī's synthesis of different philosophies and Islam was persuasive both in Islamic and, later, in European culture. Avicenna is particularly indebted to it.

Another important idea of al-Fārābī's was his theory of prophecy. This was an important issue because of the attacks of contemporary thinkers such as al-Razi (865–925 CE) who dismissed prophecy because it set up a special category of knowledge higher than reason. Developing Aristotle's thinking on dreams as an unfettered activity of the mind, al-Fārābī elevates the dreaming state to one of reflection on ideas free of material distraction. A powerful and imaginative intellect (that is, of a true prophet) is able to rise in dreams to commune with the Active Intellect and receive spiritual truths from it. The Angel Gabriel is thus identified with the Active Intellect, which becomes the messenger of God. This theory, as with al-Fārābī's Emanationism, was attacked by al-Ghazālī in *The Incoherence of the Philosophers*.

Al-Fārābī's theory of the intellect was derived from Aristotle, but he made important additions. The theory, simply put, is that there are three levels of the intellect in its upward-moving aspect. The *potential intellect* receives impressions passively; the *intellect in action* comprehends ideas within the impressions and can make use of them; and the *acquired intellect* is enlightened from

Plato and Aristotle. Al-Fārābī argued that the seeming contradiction between their philosophies could in fact be reconciled

above and moves among higher forms, akin to Platonic Ideas, that are beyond the world of matter. Although this third level of the intellect is essentially mystical in that it depends on the divine Active Intellect, al-Fārābī insists that the earlier stages must be gone through to prepare the intellect for revelation. It is easy to see why this theory should be attractive to the West, as it joins Aristotelian empiricism to Platonic gnosis. It also, within the Muslim framework,

reconciles the three aspects of Greek philosophy, Islamic theology and Sufic mysticism. In the history of ideas, al-Fārābī's remains one of the most balanced and pleasing theories of knowledge. It has been described as 'the most significant of all the theories of Muslim thinkers[38]', and the most influential. Both Averroës and, especially, Avicenna were indebted to al-Fārābī's theory and through them Christian Europe adopted it.

AL-ASH'ARI
c. 874–c. 935 CE

Abu Al-Hasan al-Ash'ari was the chief formulator of the Sunni position in Islam. As is well known, the two main strands of Islam are the Sunni and the Shi'ite; however, as the main difference between the two is political rather than philosophical, we will not enter into it here. Suffice to say that the Sunni have always been the more numerous and may be considered as the main stream of Islam. As a member of the Islamic aristocracy in Basra in Iraq and a descendant of one of the Prophet's companions, al-Ash'ari was wealthy enough to be able to devote himself entirely to the study of theology. He was the beneficiary of the growth of learning under the Abbasid Caliphs, under whose autocratic rule Greek philosophy had first been translated. He founded an important theological school that counted among its later alumni **al-Ghazālī** and **Ibn Khaldūn.**

Tomb of the Abbasid Caliphs

The rationalist theologians, the Mu'tazilah, of which al-Ash'ari was a prominent member, had established *kalam* or theological discussion and had gained considerable prominence. By the time of al-Ash'ari, however, their thinking had become arid and distant from real experience as well as from traditional Islam, and he broke with them at the age of 40. The Mu'tazilah and orthodox positions had become polarised over the years, with the Mu'tazilah questioning everything and the orthodox becoming increasingly anti-intellectual, for example asserting that all the dogmas of the faith had simply to be accepted without consideration. The orthodox position was clearly unsustainable, and al-Ash'ari developed a new approach to *kalam* that suited orthodox convictions. Essentially, the Asharites maintain the primacy of revelation over reason in *kalam* (as **al-Kindī** did in *falsafah*), reversing the rationalist position. Another aspect of this is the question of good and evil. Al-Ash'ari maintains that good and evil are not intrinsic to an action, but are determined by the Quran and by Shari'ah law – there is no good or bad, but revelation makes it so.

Al-Ash'ari found a middle course that was generally acceptable to the majority. For example, there was a debate about whether the Quran was eternal or created. The orthodox claimed that it was eternal and that to claim that it was created was an 'innovation'. Al-Ash'ari pointed out that as Muhammad had not given an answer either way, it was equally an innovation to claim that it was eternal. Having destroyed the arguments of his opponents, he offered his own solution: the Quran should be considered to be eternal with respect to its meaning, and created with respect to its words. Another important theological question of the time was whether the attributes of God (he is merciful, wise, vengeful, all-powerful) were the same as his essence or not. Again, while the rationalists held that they were the same, causing the attributes effectively to disappear or to make God bulge with contradictions, the orthodox position that they were different tended to anthropomorphize and multiply God, as in Hinduism. Al-Ash'ari's argument was for his part similar to that of the Indian proponents of *bhedābheda* (identity-in-difference)[39] – the attributes were both part of the essence and, seen another way, external to it. So for example God is not wise in his essence, but in practice his words have the attribute of wisdom. Therefore attribute and essence are neither entirely the same nor quite different.

On the question of free will Asharism has to avoid deterministic fatalism and unfettered free will. Al-Ash'ari asserts that man can choose between right and wrong, leading him ultimately to heaven or hell. However, God is strongly present in this conception of will, being the active principle in making the choice available, in empowering the individual to choose, and in fulfilling the choice and realizing its consequences. This doctrine, which was similar to that later developed independently by Malebranche as *occasionalism* (in which God acts to carry thought into action), is an attempt to combine a strong conception of God as the doer and sustainer of all with the need for individual responsibility. In this instance al-Ash'ari may be on dangerous ground, and some of his followers tended towards the old orthodox deterministic position.

As a somewhat unwilling philosopher al-Ash'ari evolved an original metaphysical system from Aristotelian roots. According to his metaphysics (or, according to some scholars, that developed and completed by his follower al-Baqillani), the world consists of momentary atoms, brought into being by God and then disappearing again. There is no causality in the normal sense and no laws of nature; it is just that we can observe that God typically and regularly does things in this way. Fire does not cause wood to burn: God produces the fire and when fire is close to wood we may observe that he habitually burns the wood. A miracle is merely an exception, but no more special from God's point of view than any other occurrence. Macdonald describes Asharite metaphysics as 'the most daring metaphysical scheme, and almost certainly the most thorough theological scheme, ever thought out'[40]. It has parallels, as we have seen, with *occasionalism*, and also with Buddhist arguments against causality and permanence, with, of course, very different aims. Al-Ash'ari's thinking was very influential in later times, particularly through al-Ghazālī, who makes use of his ideas to attack the philosophers, notably **Avicenna** and **al-Fārābī**. Al-Ghazālī's influence was decisive in making Asharism the main theology of Islam from his time onwards.

The Mosque of Omar in Jerusalem, otherwise known as the Dome of the Rock. It is an ornate shrine built on the spot where Muhammed is believed to have ascended to heaven, and the site of the Temple of Solomon.

AVICENNA (IBN SĪNĀ)
980–1037 CE

Avicenna was, with **Averroës** (Ibn Rushd) one of the two philosophers best known to the West. He was also an influential physician and author of *The Book of Healing,* and, most famously, the *Canon of Medicine*. His reputation in medicine in the Europe of the middle ages was equalled only by Hippocrates and Galen, while his philosophy was absorbed into the main stream of Scholasticism. He was, like many Islamic thinkers, encyclopaedic in his interests and, of all the Muslim philosophers perhaps the most prolific. His *Kitab al-Shifa* is a compendium of learning, encompassing logic, geometry, arithmetic, astronomy, music, natural science and metaphysics. It is said to be the largest work of this kind by any single man[41].

Avicenna was born in Persia and was the possessor of a prodigious intellect. He had memorised the Quran by the age of 10 and had mastered all of the traditional branches of Islamic learning by 21, as well as being a respected physician. His successful cure of the Samanid emperor gave him access to a magnificent library that enabled him to further his studies. In later life, however, he was less fortunate in his circumstances as the death of his father and political upheavals in the region caused him to lead an unsettled existence. Whatever his circumstances, however, Avicenna continued to work prodigiously. A full day's work at court would be followed by sessions of discussion and composition with students, often lasting most of the night. Only in the last 14 years of his life did Avicenna enjoy an uninterrupted peace to work, in Isfahan.

Avicenna's philosophy built on the work of **al-Fārābī** (870–950 CE), who argued that philosophy and religion are in harmony with each other. Al-Fārābī was the founder of the doctrine of Emanationism, which is a development from Plotinus. Intelligence, souls and matter (this triad he takes from Aristotle) are emanated from the first intelligence, God, who rules the first sphere, with the earth being presided over by the 'Active Intellect', identified with the Angel Gabriel, ruler of the tenth, sublunary, sphere. In Emanationism the intellect can rise up through the spheres to become united to the primary intellect through reasoning and contemplation, a similar process to that described by Plato in the approach to the Good. Al-Fārābī also had

Avicenna was physician, scientist and philosopher.

an original theory about the status of a prophet as a highly imaginative person who is able to connect in sleep or trance with the active intellect and thereby receive spiritual truths.

Avicenna thought of God as the only absolutely uncompound, simple entity. This creates a problem as Avicenna follows Aristotle in holding that God would know only universals, being outside of time and space, which define particulars. The orthodox criticised this as being inconsistent with the Quran, which says, 'Not a particle remains hidden from God in the heavens or on the earth'. Avicenna's way around this was to argue that God could see the whole chain of cause and effect from outside time, and would therefore be aware of each particular event in its context. This explanation was

never fully accepted and **al-Ghazālī** in particular criticized Avicenna's apparent limitation of what God could know. The rather remote and impersonal concept of God in Avicenna could be seen as one of the drawbacks in his philosophy.

His idea of a prophet is of someone with deep imaginative power, enabling identification with the active intellect. As well as this he will be charismatic and possess political gifts, and will have the ability to express philosophy allegorically, so that it can be widely understood in the form of religion.

Avicenna's psychology is interesting and in some ways original. Our five outer senses are mirrored inwardly by five inner faculties including memory, imagination and our sense of value. Like Aristotle,

Avicenna holds that the intellect is that in the individual that is godlike – indivisible, immaterial and imperishable. It is a mirror that reflects ideas from the Active Intellect (see above) and which is capable of being, as it were, polished. Avicenna is Platonic rather than Aristotelian in his view that universals are learned from above rather than from experience. To take a classical Greek example, we do not intuit the universal idea of 'triangle' from seeing

influence to decline in the Islamic world. He became symbolic of a certain kind of philosophic thinking that was not orthodox. His belief in the eternity of the creation, his idea of a prophet as a highly imaginative person, and his (private) rejection of bodily resurrection all came to be considered heterodox. In addition to this, his conception of God is rather distant and cold, as is his view of the individual intellect. So although his

Avicenna being received by the Governor of Isfahan.

many triangles, but by the revelation from higher intelligence of the supersensuous idea 'triangle' to reason. The ideal triangle is free from imperfections of any physical triangles, which only serve to prepare the reason for revelation. According to Avicenna, thought is the faculty that brings about universality in forms.

After Avicenna's time he was attacked not only by al-Ghazālī but also by Averroës and, later, **Ibn Khaldūn**, causing his

influence on Europe was huge, Avicenna did not enjoy such a wide following within his own culture. This is perhaps unfortunate as, in addition to his status as the most important of the Aristotelians, he also made efforts to found an Oriental Philosophy, a mystical theosophy that seems to prefigure later developments in Persia. Most of his works on this have sadly been lost.

AL-GHAZĀLĪ
1058–1111 CE

Abu Hamid Muhammad al-Ghazālī inherited a rich tradition of theology and mysticism and went on to develop a system of thought that was to bring the two together. His life-story was fascinating, both to his contemporaries and in subsequent history, and has contributed, some say unduly, to his influence as a thinker. He is in some ways reminiscent of St Augustine, with whom he is often compared for his formidable intellect, his internal struggles, his energy and his faith. He is also a contradictory figure, as we will see.

His father and brother were celebrated Sufi mystics, and the young al-Ghazālī underwent spiritual training, but failed to reach the mystical states he hoped for. His early bent was for scholarship and he swiftly progressed to be appointed professor of theology at Nizamihah University in Baghdad. This seems to have been equally unsatisfying, as al-Ghazālī's relentlessly questioning mind exposed the inadequacy of both theology and philosophy as it was then practised. Al-Ghazālī sets out his aims in terms reminiscent of Descartes:

> *The search after truth being the aim which I propose to myself, I ought in the first place to ascertain what are the bases of certitude. In the second place I ought to recognize that certitude is the clear and complete knowledge of things, such knowledge as leaves no room for doubt, nor any possibility of error.*[42]

At 36 the strain of being unable to find a solid foundation for truth became too much. He suffered a severe breakdown, resigned his post and left for Damascus to become a wandering Sufi. Having demonstrated to himself that neither observation nor reason were adequate to the purpose of finding truth, al-Ghazālī was instead to find a spiritual source, speaking of a light which God infused into his heart. Instead of reasoning our way to truth, it is the grace of Allah that is the key to knowledge. He spent eleven years in this way, practicing meditation and asceticism, after which he returned to teaching and writing. One reason for this return to active life was the tradition that Islam would be renewed by a true teacher every century: al-Ghazālī was persuaded by others that he was the teacher for the century beginning (in the Christian calendar) in 1106 CE[43]. His *Revival of the Religious Sciences* is a vast work dedicated to this end, and is still the most-read Islamic text after the Quran. Al-Ghazālī is credited in addition with the authorship of hundreds of works, but many have been mis-attributed. Around 40 are now considered to be authentic.

Al-Ghazālī was acutely aware of the divisions within Islam, and in an autobiographical work intended to justify his retirement from the University post he outlines four main strands in the faith. These are the al-Asharite theologians, the Sufi mystics, the *falsafyah* (philosophers) and the Shi'ite followers of the Imams. Al-Ghazālī had criticisms of all of these groups, including theologians who tried to rely on philosophical proofs and those Sufis who held to unorthodox monist doctrines[44]. However, it was the philosophers and, especially, the Shi'ite theologians that were his real targets. To deal with the latter first: Islam as a religion has traditionally been divided into the Sunni and the Shi'ite strands. These each had their beginnings in the early politics of the succession to the Prophet. In essence, the Shi'ite belief was in the Imams, the bloodline of Muhammad. For them, only a true Imam could teach Islam; while the Sunnis, on the other hand, took the pragmatic view that *Shari'ah* law should be allowed to develop as an interpretive tradition, augmenting the words of the Prophet. For al-Ghazālī the authoritarianism of the Shia was a mystical blind alley: all of the true Imams were dead and the bloodline had ended.

For our purposes, however, al-Ghazālī's attack on the philosophers is of more importance, as the first examination of Greek-influenced Islamic philosophy by a theologian. Al-Ghazālī was the first theologian equipped to offer such a critique and did so, firstly in his *The Intentions of the Philosophers*, a book which was influential in Europe and which sets out the key ideas of thinkers like Avicenna (Ibn Sīnā), and al-Fārābī and finally in his great work *Tahafut al-Falsafyah* (*The Incoherence of the Philosophers*). At the root of his antipathy to the philosophers was his conviction that theology depended on faith and not on reason, which, in al-Ghazālī's unhappy experience, had not succeeded in bringing him the answers he craved. Because reason cannot be relied upon to prove God or other truths, it

'The imponderable decisions of God cannot be weighed by the scales of reason.'

should be relegated to a secondary position. His critique of the *falsafyah* is not that philosophy should not take place, but that its findings should start and end with the Quranic revelation. Al-Ash'ari and al-Ghazālī after him both take an agnostic position towards the mysteries of God, as is seen in the example, cited twice by the latter, of a child who finds himself in heaven but in a lower place than a man. He asks God why he should be in a lower place, to which the reply is that the man did many good works. The child then asks why he had to die before he did good works, to which God replies that he ended the child's life because he knew he would have become a sinner. The cry goes up from the damned in hell as to why they were not caused to die before they sinned. Al-Ghazālī comments that 'the imponderable decisions of God cannot be weighed by the scales of reason and Mu'tazilism [Islamic rationalism]'. He was, however, in favour of logic as a discipline and promoted its use in theological training.

Al-Ghazālī attacked in particular three claims by *falsafyah* such as **Avicenna** that, according to him, are heretical. These were that the world is eternal, that God cannot know particulars, and that the resurrection of the body (mentioned in the Quran) was a myth. These ideas had grown up in the tradition of Islamic philosophy as successive thinkers built on an essentially Aristotelian set of assumptions. Al-Ghazālī said, quite reasonably, that there is a vast difference between the Quran and Aristotle. His attack on the *falsafyah* in *The Incoherence* was all the more powerful because it made use of the Aristotelians' own methods of argument. The three heresies are today of merely historical importance, but al-Ghazālī's arguments against them produce some fascinating philosophy all of their own.

One of the most important arguments advanced by al-Ghazālī is his critique of causality. The target here was the doctrine of Emanationism, which posits a vast hierarchy of cause and effect from God down to man based on Aristotelian cosmology[45]. Al-Ghazālī objects to the idea of 'natural law': that is, the view that the universe is governed by physical laws of nature. In particular, the law of causality makes God subservient to his own creation, and to the laws that affect mankind. God may do as he wishes at all times. His argument against causality is that it is based on observation and not on natural law: we may observe that fire burns, but we cannot assert that it will do so in all cases. What we have observed is not a 'natural law' but one example of many that God has his habitual way of acting. This also serves to justify miracles, which are not violations of some natural law, but merely unusual acts of God. In this he is reminiscent of the occasionalism of **al-Ash'ari**, who is the major influence, but it is intriguing to note parallels in other traditions - with the eighteenth century philosopher David Hume in the West, and with the materialism of **Chārvāka** in India. Islamic theology, in its enthusiasm for sweeping out presumptuous philosophies, here uses similar arguments to those of the atheists and the materialists – an irony that a Sufi would appreciate.

Another important question, and here again the influence of al-Ash'ari was decisive, is that of free will. Al-Ghazālī cannot accept a strong determinist argument because that

David Hume

would make heaven and hell meaningless. Instead, he posits a three-tier system: the world of matter is entirely without free will; man has a limited free will, allowing him to choose between right and wrong; and God has total free will.

On the question of what God can know, al-Ghazālī argued against the Emanationist argument that God knows only timeless universals and is above particular temporal details, asserting that this goes against Quranic statements of God's omniscience. Al-Ghazālī can be seen as a reactionary force against Hellenism, which as understood by Islam was more like a rival religion than a system of thought. Such was the influence of *al-Tahafut* that al-Ghazālī is held responsible for almost shutting down philosophy as a separate discipline in Eastern Islam, making it entirely subsidiary to religious aims. The great response to it

Such was the influence of al-Tahafut that al-Ghazālī is held responsible for almost shutting down philosophy as a separate discipline in Eastern Islam.

about half a century later came from the West when **Averroës** (Ibn Rushd), who was active in Spain and Africa, wrote *Tahafut al-Tahafut (The Incoherence of 'The Incoherence')*.

Al-Ghazālī's most constructive aspect was his integration of Sufism with the mainstream, a task to which he was uniquely suited. In *Revival of the Religious Sciences* he set out the basis of Islamic spirituality, showing how it progressed to the higher mystical states of Sufism. Later in life al-Ghazālī came to see theology as merely subsidiary, or preparatory, to mysticism. In accordance with this, the prime virtue for al-Ghazālī is love, which allows for a direct cognition of God by the soul. This strand of his thinking was very influential and culminated in the Persian school of Isfahan some three centuries later. In his *Mishkat al-Anwar* he explains, following al-Junayd, the father of 'sober' Sufism, 'the words of lovers when in a state of drunkenness must be hidden away and not broadcast'. A Sufi should not be held responsible for what he or she says in the 'drunken' state brought on by mystical experience, but should reflect on it in sobriety and modify his or her words according to reason and piety. He then quotes the famous utterances of **al-Hallāj** ('I am the Truth'), Abu Yazid ('Glory be to me') and Abu Sa'id ('Within my robe there is nothing but God'), closing with the strange sentence, 'beyond these truths there are further mysteries, the penetration of which is not permissible'. Whether that word 'permissible' indicates mysteries that are wrong to explore, or that such mysteries are considered heretical and should not be expressed openly, al-Ghazālī's position is ambiguous.

What is certain is that the 'sober' Sufism founded by al-Junayd and so successfully promulgated by al-Ghazālī puts mystical experience – the direct perception of the divine – at the centre of Islamic practice. It provides a model within which the excesses of Sufic enthusiasm are tempered by reference to scriptural authority. The mysticism that emerges is not the absolute monism or identification of the self with God suggested by the three quotations above, but a qualified monism in which the individual self disappears in contemplation of the single reality of Allah.

AVERROËS
(IBN RUSHD)
1126–1198 CE

Averroës is regarded by many as the most significant Islamic philosopher. He was born in Cordova, then a centre of learning to rival Damascus and Baghdad in the East. Raised in the traditions of *fiqh* (jurisprudence), he was a younger contemporary of the philosopher Ibn Tufail, whom he met at the court of Abu Ya'qub, then Amir in Cordova. The Amir requested that he write a commentary on Aristotle. This huge work became famous in Christian Europe, and accordingly it is with Averroës' name that Dante closes his list of pagan thinkers in the first circle of Hell:

And Linus, Tully and moral Seneca,
Euclid and Ptolemy, Hippocrates,
Galenus, Avicen, and him who made
That commentary vast, Averroës.
Inferno, IV

Avicenna is the only other Muslim mentioned here by Dante. The followers of Averroës in Christian Europe were known as the Latin Averroists and they regarded him both as a faithful transmitter of Aristotle and as a great thinker in his own right. Others, notably Thomas Aquinas, objected to those aspects of his interpretation of Aristotle that were thought incompatible with Christian teaching, especially concerning the immortality of the individual soul. Bertrand Russell regards Averroës' version of Aristotle as being generally more authentic than that of Aquinas. His ideas on the intellect were especially influential. Averroës argues that the intellect of God and that of man are radically different: God's intellect is the cause of existent things, and existent things are the cause of man's intellect. Elsewhere he says, 'Intelligence is nothing but the perception of things with their causes'[46]. The function of the intellect is to strip matter away from pure concepts, as for example when we look at a figure of a triangle and perceive its perfect mathematical form without the physical imperfections of its drawing. The concepts do not exist in a realm of pure Form, however, as Plato maintained, but only in the mind of man. Averroës takes the soundly scientific view that the world is well ordered and susceptible to reason. The world is created by the benevolence of God and the happiness of man rests in his ability to rise out of the corruption of matter into the eternity of the higher spheres (his cosmology, like that of the other philosophers before him, is Greek). Latin Averroism was influential in Europe well into the fifteenth century.

The most significant of Averroës' works for the Muslim world is his refutation of **al-Ghazālī's** *Tahafut al-Falasifah* (*The Incoherence of the Philosophers*), in the *Tahafut al-Tahafut* (*The Incoherence of 'The Incoherence'*). Unfortunately, its delightful title is not reflective of its contents, which are a thorough and systematic demolition of what was, in al-Ghazālī, a rather rambling though comprehensive argument. Averroës suffered, like many Islamic philosophers, from the antagonism of the *Ulama*, the orthodox religious teachers, whose wide popular support enabled them to influence their political rulers. He was banished from Cordova to nearby Lucena and his books were publicly burned, although he was restored to favour after a short time and lived the remainder of his life in Marrakesh. Averroës' exile and disgrace gives an indication of the political climate in which he lived. A central issue of the time was whether philosophy and religion were incompatible. According to al-Ghazālī, the philosophers were *kufr* (heretical), which meant that they could be executed for maintaining their beliefs if this charge were upheld. Averroës sought to argue against this in his work. He asks whether philosophy is prohibited, permitted, recommended or ordained by Islam. His answer is that it is at least recommended, because of Muhammad's frequent exhortations that Muslims should reflect on the universe. Averroës' definition of philosophy is that it consists

Averroës

of reflection on beings in order to gain understanding of their creator. His definition of theology is intentionally reminiscent of **al-Kindī's** definition of philosophy: true knowledge and true practice.

Averroës makes use of **al-Fārābī's** conception that there are five forms of reason (the demonstrative, the dialectical, the rhetorical, the sophistical and the poetical). Again, the highest form is the demonstrative and is the preserve of philosophers, whereas the al-Asharite theologians are restricted to dialectic. Reason and revelation should go hand in hand, but where revelation conflicts with reason its meaning must be regarded as allegorical. The hidden (*batin*) significance should be discovered through philosophy.

Averroës was forced to do penance for his intellectual temerity.

The debate between al-Ghazālī's position – theological and mystical – and that of Averroës – philosophical and scientific – is an important one not only for Islam but also for the rise of Western Europe. Broadly, Islam followed al-Ghazālī and Europe Averroës, although it is too much to say, as some Islamic scholars do, that the rise of science in Europe is therefore an outgrowth of Islamic philosophy. Relatively speaking Averroës' philosophy is scientific: he rejected astrology and doubted alchemy, of which even Newton was a practitioner. But scientists such as Galileo had to defeat Aristotelian ideas before their own ideas and methods could flourish. What is more accurate to say is that in his defence of causality against the theologians Averroës influenced modern Islam in a positive way. al-Ghazālī and **al-Ash'ari** both denied causation on the

grounds that to compel God to follow natural laws was to lessen his power. Averroës argues against this point of view, which was partly intended to establish the reality of miracles. God is the wise creator and accordingly his creation follows just laws, of which causation is an example. He does not deny the possibility of miracles, but objects to creating a whole system of thought based on such exceptional occurrences. Pointing to the instance in which Muhammad had refused to perform a miracle on the grounds that he was only a human being, he asserts that the true miracle of Islam is the Quran itself. This Averroist position is the one taken up by most modern Islamic thinkers.

On the issue of predestination, Averroës has an original position, rejecting both free will and predestination in favour of determinism. Actions are determined by causes that are external (circumstance) and internal (individual disposition). God sees all and creates the appropriate circumstances for our dispositions. Averroës is an optimist and regards humanity as generally well intentioned.

With regard to his philosophical antecedents within Islam, Averroës sided more with al-Kindī and Aristotle than with al-Fārābī and Plotinus. Al-Fārābī held that all of philosophy and religion was one, a unicity that is itself Neoplatonic and mystical. Averroës has a more analytical approach and was the first to properly distinguish between Aristotelian and Neoplatonist ideas, a confusion that had crept in with al-Kindī's mistake of crediting the *Enneads* to Aristotle. His importance is far greater to the West than to Islamic thought, however. The huge influence Averroës had on Europe in the Middle Ages and Renaissance has no equivalent in Islam, which hardly remembers him.

Averroës' teachings were condemned by Muslim theologians who made him retract them on the Koran.

RŪMĪ
1207-1273 CE

The Sufi poet Jalal al-Din Rūmī was born in Afghanistan and wrote in the Persian language, but in early adulthood he moved with his family to Anatolia, fleeing perhaps from the displeasure of the local ruler, or from the Tartars. The name 'Rūmī' means 'Roman', 'Rum' being the name of Anatolia as part of the old Empire. Rūmī was born into a prominent family and received an excellent education. At 24 he took over his father's post, teaching religious science and mysticism. A meeting with the enigmatic mystic Shams of Tabriz transformed Rūmī's life and he himself became a Sufi and a poet. The closeness of Rūmī's relationship with Shams seems to have caused discord within the circle of Rūmī's disciples and Shams was forced to flee. He was later persuaded to return but in around 1247 CE he again disappeared, possibly murdered by one of Rūmī's circle or family.

Rūmī was the author of a vast literature, mainly poetry. He is regarded as certainly the greatest literary figure in the Islamic world. His poetry is now much admired in the West. Rūmī's non-denominational, integrationist love of God is today a deeply appealing and widely acceptable form of religion. Although the literary qualities of his verse are hard to assess by a non-Persian speaker, and can seem quite bland in translation, the reader gets a strong sense of an overwhelming mystical love of God. An analogy in English is with the poetry of George Herbert, who similarly combined brilliance with devotionalism.

Like other Sufis discussed in this book, notably **al-Hallāj,** Rūmī was given to

---

Art as Flirtation and Surrender

In your light I learn how to love.
In your beauty, how to make poems.
You dance inside my chest, where
no one sees you, but sometimes I do,
and that sight becomes this art.

from *The Essential Rumi*, translations by Coleman Barks
with John Moyne, 1995.

---

unusual statements that were open to misunderstanding by the ignorant. He once proclaimed, 'as to my creed I am neither a Jew, nor a Zoroastrian, not even a Muslim as this term is generally understood'. He claimed to support all 72 sects of Islam and when accused of being an atheist and heretic, he agreed. He was also known for his unusual practices, which included playing music, song and a whirling dance that accompanied the composition of his poetry: Rūmī was the founder of the Mevlevi order of 'whirling' dervishes. Despite this he does not seem to have suffered persecution. He was critical of Greek-influenced theological dialectic, as practiced by his father's old adversary Razi: 'If dialectics alone could reveal the secrets of the spirit, Razi would have certainly reached them, but the feet of the dialectician are wooden and the wooden feet are most shaky.'

Al-Razi (864–930 CE)

Rūmī is not a philosopher, but his training and education equipped him to understand its complexities. His thought is instinctual and experiential, but a coherent philosophy emerges. He is an Emanationist after Plotinus, in the tradition of **al-Fārābī** and **Avicenna,** which is to say that the world is an emanation or overflow from God. Like Aristotle, he maintains that the motive force of the universe is the love of God. Unlike any of these, however, for Rūmī love really is greater than reason. Existence has a purpose for every soul, and that purpose is to evolve towards God. In a remarkable passage in the *Mathnawi* Rūmī sets out his philosophy of evolution:

For several epochs I was flying about in space like atoms of dust without a will, after which I entered the inorganic realm of matter. Crossing over to the vegetable kingdom I lost all memory of my struggle on the material plane. From there I stepped into the animal kingdom, forgetting all my life as a plant, feeling only an instinctive and unconscious urge towards the growth of plants and flowers ... rising in the scale of animality I became a man pulled up by the creative urge of the Creator whom one knows. I continued advancing from realm to realm developing my reason and strengthening the organism. There was ground for ever getting above the previous types of reason. Even my present rationality is not a culmination of mental evolution. This too has to be transcended, because it is still contaminated with self-seeking, egoistic biological urges. A thousand other types of reason and consciousness shall emerge during the further course of my ascent; a wonder of wonders![47]

Leibniz believed that the physical world was simply the surface of reality; ultimate reality was composed of the mind-like entities that he named monads.

Several things are worth noting here. Firstly, Rūmī believes that souls are eternal, all seeking to evolve. This might be compared with the monads of Leibniz, with Allah as the greatest of all monads. Secondly, Rūmī reports this as an experience, although it is described as taking place over 'several epochs'. Time, and also space, does not exist in the spiritual realm. Elsewhere he wrote, 'I existed when there were neither names nor the things that are named'. Thirdly, there is a version of evolutionary reincarnation here.

Fourthly, despite the comment about 'self-seeking, egoistic biological urges', the overwhelming impression is positive. One does not reach Rūmī's God through self-denial but through self-transcendence. The ego is not destroyed but purified again and again until it is fit for the company of the quality-less Supreme. In this, Rūmī shows his Islamic heart, affirming the eternity and integrity of the individual self. Life is not an illusion, but an affirmation of reality. The illusion is death.

A group of whirling dervishes. Muslim devotees of the Sufi sect perform their ritual dance barefoot.

IBN KHALDŪN
1332-1406 CE

Ibn Khaldūn is an exceptional figure within the tradition of Islamic thought, but he would have been an exceptional figure within any tradition. He saw himself as the creator of a new science, in which view he is correct. Today his field of inquiry would be known as cultural history or social science. Some of Ibn Khaldūn's insights foreshadow Western developments that did not take place until the past few decades. For this reason, although he does not fit into any of the normal categories of Muslim thought, he deserves to be regarded as one of the greatest minds of Islam. In addition to the great originality of his new science, he is also responsible for an important critique of the theology and philosophy of his time.

The life of Ibn Khaldūn is a fascinating tale and there is no doubt that he was one of the greatest figures of the fourteenth century. He was a tremendously able politician and diplomat and, if his thinking has something of Machiavelli in it, his behaviour has something of a Machiavellian prince. Born in Tunis, Ibn Khaldūn belonged to a distinguished Arab (or possibly Berber) family. As a boy he

His parents and all of his tutors fell victim to the plague, which, Ibn Khaldūn reflected sadly, 'folded the carpet with everything on it'.

learned the Quran by heart and studied theology, grammar, rhetoric and jurisprudence. The peaceful progress of his life and education was shattered by the cataclysm of the plague of 1349 CE that decimated the population of North Africa as it did Europe. His parents and all of his tutors fell victim to the plague, which, Ibn Khaldūn reflected sadly, 'folded the carpet with everything on it'. He contemplated emigrating before being summoned at the age of 20 to office by the ruler of Tunis. This was the beginning of a colourful political life in which Ibn Khaldūn demonstrated again and again over the next 25 years his willingness to pursue personal gain and fame at all cost. No sooner would a new political master be on the throne than Ibn Khaldūn would be at his side. He travelled from court to court around North Africa and Andalucia and Ibn Khaldūn wasted no opportunity for intrigue and adventure. Two years in prison and countless intrigues later, Ibn Khaldūn seems finally to have lost his taste for politics with the torture and execution of his friend Ibn al-Khatib, who was to Andalucia what Ibn Khaldūn was to Africa: its greatest scholar, poet and political intriguer. He settled down to write his great *History* and completed it in 1382 CE. His earlier life caught up with him, however, and he was forced to flee Tunis (where he had again settled) for Cairo, under the pretext of making a pilgrimage to Mecca. There he was feted by the local

Modern pilgrims surround the Al Kaaba Temple at the centre of Mecca in Saudi Arabia.

scholars and shortly appointed to one of the highest judicial posts in the city. Throwing himself into his new role, Ibn

Khaldūn displayed such passion for justice and impatience with the habitual corruption of the judiciary that he lasted less than a year in the job. He was restored to the post five times more in his life, but he never lasted long in it due to political intrigue, into which he entered with his old enthusiasm. He travelled in the East, making the pilgrimage to Mecca and also travelling to Jerusalem. At Damascus he found himself besieged in the city by the great Mongol leader Timur (Tamburlaine). With typical élan, he had himself let down from the walls and went alone to the tyrant's tent where he successfully negotiated the surrender of Damascus. He spent his last years in Cairo, still embroiled in political struggles though never again at the pinnacle of political life, and died in 1406 CE.

Ibn Khaldūn's critique of philosophy and theology is set out in the *Prolegomena* to the *History*. He takes pains to distinguish his new science from both the political philosophy of the time and the science of rhetoric, which is his term for dialectical theology. He is neither attempting to show how people *should* be governed, nor to persuade anyone that the Islamic systems are inevitable. Instead, he is attempting a scientific examination of different types of government that have existed and their relation to human nature. This will give him an understanding of how government naturally arises, of what its natural forms are, and a more accurate understanding of history based on observation of the realities demonstrable today. He writes that 'water is not so like to water as the future to the past'. His critique of previous historians includes their tendency to interpret Islamic history as inevitable and natural. Thus, the ruler has authority from God, via the Prophet. A society needs to be ruled by divine law and by prophesy. Ibn Khaldūn points out that most societies are neither Islamic nor 'People of the Book', by which term Muhammad referred to Jews, Christians and Zoroastrians. Nevertheless, they did succeed in organising themselves on rational lines. His conclusion is that there are natural propensities in man that enable society and rulership, both of which he assumes to be essential goods. He also attacks his predecessors for their failure to apply common sense: for example in recognising that many of the accounts of numbers of armies and amounts of money in traditional chronicles must be wrong.

> 'The intellect should not be used to weigh such matters as the oneness of God, the other world, the truth of prophecy, the real character of the divine attributes, or anything else that lies beyond the level of the intellect.'

Ibn Khaldūn is critical of the Greek tradition of Plato and **al-Fārābī** for similar reasons. He distinguishes between natural science and divine science (a division he takes from **Avicenna)** and maintains that the former has never been perfectly carried out with respect to mankind. Divine science aims at the good and depends on metaphysical questions as to its nature, which may be resolved either by revelation or by philosophising. Revelation is self-validating; philosophising is rhetorical, because its truths are not demonstrable. Natural science aims at what is demonstrably true. Ibn Khaldūn's critique is thus not of religion or of scientific philosophy, but of those who claim to offer reasonable proof of what is divine, whom he classes as mere rhetoricians. He writes, 'the intellect should not be used to weigh such matters as the oneness of God, the other world, the truth of prophecy, the real character of the divine attributes, or anything else that lies beyond the level of the intellect' (*Prolegomena* 3, 38). Like **al-Ghazālī** he rejects proof of God; unlike him he does support philosophy in its proper place. The one philosopher who escapes his attack is **Averroës**, another judge who distinguished between true religion and true philosophy. In philosophy Ibn Khaldūn looks forward to modern thinking, but in religion he yearns for a time before the invention of *kalam* or dialectical theology. He might on this account be expected to oppose Sufism, but he is not, adopting a similar position to al-Ghazālī. His poetry is Sufic in style.

To turn from his view of philosophy to what Ibn Khaldūn called *'ilm al-'umran*, the science of culture. *Umran*, meaning culture or civilization, is one of two key terms associated with Ibn Khaldūn's thought. The other is *'asabiya* or social cohesion, a quality he associated with the nomadic Arabs. The two main social groups distinguished by him are the nomads and the townspeople. His view of history, like that of Thucydides, is cyclical. It is also, as might be expected from his biography, a rather pessimistic view, in which instability and corruption are inevitable. The nomads are hardy, courageous and have strong *'asabiya*. The townspeople are cultured and wealthy, but weak individually and as a group. Ibn Khaldūn's theory of *Umran* is that the nomads conquer the townspeople and rule over them for about three generations or 120 years, in which time they acquire the vices of the town. The ruler is then forced to hire mercenaries to protect this authority, but his empire is ready to fall at the first attack. Ibn Khaldūn's ideas on culture, though limited in their application to the cultural epoch in which he found himself, are a successful analysis of the observed facts. Plato's theory of the decline of society from aristocracy to tyranny (to take a contrary example) is, despite some interesting observations, created to fit his metaphysics. Ibn Khaldūn's real originality lies in his radical methodology, his convictions about human nature and his conception of *'asabiya*

Arab Nomads.

Part Three

THE
FAR EAST

CHINA, KOREA
AND JAPAN

CHINESE PHILOSOPHY
INTRODUCTION

The course of Chinese philosophy is frequently seen as a dialectic, with Confucianism the thesis, Daoism and Buddhism the antithesis, and Neo-Confucianism the synthesis.

The three great Chinese teachers of spiritual wisdom – Buddha, Laozi and Confucius.

The course of Chinese thought has been strongly affected by the isolation of China from the rest of the world. To the east and south there were vast oceans and to the north and west impassable mountains, deserts and wasteland. This meant that, to an even greater degree than in India, thought in China developed independently and in isolation. This has its positive aspect: Chinese culture was allowed to maintain its integrity for millennia. On the negative side, the lack of challenge to Chinese thought meant that it developed less variety than elsewhere and became somewhat insular. Nevertheless, there is no doubt that China takes equal place as one of the three great philosophical cultures of the world.

Whereas the West emphasised the rational, and India the spiritual, China is home to the world's greatest tradition of ethics and civilization. China shows us how we ought to live with each other.

This tradition is that of Confucius, the great founder-figure of Chinese philosophy and the inspiration for much of its culture, government and law. He is the main wellspring of Chinese thought and its debt to him is no less than that of Western philosophy to Socrates. The deficiencies in Chinese philosophy are, very broadly speaking, the areas on which Confucius preferred not to focus. These are enumerated by Fung Yu-Lan as its lack of philosophical methodology, logic and epistemology, as well as a relative weakness in metaphysics.

Daoism (or Taoism), the other great Chinese contribution, is in some sense the balance to Confucianism. It characterises itself as the weak, feminine, passive and dark *yin* to Confucianism's strong, masculine, active and bright *yang*. Accordingly, it represents the contemplative aspect of life, while Confucianism represents the active principle. Confucianism in some form or other was part of the Chinese state since the Han dynasty (206 BCE – 220 CE) while Daoism sustained itself at the edges, communing with nature and developing an ascetic way of life. It is often identified with an egalitarian counter-culture. It was founded by Laozi, but an equally great figure in its early history is Zhuangzi. Its later history is patchier than that of the establishment Confucianism. Daoism seemed to degenerate easily into superstition, divination and magic. A frequent concern of Daoists was the search for the elixir of life, a pursuit totally at odds with the essential philosophy of its founders.

Buddhism, influential from around the second century CE, was the first substantial outside influence. Nevertheless, the strength of Chinese culture was such that it developed its own forms, often from the Daoism with which it has much in common. In China Zen (originally *Chan*) Buddhism was an original form that developed from Daoist sources and is distinctively non-Indian. Another important Chinese form we

consider in this book is the Huayen, as complex as Zen is anti-intellectual.

The course of Chinese philosophy is frequently seen as a dialectic, with Confucianism the thesis, Daoism and Buddhism the antithesis, and Neo-Confucianism the synthesis. The great Neo-Confucian renaissance of the eleventh and twelfth centuries saw Daoist and Buddhist concepts renew Confucianism, which then became a more balanced and robust system. This is not to say that all that was good in Daoism and Buddhism was swallowed up by Confucianism. Indeed, the suggestion of a Darwinian struggle for hearts and minds is mistaken. The Chinese saying 'three religions, one religion' reflects the relatively peaceful co-existence of the traditions. Overall, however, it would be right to say that in terms of philosophy, the Confucians are the most important, and that they are also the most important influence on Chinese society. Daoism and

A Zen garden at the Nanzenji Temple in Kyoto, Japan.

Buddhism become tributaries to the Confucian philosophical stream, despite their continuing religious importance.

It is worth noting here that a term such as 'Confucian' or 'Confucianism' is more or less unknown in Chinese thought. The Confucians were simply the *ru (ju)*, a word meaning 'literati'. Just as Socrates thought of himself as a philosopher, the *ru* were the educated elite who reflected on philosophical issues. They spoke about the Way or 'Dao', but distinguished themselves from unorthodox thinkers known as Daoists, and from the Buddhists. Just as the *astika* philosophies in India are those that accept the Veda as revelatory, the *ru* were those that took Confucian philosophy to be true. In some ways it would be more accurate to think of them not as Confucian but as the orthodox Chinese philosophers.

The twentieth century was the most traumatic period in Chinese history in over 2,000 years. Disruptions from Europe and its growing dominance had gradually rendered the old ways untenable. The Empire finally ended in 1912, being replaced first by a republic and later by the Communists of Mao Zedong, who took power in 1949. Philosophically, too, the old order has suffered its heaviest blow, with Confucianism finally removed from the centre of government and education. This was also a period that saw great interest in Zen Buddhism and Daoism in the West. In the case of Zen (which admittedly is now more identified with Japan), it caught the Western imagination with its drama, aesthetic qualities and aversion to intellectualism. Daoism on the other hand appeals strongly to the

---

Transliteration of Chinese

There are two main systems of transliteration of Chinese characters into Latin script. The older and more familiar is the Wade-Giles system, but it is generally acknowledged to be inferior to the newer pinyin method, which is also the official method recognised by China. Although some Chinese names like Lao-Tzu and Mao Tse-Tung are familiar to us in their Wade-Giles transliteration rather than the pinyin Laozi and Mao Zedong, the latter method has been used throughout, with Wade-Giles alternatives generally given in parentheses. Translations in Wade-Giles retain the original transliterations, however.

Western sensibility because of its connection with nature, its compassion, and its antagonism towards system, technology and commerce. In some ways Daoism is like Romanticism two centuries ago, but without the associated self-destructive egotism. The effect of all this on the future of Chinese philosophy remains to be seen.

CONFUCIUS (KONGFUZI, K'UNG FU-TZU)

551–479 BCE

Confucius is a Latinization of Kongfuzi, literally 'Master Kong'. His name was first known to the West through the publication of Confucian works by Jesuits who settled in Peking in 1583. 'Confucius' soon became almost a byword in the West for Chinese wisdom. We might imagine that this myth greatly exaggerates the importance of Confucius in China, but this is not so. Although there is often little relation between Confucius' philosophy and its historical impact, there is a no more influential figure in Chinese thought.

The documentary accounts of Confucius' life are relatively uncontroversial, unlike some other philosophers of the period. The *Analects*, where his teaching is to be found, was probably started long after his death and was being 'edited' for over a century or two. However, the reported 'life events' involve no supernatural or impossible claims. Leaving aside apocryphal and untrustworthy material, the accepted sketch goes like this. He was born in the state of Lu, present-day Shandong Province. His family may have been aristocratic, but by the time of Confucius' birth, they had no income from land holdings. Confucius thought he lived in turbulent times, as hinted at by a story told of his father in which he held up a portcullis gate with his bare hands to help his companions escape. However, China's 'Warring States' period had not begun. His father died when he was only three and he was raised by his mother. By Confucius' own account 'I was of humble station when I was young. That is why I am skilled in many menial things' (*Analects*, IX, 6)[48]. According to the *Mencius*, he was once employed as a 'minor official in charge of stores', and at another time 'in charge of sheep and cattle'. The upshot is that Confucius relied on educating others. He was the first documented teacher in China (though a dubious legend suggests he learned from Laozi). His learning may have stemmed from some military training – he taught his students charioteering and archery. But his intellectual passion was traditional ceremony. By the age of 27 he may have been employed at the court of Lu in some capacity. Later, he may have been involved in diplomacy and was at the court of Wei. His role ended when he refused, or was unable, to advise the Duke on military matters. In his late forties, some accounts report that he was appointed to the post of police commissioner in Lu, but he resigned after a short time. There followed 'for more than a decade' a period of travel in other states to the south-west of Lu. Confucius was then in his fifties and seems to have lived under threat of assassination. He was back in Lu in 484 BCE and seems to have been employed at court as a counsellor of low rank. Despite this there are several conversations recorded with the Duke and his prime minister from this period. Confucius died in 479 BCE.

More important than Confucius' political life, however, is his establishment of a school, perhaps in his thirties. His teaching and appealing personality had an enormous effect on his students. This gives us Confucius' own playful description of himself:

> *The Governor of She asked Tzu-lu about Confucius. Tzu-lu did not answer. The Master [i.e. Confucius] said, 'Why did you not simply say something to this effect: he is the sort of man who forgets to eat when he tries to solve a problem that has been driving him to distraction, who is so full of joy that he forgets his worries, and who does not notice the onset of old age.'*
>
> Analects, VII, 19.

The most extreme accounts credit Confucius with over 3,000 students. A significant number founded other Confucian schools with varying emphasis. Confucius is also credited with editing (or perhaps, writing) some of the books that are known today as the 'Confucian

Classics', including *The Classic on Poetry*, *The Classic on History* and *The Book of Li*. Among the huge corpus of Confucian works, however, the only one that attributes most of its teachings to 'The Master' is the *Analects* (that is, 'literary gleanings'). The *Analects* do not purport to be the writings of Confucius, but a later collection of sayings attributed to him and to some of his disciples.

As with other Eastern cultures described in this book, philosophy and religion are not rigidly delineated. Confucian philosophy, like Daoist thought, became a popular form of religion and in later times competed with the third major religion in China and East Asia, Buddhism. None of these three has a 'true church' mentality and they are often seen as non-competitive. Chinese popular practitioners say, 'three religions are one'. Confucianism was probably the first idea system to take shape in China and its long-term impact has been greater than the other two.

Confucianism can be described as humanism, principally concerned with human social life as opposed to the divine. Accordingly, its main interests are in ethics and moral psychology: how may we cultivate the character that reliably acts rightly? Confucianism concerns itself with such questions at all levels, from mundane family relations to inter-state diplomacy and rule. Daoism, by contrast, emphasizes the metaphysical, in particular meta-ethics – questions about the ultimate nature, reality and knowability of the moral *dao*. This leads some Daoists to become moral sceptics or relativists who locate human morality as a small part of the *dao* of nature. Confucius emphasises his thoroughgoing humanism by contrast when he says, 'It is man who is capable of broadening the Way (Dao). It is not the Way that is capable of broadening man' (XV, 29). Other Daoists (sometimes called 'primitivists') become anti-moral and anti-social, withdrawing from social life in quietism and solitude. A primitivist who says Confucius should follow him and 'run away from the world altogether' prompts him to comment:

> *'One cannot associate with birds and beasts. Am I not a member of this human race? Who, then, is there for me to associate with? While the Way [Dao] is to be found in the Empire, I will not change places with him.'*
>
> Analects, XVIII, 6.

Confucianism contrasts with Buddhism partly in its avoidance of discussions on eternal life, a subject on which Confucius refuses to be drawn. He seems to have been agnostic about the afterlife and pragmatically advised wariness with regard to higher beings:

> *Fan Ch'ih asked about wisdom. The Master said, 'To work for the things the common people have a right to and to keep one's distance from the gods and spirits while showing them reverence can be called wisdom.'*
>
> Analects, VI, 22.

Confucius marks a change in Chinese thinking on divine matters, even though he speaks of them very little. In the earlier dynasty, religion was concerned with God as *Shang Di* 'the emperor above'. Confucius speaks rarely, some disciples complain, of *Tian* ('Heaven' or 'Nature'), but refuses to speak, as others do, of the Way or Will of Tian. This verbal change marks an important break with the previous conception of a personal and

active moral authority. For Confucius and his successors moral authority is impersonal, and its guidance comes in the form of the constant ways enshrined in nature. It would be wrong to suppose Confucius a kind of atheist since he accepts the authority of Tian, but nonetheless his philosophy functions without a personal deity.

Similar developments were going on elsewhere in the world at around this period. New belief-systems were springing up: the *Upanishads*, Buddhism and Jainism in India; and in Greece the growth of rational philosophy. These all, in their own way, represent moves away from tribal and ritual religion, whether towards ethical and social concerns (as with Confucius and Socrates) or towards speculative forms of philosophy and religion (as with Laozi, the *Upanishads* and Buddhism). However, it should be noted that Confucius is by temperament conservative. In this his approach echoes that of Socrates or the *Upanishads*, rather than the more radical Buddhism, insisting on respect for the old religion while 'keep[ing] one's distance'.

The second factor that distinguishes Confucius is his emphasis on traditional ritual or propriety ('*li*'). If people live properly according to tradition then their behaviour will be correctly regulated. *Li* includes filial piety, respect for the ancestors, observance of rites and performing one's duties properly. Confucius is convinced that if people follow *li* it will lead to the reform of their character and that of the state. For example, Confucius maintains that a man who is loyal to both his father and his older brother – the two most important traditional relationships – will also be loyal to the state. In the same way, ritual is to be valued not for its religious significance, but simply because it gives people something refined to follow:

Confucius consults the I-ching.

> *Tzu-kung wanted to do away with the sacrificial sheep at the announcement of the new moon. The Master said, 'Ssu, you are loath to part with the price of the sheep, but I am loath to see the disappearance of the rite.'*
>
> Analects, III, 17.

Confucius' views on the importance of *li* (ritual) throughout society could be compared with Plato's ideas of justice; not as a legal system, but as everyone being in their proper place.

Another important concept in Confucius is that of *yi* which means, roughly, 'morality' or 'duty'. Confucius did not relate this concept to *li* specifically, but it supplies to his system a moral principle against which social rituals may be assessed:

> *The gentleman is not invariably for or against anything. He is on the side of what is moral (yi).*
>
> Analects, IV, 10.

Rounding out the picture of Confucian moral philosophy is the enigmatic term *ren* (humanity). *Ren* is also translated variously as 'benevolence,' 'kindness', and 'human-heartedness'. When asked about the meaning of *ren*, Confucius responded, 'Love your fellow man'. In his use of the term, Confucius makes it clear that he regards it as the most fundamental: 'What can a man do with *li* (ritual) who is not

ren?' Thus humanity or loving-kindness becomes the guiding light for social order. Although Confucius is not clear on what *ren* might be – perhaps it is a catch-all word for human virtue – his successors developed these hints so that the term became perhaps the most important in Chinese philosophy. Han Dynasty (206 BCE–220 CE) thinkers understood it more or less to mean 'love', eventually becoming 'universal love'. With the Neo-Confucian thinkers, led by **Zhang Zai** (1020–1077 CE), *ren* grew to encompass the entire universe, a concept usually expressed as 'forming one body with all things'[49].

'At seventy I followed my heart and did not err.'

For Confucius, however, *ren* is best seen as the cardinal element in the make-up of the 'superior man', a term that more than any other forms the subject matter of The *Analects*. The superior man (or in Lau's translation, the 'gentleman') is moderate, serious, respectful, loyal, and flexible: he is 'on the side of what is moral.'

Another term he uses often interchangeably with that of the gentleman is 'the benevolent man'. Propriety and goodness are intimately linked. Elsewhere he says that a gentleman possesses both native energy and refinement, another sentiment echoed by Plato. Confucius' aim in political reform centres not on legislation but on the moral leadership of society: that is, on the moral character of the leader. A ruler asks him about capital punishment and his response is instructive:

> 'In administering your government, what need is there for you to kill? Just desire the good yourself and the common people will be good. The virtue of the gentleman is like wind; the virtue of the small man is like grass. Let the wind blow over the grass and it is sure to bend.'
>
> Analects, XII, 19.

Another important aspect of Confucius' social thought is the idea of 'rectification of names', which Confucius called the first principle of government. In a narrow sense it means a conformity of the behaviour to linguistic codes, such as *li* and penal codes. In a broader sense, it comes to refer to a person's executing the role that matches his name (which also denotes rank or status) and later, to a general correspondence between appearance and actuality, the inner and the outer. The rectification of names is very important in later Chinese philosophy and is considered separately on pages 130–2.

Perhaps the best illustration of the aim of Confucius' philosophy is in one of the longest of the *Analects,* in which Confucius invites four of his disciples to speak about what they would do if they could. One would take responsibility for a small, embattled kingdom; a second would take on the management of a district; and the third the role of a minor ceremonial official. The fourth, Tien, says:

> 'In late spring, after the spring clothes have been newly made, I should like, together with five or six adults and six or seven boys, to go bathing in the River Yi and enjoy the breeze on the Rain Altar, and then to go home chanting poetry.' The Master sighed and said, 'I am all in favour of Tien'.
>
> Analects, XI, 26.

The arresting quality of this dreamy passage is its apparent contrast to Confucius' concern elsewhere for constant study, appropriate observation of ritual and the reform of society. This is the Confucius who describes his life culminating in ease and propriety: 'at seventy I followed my heart and did not err'. The effort to acquire wisdom and to cultivate oneself is undertaken not for its own sake but because it is a joy, and as this passage shows, has joy as its aim.

Although Confucius was not politically successful in his own lifetime, his ideas gradually permeated the politics of the empire after the Han dynasty displaced the Qin which unified China in 221 BCE. The Han dynasty adopted Confucianism as a state ideology in the second century CE. With the fall of the Han in 220 CE, Confucianism lost some of its appeal, but it was revived under the Song dynasty (960–1279 CE), in particular by the orthodox neo-Confucian thinker, **Zhuxi** (1130–1200 CE). Zhuxi's work codified Confucian thought and his commentaries formed the basis of the Chinese civil service examinations, set up in 1313 CE and existing in that form for some 600 years. This is perhaps the most direct example of Confucius' influence in the West, as the examinations were the model for those established by the East India Company which later became the basis of the public education-system of the British Empire and thus of the Western world.

The emperor Kao Tsu (personal name Liu Pang), founder of the Han dynasty, sacrifices a pig, a goat and a cow at the tomb of Confucius, who surely would not have approved!

THE RECTIFICATION OF NAMES

The rectification of names is discussed firstly by **Confucius** *(551–479 BCE) and is, according to Wing-Tsit Chan, 'a perennial theme in the Confucian school, as well as in nearly all other schools' of Chinese philosophy. The topic came to divide those who maintained an interest in social and ideological forms and norms, and those that sought to question or break them down. The idea of 'rectification' arises because of Confucius' view that names and actions had begun to change, corrupting everything. The process he describes is of a gradual drift of authority away from those who should exercise it – ideally the Emperor – downwards to lesser figures. Power passes from the Emperor to the nobles, from the nobles to the ministers and from the ministers to their officials. This leads ultimately to the downfall of the Empire. For Confucius the solution is the rectification of names. This has two principal meanings: firstly that the 'names' people have, that is, their job titles or roles such as minister, farmer, father, son, sister and so on, and the reality of their conduct should coincide; and secondly that words and deeds should in general coincide.*

Confucius is asked what his first measure in government would be, and his reply is 'the rectification of names'. His account is as follows:

> When names are not correct, what is said will not sound reasonable; when what is said does not sound reasonable, affairs will not culminate in success; when affairs do not culminate in success, rites and music will not flourish; when rites and music do not flourish, punishments will not fit the crimes; when punishments do not fit the crimes, the common people will not know where to put hand and foot. Thus when the gentleman names something, the name is sure to be useable in speech, and when he says something, this is sure to be practicable. The thing about the gentleman is that he is anything but casual where speech is concerned.
>
> *Analects XIII, 3.*

His other direct reference to the subject is when he says:

> Let the ruler be a ruler, the subject a subject, the father a father and the son a son.
>
> *Analects, XII, 11*

Confucius' main concern is ethical. If the 'gentleman' or 'superior man' is careful, accurate, clear and practical in his speech, then others will have a good lead to follow. If he is casual, unclear or unrealistic in what he says, then others will be confused. Furthermore there is the implication that those in authority must be responsible.

Confucius' discussion of the rectification of names is one of the more difficult areas in his philosophy. Insofar as the rectification of names is a principle of government it is easy to follow. Its other aspect, the correspondence between word and deed, knowledge and action, and name and actuality, is more complex. The difficulty is not so much in what he says as in what he does not say or merely hints at. As with the question of human nature, which he refused to discuss, the topic became one of the fundamental questions for his successors. We will now look at some of these and their divergent views.

***Hanfeizi** (280–233 BCE) makes the rectification of names into a matter for legislation. Everyone must do their duty and only their duty. Doing more than one's duty is as bad as doing less; exaggerating one's achievements and downplaying them are equally wrong. This extreme view leads to tyranny and is hardly in the Confucian spirit.*

*The Confucian **Xunzi** (298–238 BCE), Hanfeizi's teacher, examines the subject more closely. He relates it to our sense perceptions. If we see something with the eyes but fail to name it properly, 'there is no knowledge' and we are unable to make use of it. Thus, naming is part of the process of thought. For Xunzi, names are conventional rather than fundamental: ordering things is not in any way natural, though it is necessary. In this, he diverges from the mainstream view, which is that there is something fundamental about names. The sage is someone who sees how things are and so divines the correct names for them. Typical of this approach is another Confucian, Tung Chungshu (c. 179–c. 104 BCE), who is fascinated by etymology. For example, the word for people (min) is derived from the word for sleep (ming); therefore the people need to be awakened by education. Confucius did not discuss whether names were conventional or fundamental, and so he supports neither view.*

*The rectification of names was attacked by the socially radical followers of **Mozi** (c. 470–c. 391 BCE) on the grounds that one-name-one-thing was unsustainable. A similar line was taken by the 'School of Names' thinkers* *such as the paradox-maker Gongsun Long. In the chapter on Xunzi we examine how he tackles these challenges to the concept. Social order is essential to Xunzi and, for him, the growth of linguistic logic provides a way for the social order to be questioned. His development of a more subtle version of the rectification of names is nevertheless itself an excellent and rare example of Chinese logic.*

In the Neo-Confucian movement of the twelfth century onwards, the theme continued to be an important one. **Wang Yangming** *(1472–1529 CE) took the idea further than anyone had before in arguing that name (or knowledge) and actuality (action) were the same thing. Knowing about something without acting on it, or acting without knowledge, was a mistake, and to divide the two was a logical error. Again, the name is a moral injunction.*

Daoist thinkers take an opposite view. **Laozi** *(Lao Tzu), for example, opens his Daode Jing with the enigmatic words:*

> The Way (Dao) that can be told of is not the eternal Way;
> The name that can be named is not the eternal name.
> The Nameless is the origin of Heaven and Earth;
> The Named is the mother of all things.
> Therefore let there always be non-being so we may see their subtlety.

While Confucius argues for external clarity and order, Laozi emphasises the underlying mystery of life. The true teacher 'spreads doctrines without words'. Names have their power: 'the Named is the mother of all things', but the fundamental reality is precisely that which is beyond the nameable.

Zhuangzi *argues in a similar way that the Confucian view lacks clarity, subtlety and substance: 'Words are not just wind. Words have something to say. But if what they have to say is not fixed, then do they really say something?*

MOZI (MO TZU)

c. 470–c. 391 BCE

Mohism, the philosophy founded by Mozi, was with Confucianism one of the two most important early schools of thought in China during the Warring States period (403–222 BCE). It was destroyed by the Qin unification and oppression of rival thinkers and, because of its fierce opposition to Confucianism, became anathema when the Han dynasty made Confucianism the state orthodoxy. Confucians criticized it as being too idealistic in its universalism while the Daoists viewed it as being too severe and demanding with its utilitarian morality. Within 300 years of his death, Mozi's school had disappeared. Mohism was never to recover its former importance, although its utilitarianism and anti-Confucianism led to a revival of interest in China in the twentieth century.

Like many Chinese thinkers from the pre-Imperial age, Mozi's life is not well documented. He was born in either Lu or Song province, present-day Shandong. Various accounts of his life suggest that he was an artisan, a follower of Confucius and then a kind of mercenary or (as the first century BCE chronicle *Shi Ji* has it) that he was a powerful Song government official. In any case, Mozi eventually gave up his former pursuits and became a wandering teacher, attempting like **Confucius** to convince various rulers to adopt his ideas. At least three schools of disciples promulgated Mozi's ideas, others worked to end offensive warfare and some developed semantic and proto-scientific thought. In the *Mozi*, the book that sets out Mohist thought, the

'When I do what Tian wants, Tian does what I want.'

schools seem to present their rival interpretations, with three different essays on each topic. Some parts of the *Mozi* are later additions and it is doubtful that Mozi actually wrote any of the book, but it is generally accepted to be representative of his thought.

The central value in Mozi's philosophy is *li* (benefit or utility) which he develops into altruistic utilitarianism. The important virtue, therefore, is universal love or *jianai* which Mohists contrast with Confucians' emphasis on filial relations and 'graded' concern for others. Mozi's reasoning for this is that if everyone followed a doctrine of partiality to their kin, it would be worse for everyone. So the best way to make your family better off is to get people to have equal concern for all. This virtue is commended not because it is natural or good in itself, but because it produces good utilitarian consequences. However, in other places he appeals to *Tian* ('Heaven' or 'Nature') to justify his valuing utility. He observes, typically, 'when I do what Tian wants, Tian does what I want'[50]. *Tian* approves of moral action and naturally rewards it, while punishing immorality. Although Mohism has attracted interest in recent times for its similarity to Christian teaching on love, its appeal to universal utilitarianism is in reality very different.

In contrast to Confucianism with its emphasis on family piety, Mozi taught that people should do what would result in universal good for all people. Doing good (*li* or 'benefit' or 'utility') is explained mainly in material terms. We 'love' our neighbours by supplying their physical needs for food, clothing and shelter – not by showering them with some emotion. Our concern for those farther afield, even those in foreign states, should motivate us to accept peaceful policies. Mozi bitterly condemned all 'offensive' warfare. Curiously, he did not think of war as motivated by selfishness, but by moral disagreements. But the result is the opposite of what anyone would call moral. So he urges us to abide by a common, unambiguous, and measurable standard of morality – general utility. According to Mozi the main evil in society is selfishness, or partiality towards those close to us. Partial love is no love at all. Other thinkers did not dismiss this idea, but its failure to acknowledge the particular ties of family and hierarchy were felt to be its weakness. As the Confucian **Xunzi** wrote two centuries

later: 'Mozi has insight about equality (universal love), but not about inequality (distinction in human relations)'.

Mohism was opposed to anything that did not directly contribute to people's well-being. Thus he criticized Confucian preoccupation with showy rituals and ceremonies – particularly those associated with China's lavish funeral practices and the elaborate concerts and productions (music) for the rulers. Mozi thus goes much further than Confucius, who loved all these things while expressing coolness towards the primitive beliefs that had done much to put them in place. Confucius' conversation with Tzu-kung[51] on the subject of an animal sacrifice draws up the battle-lines between Confucianism and Mohism: 'you are loath to part with the price of the sheep, but I am loath to see the disappearance of the rite'. On the other hand, Mozi does maintain a commitment to Tian and argues for the utility of maintaining public discourse about spirits and ghosts. Mozi is equally critical of elaborate funerary and mourning ritual, in which fortunes could be spent and years of productivity wasted by mourners. He even criticises the tradition of celibacy during the mourning period on the grounds that people should be getting on with the duty of reproduction.

Mozi's critique of music is its wasteful extravagance – the term used for music is also translated as 'pleasure' or 'entertainment' and Confucius often pairs it with his *li* (ritual). In ancient China, the term probably referred to lavish royal concerts, complete with acrobats. In Mozi's view, the musicians could better employ their keen senses in tilling the fields or making cloth, the rulers should not waste their time attending recitals, and the state

Mozi viewed music as a wasteful extravagance.

should not spend its resources on maintaining expensive troupes of performers. Nothing in Mozi's formulation suggests he is opposed to people whistling while they work, but nowhere does he express any aesthetic sense. Confucius, by contrast, is recorded as having been so overwhelmed by a beautiful musical performance that he did not notice the taste of his food for three months afterwards. Mozi's philosophy is, in this regard, reminiscent of the caricatured utilitarianism of Dickens' *Hard Times*, judging Gradgrind-like the value of every activity by its productivity alone.

An interesting feature of Mozi's rejection of music and other cultural 'entertainment' is the absence of any hint of concepts of subjectivity. His formulation of utilitarianism does not appeal to concepts of pleasure and pain, nor happiness and unhappiness. His objection to music simply skips over weighing the pleasure it may bring. This is a surprising feature of early Chinese thought which has no theory of 'experience' or 'consciousness' or the idea of an 'inner life'

or mind-body dualism. They seemed all to be naturalists[52]. So his utilitarianism appeals to its being a measurement-like standard – which would be hard if the measures were subjective states. So for Mozi, 'the greatest good for the greatest number' is the unproblematic 'greatest goods'. Thus Mozi maintains that the only criterion of human good is an objective measurable one.

Despite its narrow utilitarian focus, there are undeniably attractive elements to Mohism. Although we may feel that, even from a practical point of view, Mohism might defeat itself through sheer joylessness, there is little to object to in its emphasis on practical charity and good governance. The universal concern for others is unprecedented and foreshadows modern liberal humanism. Mozi's emphasis on the *xiaoren* or 'inferior person' as opposed to the Confucian ideal of the *zhunzi* or 'superior gentleman' is refreshingly egalitarian. While Confucius does appeal to all levels of society his aim is to raise people to the level of *zhunzi*; Mozi's philosophy represents no such ambition.

As to the divine, Mozi appeals to the Will of Tian, which corresponds to the Daoist idea of a constant *Dao* or Way, against which judgements of good may reliably be made. We learn the Will of Tian by looking at the natural harmony designed for our benefit. We then harmonize our morality as a state by reporting what policies are beneficial and getting approval from the ruler who promulgates the policy for everyone. In common with most thinkers of his era Mozi idealizes an earlier period (in his case the Xia dynasty of 2183–1752 BCE) when good governance and universal love predominated. Unlike others, he also speaks of a 'state of nature' in which anarchy and violence predominated. We should note here that Mozi does not believe that good is innate. If anything, man naturally wants to be moral but has no common standard. Only through some natural value can we guide the formulation of a social morality that will successfully harmonize human endeavours and fit them in the natural scheme of utility for all. This is a fundamental area of disagreement with Confucianism, and in particular with the later Confucian **Mencius**.

This leads to Mozi's conception of the role of the ruler or Son of Heaven (*Tian*) Disagreement about morality leads us to decide to choose the wisest among us as arbiter of moral judgment and set him up as the Son of Heaven. Then we all harmonize our moral judgments with his and he harmonizes his with *Tian's* – which we already know is universal utility. The ruler chooses (also on moral merit and wisdom) his ministers, the nobility and finally the village leaders who organize the system of harmonized moral judgment. This removes the multiplicity of value-systems and the consequent impulse to war. Mozi sees this

process taking the form of a reform of the language we use to express judgments. Speech should reflect the utilitarian morality and have the consequence that people follow that course of action which results in universal well-being – *Tian's* goal, the natural goal.

As a socially-concerned thinker, Mozi rejects fatalism. His critique of Confucianism on this score is probably unjust, but it is plain that any doctrine of fate or divine preordination would be destructive of Mohism. Mozi argues that the public guiding discourse should include phrases such as 'there is no fate' and 'there are spirits.' Including these, rather than their opposites, in the public discourse results in better behaviour and thus more benefit for people in general. Our actions have direct consequences in advancing or degrading the good of humanity. This is not just a matter of material cause and effect, nor is it a spiritually-based causality such as the Indian law of *karma*. Mozi believes not only that our actions have consequences in the world, but also that Heaven actively intervenes to answer just prayers, reward good actions and punish the unjust.

Mozi's philosophy includes elements that we associate with early modern Western thought: utilitarianism, state-of-nature arguments for morality and authority, pragmatic theories of language and equality. His analytic terms set the stage for the development of sophisticated Daoism. Some critics have argued that Mozi's critique of the former was crucial in stimulating the refinement of Confucian thought in the work of Mencius and Xunzi. Some scholars argue that his impact may rival that of Confucius himself, despite his lack of recognition.

LAOZI (LAO TZU)
Flourished fourth century BCE?

Laozi is acknowledged, with **Zhuangzi**, as the founder of Daoism (Taoism). It is questioned whether he really existed as an individual or whether his work is by the hands of many. Perhaps, like several of the other early classical works of China, the *Laozi* or, as is better known, the *Daode Jing (Tao Te Ching)* represents Laozi's thought but is the creation of his followers. The *Daode Jing*, literally *The Classic of The Way (Dao) and Its Power (De)*, is a short work in poetic form that has inspired more commentary and more translation than any other in Chinese. Its influence on virtually all aspects of Chinese life from government to cookery is immeasurable.

One of the controversies surrounding Daoism is its claim to be the primeval 'Way'. Most of the Chinese philosophers idealise some earlier golden age in which, they assert, the principles of their philosophy were practised naturally. The emperors and teachers of these golden ages are generally thought to be mythical. It is particularly important to Daoism to establish itself as the embodiment of the natural order, as opposed to the unnatural (to the Daoists) civilization represented by the 'Confucian' virtues such as *ren* and *yi*:

> *When the great Dao declined,*
> *The doctrines of humanity (ren)*
> *and righteousness (yi) arose*
> *When knowledge and wisdom appeared,*
> *There emerged great hypocrisy.*
> *When the six family relationships are*
> *not in harmony,*
> *There will be the advocacy of filial piety*
> *and deep love to children.*
> *When a country is in disorder,*
> *There will be praise of loyal ministers[53].*

The Daoist critique is that if there really was virtue, there would be no need to keep talking about it. Confucius' key virtue is *ren*, 'benevolence' or 'human-heartedness'. Laozi writes dramatically:

> *Heaven and Earth are not humane [ren]*
> *They regard all things as straw dogs.*
> *The sage is not humane*
> *He regards all people as straw dogs.*

Neither the sage nor the universe is *ren* because they are impartial. Daoism promises to restore us to the Garden of

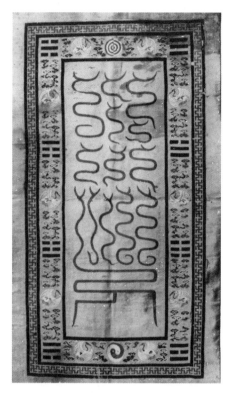

Taoist sacred diagrams on a wall hanging from the Ming period (1368–1644 CE).

Eden, while, according to this view, Confucianism struggles in a fallen world.

Traditional accounts of Laozi's life vary. According to one he was born in Juren in the state of Chu. He worked as an archivist for the state of Zhou before deciding to retreat from the world and to leave China. Travelling westward on a water buffalo's back, Laozi was recognized by a border guard who refused to let him pass until he had written down his wisdom. Over two to three weeks he composed the 81 short chapters of the *Daode Jing*, which satisfied the guard. He was apparently never seen or heard from again. Other highly improbable legends that find Laozi instructing Confucius in ritual and enlightening the Buddha merely serve to confirm the importance to Daoism of a claim to be the first teaching.

Daoist sources tend to place Laozi in around the sixth century BCE, perhaps as an older contemporary of Confucius. Others date Laozi to as late as the fourth century BCE. Fung Yu-Lan in *A History of Chinese Philosophy* points to the account of Daoism in the *Shi Ji* chronicle:

> *The Taoist school urged men to unity of spirit, teaching that all activities should be in harmony with the unseen, with abundant liberality toward all things of nature. As to practice, they accept the orderly sequence of things from the Yin-Yang school, gather the good points of the Confucians and Mohists, and combine with these the important points of the (school of) Names and Law. In accordance with the changes of the seasons, they respond to the development of natural objects. Their achievements fit everywhere. Their ideas are simple and easily carried out. They perform but little, but their achievements are numerous.*

If this is correct, Laozi is after not only Confucius (551–479 BCE) but also **Mozi** (founder of the Mohist school), who died around 391 BCE. He is certainly earlier than **Zhuangzi** (369–286 BCE) and **Mencius** (371–289 BCE), both of whom are familiar with the *Daode Jing*.

The summary of the Daoist school given in the *Shi Ji* seems very believable. The *Daode Jing* is a reaction to an existing orthodoxy

Laozi riding an ox.

rather than (or perhaps as well as) being the ancient, timeless Way its adherents claim. The strength of Laozi's criticism proves the point that in his time, at least, the *Dao* is not the single, natural Way of yore but a radical alternative to a much more prevalent philosophy. It derives much of its strength from the ethic of opposition.

The symbolism of *yin* and *yang*, the two contrasting but complementary principles in Chinese philosophy, are another way Daoism positions itself in relation to 'Confucian' values. From the Daoist perspective, Confucianism is *yang* in its concern with masculinity, structure, growth, externality and enlightenment, while Daoism is *yin* in its femininity, flexibility, quietism, internality and passivity. In its positive view of femininity, Daoism is almost unique in ancient philosophy. Even the most progressive tendencies in Greek or Indian thought of similar vintage do not come close. The three most common analogies for the *Dao* in Laozi are those of the woman, the infant and water. All have the *yin* qualities of passivity, weakness and potentiality. Fittingly, although Daoism has never attained the status of Confucianism in Chinese public life, it has exerted its influence in a more covert fashion. To Daoism and Laozi can be traced many of the important characteristics of Chinese Buddhism, in particular Chan (Zen) Buddhism, as well as of Neo-Confucianism.

Laozi's key principle is of course that of the *Dao* or Way. There are two main aspects to this: the *Dao* is the way to be and behave; and it is the way things are. It is something like the idea of natural law as used in some Western philosophy – a single principle underlying both moral conduct and physical reality. By according with the Dao rather than selfish desire, a human being is fulfilled. The *Dao* is an important principle in all of the early Chinese philosophers, but the emphasis of thinkers such as Laozi and Zhuangzi on the idea is such that they became known as the Daoists.

The variety of translations and interpretations of the *Daode Jing* attest to its brevity and difficulty. From its very opening words, the *Daode Jing* sets out a view radically different to rival Chinese philosophies:

> *The Way (Dao) that can be told of is*
> *not the eternal Way;*
> *The name that can be named is not*
> *the eternal name.*
> *The Nameless is the origin of Heaven*
> *and Earth;*
> *The Named is the mother of all things.*
> *Therefore let there always be non-*
> *being so we may see their subtlety.*

'The rectification of names' is a key theme in many of the other thinkers we consider in this book, going back to Confucius[54]. By this is meant a correlation between word and deed, classification and reality. Philosophers as diverse as the idealistic **Mencius** and the tyrannical **Hanfeizi** agree that the reform of society depends on a clear definition of names. Laozi, on the contrary, maintains that what can be named passes away. The eternal *Dao* or Way is beyond name.

Another perspective Laozi gives on this is that:

> *The sage manages affairs without*
> *action (wuwei)*
> *And spreads doctrines without words.*

The principle of *wuwei* is, after the *Dao*, the most important in Laozi. It is not to be understood as inaction, but as doing nothing contrary to nature, going with the flow of the Way.

Another Daoist term that challenges Confucianism is *xu* (*hsu*) or emptiness: 'Dao is empty'. Again, the emptiness of *Dao* is not that of something that has no substance or reality, but the emptiness of a bowl of infinite capacity, an infinite womb. It is easy to see how Daoism prepared the way for the arrival of Buddhism in China, from around the second century CE. *Xu* is close to the *shūnyata* or emptiness of Madhyāmika Buddhism, although it would be a mistake to equate the two. Perhaps the key difference is that Daoism consistently affirms the world while Buddhism reaches beyond it. Although Daoism is associated with hermitage and withdrawal, the withdrawal is regarded as the most effective means to achieve worldly ends, or perhaps is regarded as consistent with worldly ends: 'because he has no personal interests. . . . His personal interests are fulfilled'. Tranquillity is important to Laozi, but does not imply a retreat from the activity of the world. Rather, the retreat is from belief in the efficacy of activity. Confucius on the other hand speaks frequently of his indefatigability.

Another important difference between Laozi and Buddhism is the degree to which he affirms the spiritual reality: 'the essence is very real; in it are evidences'. If Buddhism as a philosophy tends to say 'no' to everything, Daoism says 'yes'.

> *… the great man dwells in the thick*
> *(substantial), and does not rest with the*
> *thin (superficial).*
> *He dwells in the fruit (reality) and does*
> *not rest with the flower (appearance).*

To Laozi, the reality of the Dao is not achieved through the superficial constructs of learning. Living in the reality differs from thinking about its appearance. This theme is developed further in the chapter on Laozi's fascinating successor Zhuangzi.

ZHUANGZI (CHUANG TZU)

369–286 BCE

Zhuangzi is, with **Laozi** (Lao Tzu), regarded as the co-founder of what came to be known later as Daoism (Taoism). As with Laozi, there are many who question whether he really was an individual, or whether his works, the *Zhuangzi*, are an anthology of what were later labelled as 'Daoist' sages. There is even a tradition that refers to the two sages as one, but this only began several centuries after the *Zhuangzi* and the *Daode Jing*. In addition to this, there are several key differences between the two and if they are not real individuals then they do represent real and distinct schools of thought. We will assume here that there was a historical Zhuangzi, although not all of the

Zhuangzi is written by him. The current version of the *Zhuangzi* was compiled by Guo Xiang around 300 CE. Guo Xiang is important both for his arrangement of the Zhuangzi and for his editing out of what he regarded to be inauthentic material. An earlier recension of the Zhuangzi is known to have comprised 51 chapters, but the extant one, by Guo Xiang, has only 33. For some reason – perhaps judicious editing – the 33-chapter version entirely replaced the older one, which is now lost. The *Shi Ji* chronicle seems to refer to an earlier version of 100,000 words which was impractical due to the variety of doctrines it seemed to propound.

Only the first seven chapters, the 'Inner Chapters' are regarded by most scholars to be the work of Zhuangzi. Chapters 8–22 are traditionally known as the 'Outer Chapters', while Chapters 23–33 are the 'Miscellaneous Chapters'. Some scholars divide the *Zhuangzi* even more, detecting at least five different authors within the Zhuangzi. It is beyond the scope of this chapter to distinguish between these, and we will therefore treat the entire book as a repository of Zhuangist thinking, with special reference to the Inner Chapters. The Inner Chapters do not mention Laozi, but the authors of the Outer Chapters evidently know and draw upon the *Daode Jing*.

What we know of the life of Zhuangzi is drawn from sources centuries later. These accounts tell us that he was a civil servant in the Meng (present-day Henan) province. He apparently gained a great reputation for wisdom and turned down King Wei's request that he become his prime minister. A version of this story is in chapter 17 of the *Zhuangzi:*

Once, when Chuang Tzu [Zhuangzi] was fishing in the P'u River, the king of Ch'u sent two officials to go and announce to him: 'I would like to trouble you with the administration of my realm.'

Chuang Tzu held on to the fishing pole and, without turning his head, said, 'I have heard that there is a sacred tortoise in Ch'u that has been dead for three thousand years. The king keeps it wrapped in cloth and boxed, and stores it in the ancestral temple. Now would this tortoise rather be dead and have its bones left behind and honored? Or would it rather be alive and dragging its tail in the mud?'

'It would rather be alive and dragging its tail in the mud,' said the two officials.

Chuang Tzu said, 'Go away! I'll drag my tail in the mud!'[55]

Whether or not there is any literal truth in this story, Zhuangzi is made to symbolize here several of the priorities of the 'primitivist' strand of Daoism. He prefers nature to civilization; lived life, though unrespectable, to the living death of venerated formality; and simplicity to sophistication. Having said this, even in translation it is clear that the *Zhuangzi* is a work of considerable poise and

sophistication. Its literary style is delightful and represents an advance on the *Daode Jing*.

The *Zhuangzi* and *Daode Jing* share common conceptions of the terms *Dao* (the mystical and transcendent Way) and *De* (the Virtue or power of the Way in manifestation). Zhuangzi develops from this a far more explicit mysticism, including the meditative techniques described in the Inner Chapters. He attributes this instruction to Confucius, who is playfully transformed in the *Zhuangzi* to a Daoist:

Unify your attention. Do not listen with the ears, listen with the mind. Do not listen with the mind but listen with the vital breath (qi). The ears only listen to sounds. The mind is only aware of its objects. But to focus on the vital breath is to be empty and await the arising of objects. It is only the Way that settles in emptiness. Emptiness is the fasting of the mind.[56]

What this hints at is a Daoism rooted in transcendental meditative experience, with parallels to the Indian Vedic concept of meditation on the *prana* or 'breath'. The meditation allows the adept to 'merge with the Great Pervader', to become one, as it were, with the Dao. Like many Daoists, however, Zhuangzi is not content with this inner experience: he makes 'Confucius' say, 'to stop making footprints is easy but it is difficult to walk without touching the ground.' In other words, sitting in meditation (where one makes no footprints) is the easy part; much harder and more important is the living, participating meditation of ordinary everyday life. As we noted in the chapter on Laozi, this outward-looking mysticism is important in distinguishing Daoism from Buddhism, although it would later influence the development of the distinctively Chinese form of Chan or Zen Buddhism.

Whether inward or outward, it is clear that Zhuangzi's reliance on mystical experience is key to both the sceptical and primitivist tendencies in his thought. The faith in a monistic Dao gives Zhuangzi the absolute security to dismiss both the intellectual and the social constructs of those who are less flexible. One of his most important passages in Chapter 2 questions whether we can know anything to be real:

> *Once Chuang Chou dreamt he was a butterfly, a butterfly flitting and fluttering around, happy with himself and doing as he pleased. He didn't know he was Chuang Chou. Suddenly he woke up and there he was, solid and unmistakable Chuang Chou. But he didn't know if he was Chuang Chou who had dreamt he was a butterfly, or a butterfly dreaming he was Chuang Chou. Between Chuang Chou and a butterfly there must be some distinction! This is called the Transformation of Things.*

Zhuangzi questions the reality of both waking and dream states by indicating their inconstancy, just as the Indian Vedāntin thinker **Gaudapada** would do

some centuries later. Another passage from the same chapter examines whether we have a consistent self:

> *Joy, anger, grief, delight, worry, regret, fickleness, inflexibility, modesty, wilfulness, candour, insolence – music from empty holes, mushrooms springing up in dampness, day and night replacing each other before us, and no one knows where they sprout from. Let it be! Let it be! [It is enough that] morning and evening we have them, and they are the means by which we live. Without them we would not exist; without us they would have nothing to take hold of. This comes close to the matter. But I do not know what makes them the way they are. It would seem as though they have some True Master; and yet I find no trace of him. He can act - that is certain. Yet I cannot see his form. He has identity but no form.*

Wing Tsit-Chan in *A Source Book of Chinese Philosophy* points out that this passage has 'fortified the long tradition of agnosticism' in China. Confucius is also agnostic on regions beyond common experience, suggesting that we stick to what we can know; Zhuangzi is very different in hinting that we should consider such questions and dwell in their mystery. Compared to other thinkers from the classical period of Chinese thought, Zhuangzi is unusually concerned with subjective, inner experience.

Zhuangzi's agnosticism extends to language:

> *Words are not just wind. Words have*
> *something to say. But if what they*
> *have to say is not fixed, then do*
> *they really say something? Or do*
> *they say nothing? People suppose*
> *that words are different from the*
> *peeps of baby birds, but is there any*
> *difference, or isn't there?*

This could be wrongly taken as a purely destructive scepticism, but Zhuangzi here attacks the grounds for certainty of the Confucian and Mohist thinkers who argue back and forth about terminology:

> *When the Way relies on little*
> *accomplishments and words rely*
> *on vain show, then we have the*
> *rights and wrongs of the Confucians*
> *and the Mo-ists. What one calls right*
> *the other calls wrong; what one*
> *calls wrong the other calls right.*
> *But if we want to right their wrongs*
> *and wrong their rights, then the best*
> *thing to use is clarity.*

Zhuangzi seems to argue here that the concern of, for example, the Confucians with ritual misses the real point. Such 'little accomplishments' are not enough, they are not the Way. In the same vein, it is important to dwell with the meaning, the 'something to say', even if that something changes from moment to moment, than to hang on to words that are constantly being undermined by the inconstancy of their subject-matter. Elsewhere Zhuangzi says that words are like a net for catching fish. The meaning is the main thing (the fish), and when we have caught it, the words are set aside. It is not possible to determine the meaning of words in themselves, any more than we can catch a fish in the street. Meaning is always contextual.

Another well-known story illuminates Zhuangzi's view on knowledge:

> *Chuang Tzu [Zhuangzi] and Hui*
> *Tzu [Huishi] were strolling along the*
> *dam of the Hao River when Chuang*
> *Tzu said, 'See how the minnows come*
> *out and dart around where they*
> *please! That's what fish really enjoy!'*
>
> *Hui Tzu said, 'You're not a fish - how*
> *do you know what fish enjoy?'*
>
> *Chuang Tzu said, 'You're not I, so*
> *how do you know I don't know*
> *what fish enjoy?'*
>
> *Hui Tzu said, 'I'm not you, so I*
> *certainly don't know what you know.*
> *On the other hand, you're certainly*
> *not a fish - so that still proves you*
> *don't know what fish enjoy!'*
>
> *Chuang Tzu said, 'Let's go back to your*
> *original question, please. You asked*
> *me how I know what fish enjoy - so*
> *you already knew I knew it when you*
> *asked the question. I know it by*
> *standing here beside the Hao.'*

A Chinese Taoist monk.

Although we may feel some sympathy with Huishi's suspicion, the point comes across forcefully. Zhuangzi holds that reality can be known through immediate experience, but not through speculation. Huishi speculates about what Zhuangzi knows or does not know; Zhuangzi *knows* the happiness of fish. The critique is not of knowledge, but of the desire to give it a fixed and objective form. Similar discussions were taking place in Indian philosophy, perhaps at about the same time: 'That which is not uttered by speech, but that by which speech is revealed, know that alone to be Brahman, and not what people worship as an object[57]'. By comparison with the East, Western philosophy has had no such subtlety with regard to knowledge and language until very recent times.

Zhuangzi's politics, like those of **Laozi**, are guided by the principle of *wuwei* (action through inaction). A government should do as little as possible, not just in the sense that it should render itself unnecessary through good governance but in the more radical sense that it is better for the government to rule through passivity:

> *There has been such a thing as letting mankind alone and tolerance; there has never been such a thing as governing mankind. Letting alone springs from the fear lest men's natural dispositions be perverted and tolerance springs from the fear lest their character be corrupted. But if their natural dispositions be not perverted, nor their character corrupted, what need is there left for government? ... From the Three Dynasties downwards, the world has lived in a helter-skelter of promotions and punishments. What chance have the people left for living the even tenor of their lives?[58]*

MENCIUS
(MENGZI, MENGE K'E)
371–289 BCE

Mencius[59] is traditionally regarded as the 'Second Sage' of Confucianism. He stands in roughly the same relation to **Confucius** as Plato did to Socrates. Just as Plato is responsible for making Socrates a central figure in Western thought, it is unlikely that without Mencius Confucianism would have had anything like as much of an impact. Mencius also added to Confucius' ethical teaching a metaphysical dimension, just as Plato did to that of Socrates. Mencius was not a direct pupil of Confucius, but was taught for a time by his grandson. He is one of the few reliable authorities we have for the teaching of Confucius. His

own work, known as the *Mencius*, is one of the Four Books that formed the Confucian education system formalised after 1313 CE.

Mencius was born in the state of Zou, present-day Shandong. His father, like that of Confucius, died when he was three. He was raised by his mother, who went to extraordinary lengths to secure an ideal education for her son. First employed as a teacher and then, in Qi, as a government official, he then took to the roads, like Confucius and Mozi before him, to attempt to promote his ideas to a succession of rulers, with a similar lack of success. He seems to have ended his life

> *'Moral principles*
> *please our minds*
> *as beef and mutton*
> *and pork please our*
> *mouths.'*

in seclusion with a number of students, perhaps then composing the *Mencius*, although at least some of that work dates from after his death. Mencius seems to have been almost exactly contemporaneous with **Zhuangzi**, but neither mentions the other. This may have been, as Fung Yu-lan speculates, because Mencius regarded Zhuangzi as a mere follower of Yang Zhu[60], while Zhuangzi saw Mencius as just another Confucian. If so, neither could be said to have studied the other's philosophy closely.

An important factor in understanding Mencius is his relation to other philosophers of the period, which was one of great fertility in Chinese thought. Just as the critique of Brahmanism in India by figures like **Chārvāka** and the **Buddha** led to the rise and refinement of Indian philosophy, in Mencius we see Confucianism define itself in response to its detractors. One of the principal oppositions is to Legalism (see the chapter on **Hanfeizi**), an influential philosophy that maintained that man was self-centred and untrustworthy. Against this Mencius argued that man was innately good. The demonstration of this is the example of a toddler going towards an open well: Mencius argues that anyone will naturally move to prevent calamity. This goes back to the Confucian notion of *ren*, normally translated as 'benevolence' or 'human-heartedness'. The latter translation seems, in Mencius, far more appropriate[61]. It would perhaps be naïve to suppose that people are naturally benevolent; Mencius is subtler in referring to our unconditioned human responses. He makes clear elsewhere that the natural response of the heart can be either corrupted or refined: 'Slight is the difference between man and the brutes. The common man loses this distinguishing feature, while the gentleman retains it[62]'. In his conviction as to the germ of goodness in man, Mencius is opposed by another Confucian philosopher, **Xunzi,** who held the opposite belief.

Another important dispute is between Mencius and the Mohists, the followers of **Mozi**. The latter was a utilitarian thinker who opposed Confucius' regard for tradition and ritual. Mencius again bases his defence on the natural responses of the human heart. To the Mohist critique of

elaborate funeral rites, he goes back to an imagined state of nature (here he makes use of Mozi's own methods) and to the origins of burial. Primitive man is pained to find his father, whose body he left in a ditch, being eaten by scavengers. From this instinctive response comes the burial rite, carefully designed to honour the dead and console the living. It is difficult not to feel that Mencius' argument is more psychologically convincing. His view of the innate goodness of human nature eventually prevailed in Chinese thought, persisting down to the present day. Mencius teaches the doctrine of the Four Beginnings to illustrate how the virtues emerge naturally from instinctual responses:

The feeling of commiseration is the feeling of humanity; the feeling of shame and dislike is the beginning of righteousness; the feeling of deference and compliance is the beginning of propriety; and the feeling of right and wrong is the beginning of wisdom. Men have these Four Beginnings just as they have their four limbs.[63]

Accordingly, the sage or absolutely wise person teaches men what they have innately. Mencius uses the analogy of a renowned chef who established the principles of good flavour. Just as the chef did not invent good flavour but understood what it is that all people enjoy in food, 'the sage is the first to possess what is common in our minds. Therefore moral principles please our minds as beef and mutton and pork please our mouths.' Confucian ethics are considerably developed by Mencius. In particular, he developed the idea of *yi*, which he defines as 'the path a man ought to follow'. This, a minor element in Confucius, becomes in Mencius' teaching a categorical imperative like that of Kant, a command that must be followed even to the point of death: 'I like life and I also like righteousness. If I cannot have both of them, I shall give up life and choose righteousness.'

Politically, Mencius is the most democratic of Confucian thinkers (the Mohists' justification of the state hints at democratic choice and Mohist groups apparently chose their leaders democratically – then followed them to the death). Confucius followed the traditional doctrine of the Mandate of Heaven: the natural authority of kings was withdrawn when the king lost virtue. Mencius, again probably influenced by Mohism, interpreted this to be judged by people 'voting with their feet.' If a king is benevolent, people will flood to his kingdom, filling his coffers and his army. Mencius calls this 'winning the people's heart-minds':

> *If a ruler regards his ministers as his hands and feet, then his ministers will regard him as their heart and mind. If a ruler regards his ministers as dogs and horses, his ministers will regard him as any other man. If a ruler regards his ministers as dirt and grass, his ministers will regard him as a bandit and an enemy.*

As was already mentioned, Mencius added a metaphysical dimension to Con-fucianism. A traditional belief of Chinese philosophy with its roots in the old folk religion was that the universe consisted of *qi (chi)*, a substance that was graded from coarse to fine, from the heaviness of the earth to the lightness of the heavens. A human being, according to Mencius, is made of a mixture of the coarse and the fine *qi* and the spiritual path is a matter of 'cultivating one's own *qi*':

> *Nourish it with integrity and place no obstacle in its path and it will fill the space between Heaven and Earth. It is a qi which unites rightness and the Way ... it is born of accumulated rightness and cannot be appropriated by anyone through a sporadic show of rightness ... whenever one acts in a way that falls below the standard set in one's heart, it will collapse ... you must work at it and never let it out of your mind. At the same time, while you must never let it out of your mind, you must not forcibly help it grow either.*[64]

The Confucian tradition before Mencius emphasises the active and public life in a way that is somewhat alien to contemplation. While Daoism and, later, Buddhism, emphasise being, the Confucians emphasise doing. But by uniting morality with metaphysics, Mencius hints at the beginnings of a Confucian mysticism. His example would be crucial in the new direction taken by the Neo-Confucian thinkers of the eleventh century onwards, who incorporated Daoist and Buddhist ideas to strengthen and renew Confucianism.

XUNZI (HSUN TZU)

c. 320–c. 230 BCE

Confucius had two important successors in the Time of the Warring States period (403–222 BCE). The first was **Mencius**, who developed Confucius' ideas on *ren* (human-heartedness) and added a

'Man's nature is evil; goodness is the result of conscious activity.'

metaphysical dimension, teaching that human nature is essentially good. Xunzi, the second, focused instead on Confucian *li* (ritual) and the agency of society in forming character. He dramatically emphasised the importance of social convention by maintaining that 'man's nature is evil; goodness is the result of conscious activity'. It is not surprising that the debate on 'nature versus nurture' should have become central. Confucius' emphasis was on outward behaviour such as ritual, government and culture. He seems to have been deliberately silent on human nature, but the question was taken up by both his main successors. Xunzi was the more influential figure in the Qin and Han dynasties (ending 220 CE). Centuries of Buddhist domination of Chinese thought followed, after which Mencius emerged as the model for a system that could fuel a Confucian renaissance. It was to be his version of Confucianism that dominated China for the remainder of the Imperial system from the eleventh to twentieth centuries. Xunzi, on the other

hand, was neglected in Chinese philosophy until the nineteenth century, since when he has enjoyed a revival of interest. Xunzi is the most important critic of early Chinese philosophy, and delivered attacks on Mencian Confucianism, Mohism, Daoism and on a range of other less well-known systems of thought.

According to the *Shi Ji* chronicle Xunzi was born in Zhao, now Shanshi and Henan. At 50, he was attracted, along with many other intellectuals, to the court of Ji on the east coast, where he was acknowledged as the most brilliant scholar. The jealousy of his rivals led to his flight to Chu in the south, where he became the magistrate of the city of Lanling before a coup against the local ruler led to Xunzi's removal. Not much is known for certain about when Xunzi lived, but he was certainly active between 298 and 238 BCE. He also kept a school, including among his pupils the Legalist

Li Si

'The superior man is serious about what lies in himself and does not desire what comes from Heaven. The inferior man neglects what is in himself and desires what comes from Heaven.'

philosopher **Hanfeizi** and Li Si, later to become the Prime Minister of Qin and, after its final victory, of the Empire. It was Li Si who recommended that all books in the Empire be burned, to defeat all non-Legalist thinking, in particular Confucianism. How far Xunzi can be held responsible for the authoritarian attitudes of his two disciples[65] is impossible to decide. As the teacher of two such influential figures, his own authoritarianism was clearly a substantial influence on them. Xunzi did maintain that the ultimate authority rested with the *junzi* or 'cultured Confucian gentleman'. His pessimism about human nature has some affinities with Hanfeizi's cynical 'class interest' analysis. He also advocated a positive effort to manipulate human nature which Legalism extended to an extreme. However, compared to the strong, not to say extreme, anti-traditionalism and anti-moralism of both his students, Xunzi's reflective philosophy was rather moralistic and constituted a sophisticated argument for tradition. Their ideas and practices represent a continuation of his dogmatic assertiveness but a radical break with his sometimes very careful reflective argumentation.

Xunzi's philosophy is based on the fundamental conviction that man needs socialization in order to be good. Hanfeizi's cynicism about role interests led him to acute paranoia directed at ministers and high officials. Xunzi sought to promote education and clarity of thought: 'the superior man is serious about what lies in himself and does not desire what comes from Heaven. The inferior man neglects what is in himself and desires what comes from Heaven[66].' The word *Tien*, normally translated as Heaven, is a useful barometer of Chinese philosophy of this period. For **Mozi** it means a God who responds to prayer and the actions of men. For Confucius and Mencius, it represents something like the abstract will of God: how things should be. For the Daoists it is more like 'Nature': how things are under natural law. Xunzi's critique of the view of the inferior man is that he looks for an outside, possibly supernatural agency to come to his aid. In this he develops Confucius' emphasis on self-reliance: 'it is Man who is capable of broadening the Way; it is not the Way that is capable of broadening Man.' Xunzi writes as a pragmatic naturalist: 'if the foundations of living [i.e. agriculture] are strengthened and economically used, then Nature [*Tien*] cannot bring impoverishment.'

As with his pupil Hanfei, Daoist thinking proves a useful source for a philosophy that is in many ways alien to it. Xunzi is not in the least mystical, but uses Daoism as the starting point for a naturalistic and scientific approach. On the subject of fortune he writes, 'it is good fortune to regard [rites and sacrifices] as ornamental but it is evil fortune to regard them as supernatural'. In other words good fortune is having the right attitude and education. This is an extrapolation of Confucius, but while the latter refuses to speculate on the supernatural, Xunzi disregards it entirely.

Xunzi's view of the physical universe is a natural continuation of Confucianism. It is a triadic system as found in *The Doctrine of the Mean* of Heaven, Earth and Man. Xunzi writes, 'Heaven has its seasons, earth has its wealth, and man has his government'. The first two we have no control over; the third is our only proper area of concern. Perhaps Xunzi's most original contribution to Chinese thought is his view of man as an agent within nature:

> *Instead of regarding Heaven [or Nature] as great and admiring it*
> *Why not foster it as a thing and regulate it?*
> *Instead of obeying Heaven and singing praise to it,*
> *Why not control the Mandate of Heaven and use it?*
> *Instead of looking on the seasons and waiting for them,*
> *Why not respond to them and make use of them?*
> *Instead of letting things multiply by themselves,*
> *Why not exercise your ability to transform them?*
> *Instead of thinking of things as things,*
> *Why not attend to them so that you don't lose them?*
> *Instead of admiring how things come into being,*
> *Why not do something to bring them to full development?*

Such a view was too radical to have a profound influence on Chinese thought, but it could have been the beginning of the world's first scientific tradition. It is reminiscent of Western Enlightenment thinking from the eighteenth or nineteenth century in its enthusiasm for utilizing nature. Today, we would have reservations about the lack of respect for nature in Xunzi and perhaps more enthusiasm for the enjoyment of 'thinking of things as things' rather than as mere means to an end. In this our instincts are closer to the traditional Chinese view of the harmony between man and nature, even if our economics are not. If the Daoist term *wuwei* is translated as 'taking no action contrary to Nature', it will be seen that Xunzi is no Daoist.

Another important contribution of Xunzi was his consideration of the traditional question of 'the rectification of names'. This was Confucius' solution to the problem of a breakdown in the social order and implies firstly that each will play his allotted part in society, and secondly that the 'superior men' set the pattern for others to follow through understandable and sincere speech. Xunzi is aware of two attacks on Confucius' principle. The first was that of Later Mohists who had rejected rectification of names on the ground that a given thing could properly be called several things – thing, living thing, animal, mammal, primate, human, male, father, and so on. The second critique came from the linguistic paradoxes created by the so-called School of Names. The most notorious is Gongsun Long's 'a white horse is not a horse'. Gongsun Long argued that if one specified a white horse and was given a yellow horse, one would reject it.

Therefore a 'horse' is not a 'white horse'. This makes the point that rectifying names entails a principle of one-name-one-thing and thus leads to paradox.

Xunzi has to accept that the Confucian system will not work on a one-name-one-thing basis, and so makes use of the Mohist theory to redevelop it. The word 'horse' is a 'simple name' while 'white horse' is a 'compound name'; 'knowing that different actualities have different names, one should let different actualities always have different names'. Xunzi is at best an unwilling logician, however. Having established that the logical paradox does not destroy Confucian thinking, he quickly moves to assert that semantic theorizing should be forbidden because it uses names to confuse names and thereby sows disorder. Xunzi advocates the ruler prohibit such activities as they are the ultimate seeds of disorder – which like most Confucians he sees as the entire kingdom accepting the same discourse. The judgement of the superior man or sage, rather than logic, is sufficient to decide in what way a name is used. It is this attitude, or one close to it, that Li Si called on in burning books and burying scholars.

Xunzi's view of the untrustworthiness of human nature is essential to his thinking, because from this he demonstrates the importance of education, training and social propriety. In Mencius' writing they were merely ways of training the heart in its existing humanity, but in the *Xunzi* the ritual becomes an external system of social control of which desires are appropriate to pursue in an ordered society. Only if society is structured so that different ranks have different appropriate values can one allocate scarce natural resources in a way that can satisfy everyone. The difference between Confucius' two successors is brought out in their views as to the attainability of ultimate wisdom. Both argue that anyone has the potential to become a sage, but while Mencius holds this out as a real possibility, Xunzi is characteristically sceptical: 'it is possible for a man with feet to walk all over the world and yet so far there has not been any who is actually able to do so.' The reason why we do not walk all over the world, or become sages, is that the motivation is lacking. Xunzi's awareness of the natural context in which man exists is, in the final analysis, his greatest strength and weakness. Xunzi is, by the standards of his time, without parallel as a scientific mind and as a critic of philosophy; but his safety-first pragmatism always wins out over philosophical daring. There is much in the *Xunzi* to admire, but little to delight in. For Confucius, as for Mencius, the social controls and the rituals finally bear fruit, and their fruit is tranquillity, easy action and joy: 'at seventy I followed my heart's desire, without overstepping the line'. But for Xunzi, social control will always be necessary.

HANFEIZI
(HAN FEI TZU)

c. 280–233 BCE

Hanfeizi, or Master Hanfei, was a unique and pivotal figure in the history of Chinese philosophy. A pupil of **Xunzi**, the leading Confucian of his day, Hanfei nevertheless rejected the Confucian commitment to conventionalism. Although he was an aristocrat, Hanfei's philosophy justified the emperor in treating the aristocracy by the same objective standards applied to everyone else – except of course the emperor himself. Like the early Daoists he is regarded as being a member of a group – known as the Legalists – that exists only as a projection of later historians. Neither Daoism nor Legalism was an actual association in the classical period.

Living during the violent and unsteady period known as the Time of the Warring States, Hanfei proposed a practical solution to the problem of how to achieve and retain power. He credited Lord Shang, a prime minister of the state that finally unified China (who almost certainly was not the author of *The Book of Lord Shang*), as well as Shenzi (350–275 BCE) and Shen Pu-hai (d. 337 BCE) with the three core concepts of his theory. The most important of these were objective standards of reward and punishment, promotion and dismissal. Its fundamental motivation, at least in Hanfei, is self-interest. Hanfei recognized that the threat to the ruler comes from his ministers. By holding them to measurement-like standards of performance, he could keep them from controlling him by 'persuasion.' At the same time, it would

protect the people by giving them clear guidelines for avoiding punishment and preventing officials from using punishment to reward loyalty to them. Hanfei developed the ideas of Legalism to their logical (and extreme) conclusion. No-one is above the law, and the law never shows mercy. The Confucian doctrine of 'rectification of names', which for **Confucius** is a corrective measure to restore natural order – 'let the ruler be a ruler, the subject a subject, the father a father and the son a son' (*Analects*, XII, 11) becomes in Legalism a measure governing (and threatening) the high officials by preventing them from acting outside their strict job-description. Confucians tell numerous stories of the injustices they perceived implicit in this idea. An officer who spontaneously undertook a daring and successful raid on the enemy was executed for insubordination. A tavern-keeper who covered the king with his coat as he slept met the same fate. Hanfei writes of ministers who present their achievements modestly:

> *It is not that the ruler is not pleased with the big accomplishments [of his minister], but he considers the failure of the big accomplishments to correspond to the words worse than the big accomplishments themselves. Therefore he is to be punished.*[67]

Hanfei's writing is full of energy and hard-headed pragmatism. He rejects the backward-looking Confucians and the moralizing Mohists, taking instead the approach that any way of achieving total order was as good as any other. Although it would be wrong to overemphasise the influence of his master Xunzi, Hanfei draws heavily on his arguments for preventing people from disagreeing with the way of the empire. This became the justification for killing philosophers and burning books. Further, he follows Xunzi's theory that human nature is evil. Xunzi observed that goodness was not innate in man, any more than straightness is innate in wood. For Xunzi this supports the argument for education and training by a wise master. Hanfei uses the same illustration, but to different purpose:

> *Although there is a naturally straight arrow or a naturally round piece of wood*[68] *[once in a hundred generations] ... the skilled worker does not value it. Why? Because it is not just one person who wishes to ride and not just one shot that the archer wishes to shoot. Similarly, the enlightened ruler does not value people who are naturally good and do not depend on reward and punishment. Why? Because the laws of the state must not be neglected and government is not for only one man.*

Not only is it not possible to rely on people being naturally good, Hanfei argues that the naturally good person is of no value. Precisely because Hanfei's 'two handles' of punishment and kindness do not manipulate them, the naturally good person should be got rid of. The entire system of Legalism depends on an ethic of manipulation. Do not trust people, says Hanfei, trust your ability to force them to obey you.

The *Hanfei* contains a commentary on Laozi who advocates passive, laissez-faire small government. Hanfei argues that when objective standards are in place and working, there is no need for the ruler to do anything. His people are already acting at all times according to common standards. The *wuwei* (or action through inaction) of the Daoists arises from the conception of a transcendent Dao as well as scepticism about moral doctrines working reliably. The *wuwei* of the Legalists comes about because the state consists of self-enacting standards of behaviour – total acceptance of the ruler-instituted ways of measuring, judging and acting: 'Like water flowing and like a boat floating, the ruler follows the course of Nature and enforces an infinite number of commands.'[69] Hanfei also followed Xunzi's advocacy of brutal punishment arguing that the more brutal they are, the less they will be used. Needless to say, that did not work out in practice and the Legalist dynasty has few equals in history in either the frequency or severity of its punishments. Neither Machiavelli nor the Islamic social theorist **Ibn Khaldūn** approach Hanfei's cold-bloodedness and perhaps only in the writing of Orwell and Kafka do we find something that exceeds it. It hardly needs to be said that despite the appropriation of *wuwei* by Hanfei, he is totally at odds with the spirit of **Laozi** and **Zhuangzi**. Nevertheless, Hanfei's interpretation of Laozi reminds us that the text was read and used by many besides the students of Zhuangzi. Hanfei created an artificial Dao to engineer a man-made paradise.

Hanfei had a slightly different view of human nature than Xunzi. Rather than thinking of people as motivated by selfish desires, Hanfei characterized them as adopting the values of their status or rank. Thus he believed that no-one could be trusted to judge objectively, for example writing that 'consorts and concubines long for the early death of the ruler'. This insight into the communitarian shaping of our self-identity flows neatly out of the social conception of man shared by Confucianism and Mohism, given Hanfei's innate pessimism. Its truth was borne out in his own life. He lived in the state of Han and petitioned King An with an outline of his ideas. They were rejected, but the rival

Qin Shi-huang-di

king Qin Shih-huang-di was impressed. One of Hanfei's fellow students at the school of Xunzi was Li Si, who went on to become the Qin ruler's Prime Minister. When Hanfei attempted to enlist as an advisor of the Qin, Li Si argued that he could not be trusted and had him

imprisoned. Li Si then sent Hanfei poison which he took, realising his position to be impossible.

Li Si put many of Hanfei's ideas into practice himself. The rigorous discipline introduced into Qin was one factor helping them to conquer all other states and unify China for the first time in 221 BCE. This achieved, Shih-huang-di set about establishing the fledgling Empire on Legalist grounds. The scale of the ambition and single-mindedness displayed by Shih-huang-di and Li Si was remarkable. The problem of Northern invaders was dealt with by ordering the construction of the Great Wall in 214 BCE. The problem of rival, non-Legalist philosophies was dealt with by ordering all books to be burnt, to 'make the people ignorant'. Li Si wrote:

> *In the past the empire was divided. Because there was no emperor, the feudal lords were active and in order to confuse the people they harped on antiquity ... Now Your Majesty rules a unified empire in which distinctions of right and wrong are as clear as your own unapproachable authority. Yet there are those who unofficially propagate teachings directed against imperial decrees and orders. When they hear of new instructions, they criticize them in the light of their own teachings ... the people are thus encouraged to be disrespectful ... Your servant therefore requests that all persons possessing works of literature and discussions of the philosophers should destroy them. Those who have not destroyed them within thirty days after the issuing of the order are to be branded and work as convicts.*[70]

Ch'in Emperor Shi-huang-di burns books which oppose his views.

The consequences of this were that much of the literature of the early period was lost. The only remaining copies of many works were held in the imperial library, burnt by a rebel army in 206 BCE. Hanfei directly influenced Li Si in this, who wrote that 'in the state of the enlightened ruler, there is no literature of books and records but the laws serve as the teaching.'

The reign of Shih-huang-di demonstrated with breathtaking strength of purpose the value of unity in law, philosophy, politics, economics, and military strength. The Argentinean writer Borges remarked admiringly on the Emperor's unique qualities: a mind that could conceive of destroying all human knowledge, and of putting a wall around an empire. His success was undoubtedly due in large measure to the influence of Legalist thinking. The rapid decline of the Qin Empire after the death of the Emperor was the perfect illustration of the weakness of extreme Legalism. Hanfei was right that it was possible to rule an Empire with the iron fist of law; but he was wrong that the people would accept 'an infinite number of commands' and punishments. In retrospect, the Confucian concept that the Emperor ruled courtesy of the Mandate of Heaven, which depended on justice and righteousness, was more sustainable as well as more humane.

HUINENG
638–713 CE

The earliest record of Buddhism in China dates to as early as 2 BCE. About 150 years later the first Chinese translations of Buddhist texts were made, and by the third century CE, two main schools were active, distinguished by the Sanskrit names *prajna*, meaning 'knowledge' and *dhyana*, meaning 'meditation'. The school of *dhyana* was later to develop into the most distinctively Chinese form of Buddhism, *dhyana* being transformed into *Chan* or, as it is more commonly known, Zen.

Meditation in China was not very similar to its Indian cousin. In India meditation is typically associated with sitting still and concentrating one's mind inwardly by a variety of methods including breath-control and the silent mental chanting of *mantras*. In China it was understood through Daoism and associated with more outward-looking states. By the time of Zen, however, it had come to mean simply 'enlightenment'. Zen is known as the 'sudden-enlightenment' (*satori*) method, as distinguished from the 'gradual-enlightenment' method.

The first Zen Patriarch is traditionally Bodhidharma (460–534 CE). More is known, however, about a later figure, Hongren (601–674 CE), the Fifth Patriarch. He was the first in China to advance the *Diamond Sūtra*, subsequently regarded as China's key Buddhist text. The *Diamond Sūtra* is part of the 'Perfection of Wisdom' tradition that emphasises the mind.[71]

Huineng's story is recorded in *The Platform Sūtra of the Sixth Patriarch*, which seems to be a collection of stories about him, assembled by his followers. He was born into a poor family in the Guangdong province, something of a backwater. Although allegedly an illiterate wood-pedlar, Huineng seems to have read the *Diamond Sūtra* in his twenties and then set off to study under the Fifth Patriarch Hongren. The scripture tells how he successfully argues with Hongren that he should be allowed to stay despite his 'barbarian' origins, although he is given only a menial position pounding rice in the kitchens. Hongren announces that he will give the title of Sixth Patriarch to whoever can write a verse that expresses 'the basic idea' of Buddhist teaching. The leading disciple Shenxiu's attempt is as follows:

> *The body is the tree of perfect wisdom*
> *The mind is the stand of a bright mirror*
> *At all times diligently wipe it*
> *Do not allow it to become dusty.*
>
> *Hongren declares that this is the best*
> *of the entries, but that it is not enough.*
> *Then Huineng writes his verse:*
>
> *Fundamentally perfect wisdom has*
> *no tree*
> *Nor has the bright mirror any stand*
> *Buddha-nature is forever clear and*
> *pure*
> *Where is there any dust?*

Needless to say, Hongren acclaims the verse as evidence of Huineng's wisdom. Hongren does not, however, proclaim Huineng's success openly. He gives him instruction in the *Diamond Sūtra* and Huineng achieves immediate enlightenment. Hongren then advises him to leave secretly to avoid the jealousy of the others.

The story should be understood in the light of the political fighting that was to follow. Huineng's disciple Shenhui engaged in a bitter struggle after Huineng's death with the Northern School of Shenxiu over who was the true Sixth Patriarch. It seems possible from the story of *The Platform Sūtra* that Shenxiu was accorded the title and that Hongren never accepted Huineng. All of Hongren's compliments to Huineng are made privately, while publicly he is hostile to the barbarian Huineng. On the other hand, it may be, as the tradition of the Southern School holds, that Huineng was indeed proclaimed the Sixth Patriarch in

661 CE. Shenhui's possession of the apparent relics of Hongren eventually seems to have settled the matter. *The Platform Sūtra* is now regarded as the original classic of Zen Buddhism.

There is no evidence that Huineng ever tried to promote his own claims. He seems, from the evidence of his words, to have been an extraordinary genius, the possessor of a rare mind akin to that of the Indian Madhyāmika Buddhist **Nāgārjuna**. The two verses encapsulate the difference between Huineng's new approach and that of Shenxiu. The traditional way to enlightenment involves a constant effort to purify the mind in preparation. Huineng denies even the possibility that the Buddha-nature can be defiled. In a fundamental sense, we are already Buddhas. This is why enlightenment can be sudden. Rather than adhering to the traditional path of formal meditation, Huineng argued for a free meditation, with the aim of achieving *samadhi*, which in the Chinese tradition means 'calmness'. In the words of *The Platform Sūtra*:

> *Good and learned friends, calmness*
> *(samadhi) and wisdom (prajna) are*
> *the foundations of my method. First of*
> *all, do not be deceived into thinking*
> *that the two are different. They are one*
> *substance and not two. Calmness is*
> *the substance of wisdom and wisdom*
> *is the function of calmness. Whenever*
> *wisdom is at work, calmness is within*
> *it. Whenever calmness is at work,*
> *wisdom is within it … do not say that*
> *wisdom follows calmness or vice versa,*
> *or that the two are different.*

If Nāgārjuna is Huineng's forefather in Buddhism, perhaps more important is the influence of Daoism. Like the Daoists, Huineng insists on a monistic view. The knowledge of enlightenment and the effect of enlightenment are simply different ways of looking at the same thing. Another Daoist idea is called absence-of-thought: 'Absence-of-thought means not to be defiled by external objects.' The idea here is not that the mind is unconscious, but that it is free of attachment to things. A criticism Huineng had of the Northern School was that they

'Our nature is originally pure.'

emphasised inactivity to the point of stupefaction, which he said was inconsistent with the Way (Dao). The Southern Zen master, on the other hand, would be able to go about his business normally, dwelling constantly within the Buddha-mind and unattached to any object, either external or within the mind. The Daoist ethic of activity through inactivity is thus given a Buddhist form. Another concept alien to Indian Buddhism but which is reminiscent of Daoism is the idea of 'becoming a Buddha in this very body'. Where Buddhism traditionally regarded the body as an obstruction, Zen follows the Daoist path of acceptance of all things as they are. Huineng's frequent refrain that 'our nature is originally pure' means that to reject anything is to create a false duality.

It should be said that although the enlightenment of the Northern School can be characterized as gradual and the Southern as sudden, both schools acknowledge both methods. As Huineng says, 'those who are deluded understand gradually, while the enlightened achieve understanding suddenly. But when they know their own minds, then they see their own nature, and there is no difference in their enlightenment.' The fundamental difference between the two is not really the speed of enlightenment but, as we have seen, in their conception of the mind. The Northern School emphasise the constant effort at purification, while the Southern School teach that the effort is to see the mind's original purity.

Huineng's Zen became known as the Zen of the Patriarchs, while the older tradition that traced its ancestry to Bodhidharma was known as the Zen of the Perfected One. They coexisted amicably, although Huineng's *satori* Zen grew in popularity before the revival of Confucianism in the eleventh and twelfth centuries caused its decline. Just at this point Zen became popular in Japan, where it developed its modern forms. Huineng's Southern School corresponds to the Rinzai Zen of **Eisai** and Shenxiu's Northern School to **Dōgen's** Soto Zen. In the twentieth century Zen caught the imagination of the West, where its combination of the sophisticated understanding of the mind and simple experience have proved increasingly popular.

FAZANG (FA TSANG)

643–712 CE

Fazang was born in Zhangan, present-day Sian in central China, descended from an Uzbekistani grandfather. He was a Buddhist and attempted to synthesize the previous forms of Chinese Buddhism. His own tradition is a form of Mahāyāna Buddhism based on the *Avatamsaka ('Garland') Sūtra*. The sūtra was first known in China in the sixth century, where it produced a school of adherents called the Huayen, normally translated 'Flowery Garland' school. Its popularity in China was far greater than it had been elsewhere. The school is known as Kegon in Korea and also has followers in Japan.

Fazang became a monk at the age of 28 and was a follower of the Huayen founders Dushun and Chihyan. Like other Buddhists of the time[72], he was invited to the court of Empress Wu, where he lectured to her on Buddhist philosophy using the statue of a golden lion as an illustrative device. His summary of Buddhist philosophy is illuminating, although one can easily see why the Empress found Fazang hard going. He distinguishes five classifications in Buddhism. The first is Hīnayāna (or Theravāda), the earliest teaching of Buddha, which would say that because the lion is dependent on its cause, it has no real character or nature[73]. The second is Mahāyāna, which states that the lion not only has no character, it also has no substance or existence: it is empty[74]. The third is the Chinese branch known as Tiantai, which states that although the lion has neither character nor existence, even so it has a qualified reality. The fourth is Zen (see the chapter on Fazang's contemporary **Huineng**), which declares that on enlightenment the consciousness goes beyond both emptiness and existence and finds rest. Finally, the Huayen school declares that the final enlightenment or 'Perfect Reality' is a vision of the universe as an undifferentiated and interfused mass. Everything is seen clearly as unreal, which unifies all with one and one with all. The aim of Huayen is to reach the state known as *Bodhisattva* or Buddha-to-be. Fully enlightened, the *Bodhisattva* nevertheless retains physical form and puts off full Buddhahood out of compassion for others.

A young Buddhist monk.

Fazang uses a number of other images in his work to illustrate the difficult concepts of Huayen. Most importantly there is the Net of the god Indra, studded with jewels. Each jewel reflects every other jewel and the net itself, so that the whole is reflected in every part just as every part is contained within the whole. By knowing any one 'fact' all may be known. In addition to this, every fact is interlinked to every other and cannot exist in isolation. Beneath this reality of the 'factual' world, there is another reality of 'principle' which might correspond to the noumenal realm of Kant or to the world of Ideas of Plato. The realm of fact is produced by the realm of principle, which is that of the mind. Thus

Fazang is an idealist philosopher, asserting the primacy of the mind. Like Plato, he maintains that the world of principle is eternal and unchanging, although it has no reality after enlightenment.

Fazang's ideas were to have a great influence on Neo-Confucianism. As in India at about the same time, Buddhist concepts were proving their usefulness in non-Buddhist philosophy.

An exterior of a Buddhist temple at Tatung.

ZHANG ZAI
1020–1077 CE

Zhang Zai was a pivotal figure in Neo-Confucian philosophy and taught both of the Cheng brothers as well as strongly influencing **Zhuxi**, the greatest figure of the period. A key concept for Zhang Zai that was massively influential on Neo-Confucianism is that the universe is one but manifestations are many. The Great Ultimate, a term meaning the fundamental reality in the *Book of Changes* (*Yi Jing* or *I Ching*) is said by Zhang to be the same as the material force or *qi* that is the substance of the physical world. Even more important, however, is the idea of humanity (*ren*) 'forming one body with all things'. This has been described as the most significant Neo-Confucian concept of all and is worth considering in detail.

Although it is an idea implicit in early Confucian thinkers, especially Mencius, Zhang's formulation inspired Neo-Confucianism. The 'Western Inscription', engraved on the west window of Zhang's lecture hall, is his most important text. This is part of it:

> *Heaven is my father and Earth is my mother, and even such a small creature as I finds an intimate place in their midst.*
> *Therefore that which fills the universe I regard as my body and that which directs the universe I consider as my nature.*
> *All people are my brothers and sisters, and all things are my companions.*

Cheng Yi, who said accurately that nothing like it has been written since **Mencius**, acclaimed this revolutionary text. However, it goes beyond Mencius in its extension of *ren* to the entire universe. Zhang seems to be influenced by the Buddhist ethic of universal compassion, and it inspired Neo-Confucianism for centuries to come. Zhang differs from the Buddhists, however, in his insistence on the traditional Confucian relationships and hierarchies, which he emphasises in a series of exemplars of right conduct. Love for all is manifested through, though not limited by, particular relationships.

What 'forming one body' means is that our humanity cannot help responding compassionately to the suffering of anything. The classic example given by Mencius (371–289 BCE) is that of someone who witnesses a small child about to fall into a well. According to **Wang Yangming** (1472–1529 CE), 'This shows that his humanity (*ren)* forms one body with the child'. The argument continues to take in the suffering of animals, broken plants, and even damaged objects: 'even when he sees tiles and stones shattered and crushed, he cannot help a feeling of regret. This shows that his humanity forms one body with tiles and stones.' It is as if harm to an apparently separate person, animal or thing were harm to our own body. Plainly our own body is not harmed, but our humanity (*ren*) is conceived as a universal body: 'that which fills the universe I regard as my body.'

Even a petty or mean person, a 'small man', feels this same impulse. Wang Yangming goes on: 'although the mind of the small man is divided and narrow, yet his humanity that forms one body can remain free of darkness.' Problems arise when the small man's mind is 'aroused by desire and obscured by selfishness … compelled by greed for gain and fear of harm, and stirred by anger, he will destroy things, kill members of his own species, and will do everything. In extreme cases he will even slaughter his own brothers, and the humanity that forms one body will disappear completely'.

The Mausoleum of Confucius, China.

ZHUXI (CHU HSI)
1130–1200 CE

Zhuxi is the most influential philosopher in Chinese history since **Mencius**. As a Neo-Confucian he reshaped Confucian thought and further formalised it at the heart of Chinese culture. In particular, he established the canon of Confucian works, primarily the Four Books: the *Analects* of **Confucius**, the *Mencius, The Great Learning* and *The Doctrine of the Mean*. These Four Books were to become in 1313 the basis of the examination system for entry to the Civil Service, a system that survived until 1905 and formed the model for Western public examinations. As well as establishing the Confucian canon, Zhuxi's view of the true Confucian bloodline became the norm. This began with the authors of the Confucian Classics and was revived in the eleventh century in

Zhou Dun Yi, Zhang Zai and the Cheng brothers, all discussed below.

Zhuxi edited Confucian thought, pruning out ideas that he thought alien to the tradition. His philosophy brings together Confucius, Mencius, the ancient Chinese metaphysics of *yin* and *yang* and the five elements or agents, and some Daoist and Buddhist ideas. A similar figure in India would be **Shankara**, who had the decisive influence in reviving and editing the philosophical classics of the Vedānta. Zhuxi saw himself as a transmitter rather than an originator, but his 'great synthesis', in the phrase of Wing-Tsit Chan, is a major development in Confucian thought and Chinese culture alike.

Confucianism went through a long period in which it did not advance or develop greatly. In this time, although it was often the most important philosophy from an official perspective, Daoism and Buddhism had greater vitality and continued to advance. Its new birth, Neo-Confucianism, began a couple of centuries before Zhuxi and flourished with five philosophers who lived in the eleventh century, who deserve some attention here. The five were all closely linked and knew each other.

Zhou Dun Yi (Chou Tun-I) (1017–1073) was an unusual character who gave the impression of being a kind of Zen monk, but who was really much more influenced by Daoism. He introduced many of the ideas that were to be important to Neo-Confucianism. One of Zhou's statements gives a flavour of his approach: 'having no desire, one is vacuous while tranquil and straightforward while in action'. Confucianism had always been more concerned with activity than tranquillity. This was not surprising, given Confucius' concern with the ethical and social side of life and his refusal to entertain metaphysical speculation. However, in practice the contemplative side of life had been effectively ceded to Daoism and Buddhism. Zhou's vision in a sense reclaimed this important aspect of life for Confucianism. The short sentence above is full of challenges to orthodoxy: desirelessness, vacuity, tranquillity all sit uncomfortably with traditional Confucianism. In so doing he set the scene for the thinkers that were to follow.

Zhang Zai (1020–1077) had two particularly influential ideas. The first was his conception that the universe is one but its manifestations are many. The second, and most important, is his idea of *ren*, human-heartedness or love, 'forming one body with the universe'. This is perhaps the key concept in Neo-Confucianism and is treated separately in the chapter on Zhang. As we will see below, Zhuxi adopted Zhang's ideas on the subject. As with Zhou Dun Yi, we can see Zhang developing a more holistic and unitive philosophy.

Cheng Hao (1032–1085) and Cheng Yi (1033–1107) are perhaps the only documented example of brothers who were major philosophers[75]. They were students of both Zhou Dun Yi and Zhang Zai and were friendly with the fifth great thinker of the time, Shao Yong (1011–1077) (as Zhuxi rejected most of his ideas they will not be considered here). Remarkably, the Cheng brothers' ideas are widely different, with Cheng Yi being the founder of rationalism in Neo-Confucian thought, and Cheng Hao the first of the idealists. In common with each other,

however, they based their philosophies on principle or *li*.[76] Principle is the uniting factor in the universe, unchanging everywhere. Their concept of *Tien Li* ('the Principle of Heaven') encompasses both moral and natural law – how we should behave and how things are. Cheng Hao

> *'Fundamentally there is only one Great Ultimate, yet each of the myriad things has been endowed with it and each in itself possesses the Great Ultimate in its entirety.'*

emphasised the former aspect, while Cheng Yi explored the latter.

Of these five philosophers, Cheng Yi is the real forefather of Zhuxi and it was his rationalism that influenced later Neo-Confucianism above all. Their tradition was known in later times as the Cheng-Zhu (Ch'eng-Chu) School. Cheng Yi's ideas, though influential, were by no means universally accepted and he suffered from official censorship. An indication of the climate of the times is that when he died only four people were brave enough to attend his funeral. Zhuxi too was often in trouble with the authorities. Zhuxi's genius brought him many appointments, but generally he was too radical to keep a job. For example, in 1179 he was appointed to the post of Prefect, but in 1182 he was demoted to a lowly position having written to the

Emperor denouncing official corruption. Similar appointments in 1190 and 1194 ended in similar ways, and he was finally threatened with execution. The only job Zhuxi held down consistently was that of temple guardian, which suited his studious temperament. However, over a thousand mourners attended his funeral, in contrast to Cheng Yi's.

Perhaps the most important idea in Zhuxi's philosophy is that of the Great Ultimate. This he took from Zhou Dun Yi (see above) and is akin to the idea of the Absolute in Indian philosophy or the Good in Greek. Zhuxi says, 'The Great Ultimate is nothing other than principle'. In this way he unites Zhou's Great Ultimate with the idea of principle that, as we have seen, he derived from the Cheng brothers. 'Fundamentally there is only one Great Ultimate, yet each of the myriad things has been endowed with it and each in itself possesses the Great Ultimate in its entirety.' Zhuxi uses the image of moonlight falling on rivers and lakes to illustrate how the Great Ultimate manifests in many places and forms. The Indian Vedānta tradition uses a very similar illustration with sunlight reflecting in pots of water. It is interesting to note, however, that Zhuxi's image emphasises the unity of the light even in its manifestation, whereas the Indian one emphasises the separate individuality of the pots. Perhaps this expresses the Chinese feeling for people as part of society, or a corresponding lack of feeling for the individual soul. It more closely recalls **Fazang's** image of the universe as a bejewelled net, with each gem reflecting every other. Wing-Tsit Chan indeed traces the Neo-Confucian idea of principle to Fazang's Huayen Buddhism, which has a

world of 'principle' underlying the ordinary mundane one of 'fact'[77].

The question that arises is how the world manifests itself. Zhuxi characterises manifestation as a meeting between principle (*li*) and material force (*qi*). As we saw in the chapter on Mencius, *qi* (or *chi*) is the ancient Chinese concept of an energy or life force flowing through the universe. Good and evil are not in the Great Ultimate, but come into existence in manifestation. Like all Confucians apart from **Xunzi**, Zhuxi believes good to be essential and natural and evil incidental and unnatural.

A further passage explains more about the Great Ultimate and its relationship to the duality of *yin* and *yang* and to the Five Agents:

The Great Ultimate is similar to the top of the house or the zenith of the sky, beyond which point there is no more. It is the ultimate of principle. Yang is active and yin is tranquil. In these it is not the Great Ultimate that acts or remains tranquil. It is simply that there are the principles of activity and tranquillity. Principle is not visible; it becomes visible through yin and yang. Principle attaches itself to yin and yang as a man sits astride a horse. As soon as yin and yang produce the Five Agents, they are confined and fixed by physical nature and are thus differentiated into individual things, each with its nature. But the Great Ultimate is in all of them.

Zhuxi's view of *ren* is interesting and derives from Zhang Zai: '*Ren* is the principle of love, and impartiality is the principle of *ren*. Therefore if there is impartiality there is *ren*, and if there is *ren,* there is love.' We saw in **Mozi** the earliest appearance of impartial love, and how the Confucians criticised his lack of respect for loving relationships. In Zhuxi impartiality is the principle underlying love, and just as the Great Ultimate is fully embodied in each individual, so universal love is fully embodied in filial, fraternal or matrimonial love. So universal love is realised in Zhuxi to be the source of loving relationships.

Human nature is considered by Zhuxi to be one with principle. The Way or principle is the nature of the universe as a whole and in individual people or things it becomes their nature.

Zhuxi, as has been said, was the inheritor of Cheng Yi's rationalism. His brother Cheng Hao's idealism was taken up by Zhuxi's contemporary Lu Xiangshan (Lu Hsiang-Shan) (1139–1193), who emphasised the primacy of the mind. For Zhuxi the old Confucian injunction to undertake 'the investigation of things' means rational exploration. For the idealists, everything is contained within the mind and therefore the exploration of the mind is all that is necessary. Zhuxi was far more influential than Lu Xiangshan on the subsequent course of Chinese thought and cultural life and it was not until Wang Yangming (1472–1559) that idealism found a wide audience once more.

Pictorial representation of the duality of yin and yang.

WANG YANGMING

1472–1529 CE

The most influential Chinese philosopher in the last thousand years was **Zhuxi**. His rational Neo-Confucianism became normative, and after 1313 his selection of the Confucian Classics formed the basis of the civil service examinations. Opposition in his time had come from the idealist Neo-Confucian Lu Xiangshan (1139–1193), but it was to be three centuries before a philosopher could mount a serious challenge to Zhuxi. This came from Wang Yangming, who was an idealist like Lu, which is to say that they held the mind to be the fundamental reality. The school of philosophers that followed Wang is known as the Wang-Lu School, in opposition to that founded by Zhuxi on the basis of Cheng Yi's philosophy, which is known as Cheng-Zhu[78].

Wang was an energetic and effective figure, better known in his time for his abilities as an administrator and military leader than as a philosopher. Struggling against the tide of corruption and nepotism, Wang suffered frequent setbacks. For example, in 1506 he was exiled to a semi-barbarous region for two years for offending a eunuch. Between 1510 and 1521 he had a glorious and remarkable career that included economic

On his wedding day Wang became so absorbed in a discussion with a Daoist priest that he did not return home until the following day.

reform, fighting rebellions, administering justice and establishing schools. From 1521 to 1527 he was again sidelined, this time in his native state, before being recalled for one last (successful) campaign to put down a rebellion. He died in 1529.

Wang Yangming's philosophy was very influential in its time and for 150 years after his death. Although he fought against the prevailing orthodoxy, Wang did not have a serious philosophical rival. The political situation in the Ming dynasty was very difficult and scholarship was at a low ebb. When he was young, Wang tried out most of the various options for intellectual endeavour, including Zhuxi's Confucianism (then in decline), literary

The Drum Tower, built during the Ming dynasty, on Peking's northern boundary (now Beijing).

composition, the science of war and the Daoist search for the elixir of life. Wang's energy was evident from the beginning. He and a companion, for example, are said to have sat down before a bamboo grove for seven days in a Zhuxian attempt to 'investigate the principles' in it. He eventually became sick and gave up. Like Confucius, he had a reputation for forgetting what he was doing when engaged in learning: on his wedding day Wang became so absorbed in a discussion with a Daoist priest that he did not return home until the following day. Progressively, Wang developed his own philosophy. His first major breakthrough came while in

exile in 1508 and he continued to refine it until 1521, when at the age of fifty he completed the essentials of his philosophy.

Wang argued against Zhuxi's identification of principle with things, maintaining instead that principles were in the mind. A demonstration of this (which may seem self-evident to us) is that filial piety continues after the parents are dead and gone. The principle is not to be found in the things themselves (i.e. the parents) but in the mind of the individual. Zhuxi's rationalism had, in Wang's opinion, the effect of fragmenting and disturbing the mind:

People fail to realise that the highest good is in their minds and seek it outside. As they believe that everything or every event has its own definite principle, they search for the highest good in individual things. Consequently, the mind becomes fragmentary, isolated, broken into pieces; mixed and confused it has no definite direction.

On the other hand Wang's idealism would have the opposite effect:

Once it is realised that the highest good is in the mind and does not depend on any search outside, then the mind will have definite direction and there will be no danger of its becoming fragmentary, isolated, broken into pieces, mixed, or confused. When there is no such danger, the mind will not be erroneously perturbed, but will be tranquil.

Wang's solution to the philosophical impasse that had resulted from over-emphasis on 'the investigation of things' and philology in Zhuxi's followers was what he called 'the extension of the innate knowledge of the good'. Instead of working from the outside in – that is, from observation and study towards inherent principle – Wang said that the basis should be the innate knowledge of the good, which is identified with the Principle of Nature. Wang's philosophy is a

reconnection with **Mencius** (371–289 BCE) and with his concern to demonstrate that man's nature is originally good.

Wang centres, like nearly all Confucian thinkers, on ethics. This focus works well for Wang, because ethical concepts (for example, filial piety) are in an important sense mental. His exposition of 'forming one body with all things', for example, is a pleasing and clear account of the topic[79] and demonstrates the strength of his approach. So in terms of his concern with a decline in morality, the fragmentation of philosophy and the loss of connection with the Confucian tradition, Wang's idealism was a success.

By comparison with Western idealism, however, Wang's philosophy of mind is very undeveloped. Metaphysically, Wang struggles to account for phenomena. His claim that 'there is nothing under Heaven external to the mind' was challenged by someone who pointed at some blossoming trees on a cliff and asked what they had to do with the mind. His reply, that the colours show up when one looks at them is, at best, inadequate. Although Wang is a philosopher of the mind, he is not really interested in intellectual matters, but in moral reform. His philosophy argues that knowledge and action are the same thing, and his life illustrated this. So Wang could be said to be, in every sense, an exemplary philosopher.

Wang's view of the practicality of knowledge in action was an important theme in subsequent philosophy. It could be said to be carried to its logical conclusion in **Mao Zedong** (Mao Tse-Tung) in the twentieth century: despite Mao's materialistic philosophy, his theory of mind echoes Wang.

DAI ZHEN (TAI CHEN)

1723–1777 CE

The two main schools of thought in Neo-Confucianism were the rationalism of **Zhuxi** (1130–1200) and the idealism of **Wang Yangming** (1472–1529). Zhuxi used reason to discover principle within things, while Wang looked within the mind. Although by comparison with Wang, Zhuxi was relatively interested in 'the investigation of things', he did so in order to find out principle and thus the Great Ultimate. A Western parallel would be with Plato: the 'things' were of importance only insofar as they pointed the way to the truth, which was determined by pure reason.

A second challenge to Zhuxi came from Dai Zhen. He criticised the Zhuxians for treating principle (*li*) as a 'thing'. Dai Zhen was part of a tradition known as Han Learning, because they went back to the thinkers of the Han Dynasty (206 BCE–220 CE), the first scholars to explore the Confucian Classics such as the *Analects*, the *Mencius*, the *Doctrine of the Mean* and so on. Dai Zhen's party were also known as the school of 'Investigations Based on Evidence', that is to say they were Empiricists. The Han Learning school liked to devote themselves to objective and critical reasoning on subjects such as philology, history and mathematics. Dai Zhen stood out because he regarded such study as only a means to an end, which, as a good

Ching-Hai: first entrance gate to the Temple of Confucius.

DESIRE

One of the most interesting questions in Chinese philosophy is that of desire. Desire is not a major issue for the early thinkers. **Confucius** does not condemn it, but seems to regard it as in need of management: the final step of his learning is, 'at seventy I followed my heart's desire and did not err'. **Mencius** advised a king who confessed to a weakness for sex, 'If your majesty love sex, let your people enjoy the same, and what difficulty will there be for you to become the true king of the Empire?' Mencius speaks a great deal about desire and makes it a central plank of his philosophy: for example, our desire for honour is the seed of propriety. The superior man neither insists on fulfilling his desires nor on suppressing them. They are natural and therefore, on the whole, good, although 'For nourishing the mind there is nothing better than to have few desires.' **Xunzi** has an interesting comment on a philosopher who he said understood about having few desires 'but not about having many'. The importance of the latter was that it helped a king to rule by giving him an understanding of what people want.

Daoism, on the other hand, is more censorious. **Laozi**, who speaks a great deal about desire, says 'do not display the objects of desire, so that people's hearts shall not be disturbed' and that 'the sage desires to have no desire'. The Daoists saw the ideal of vacuity as being a desireless, empty state. Overall, it would be accurate to say that Daoism is against desire. Nevertheless, there is a strong and surprising tendency in Daoism towards hedonism and self-preservation at all cost, as in the words attributed to Yang Chu (440–360 BCE). This also emerged in the Neo-Daoist 'Light Conversation' school of the third century CE, whose iconoclasm extended to moral conventions.

Buddhism is of all Chinese philosophies and religions the most opposed to desire, as would be expected. It was a core belief of Buddha that desire, or thirst (tanha), was the cause of suffering.

Desire became a hot topic in Neo-Confucian thought when Zhou Dun Yi (1017–1073 CE), influenced by Buddhist and especially Daoist thought, was the first orthodox Chinese thinker to speak of desireless vacuity as a virtue. Zhang Zai (1022–1077 CE) was the first to oppose principle and desire: 'those who understand the higher things return to the Principle of Nature, while those who understand lower things follow human desires'. He related *yang to the moral nature and* yin *to material desire. Zhuxi (1130–1200 CE) crystallized Neo-Confucian thinking on the subject, writing extensively on it to establish the polarity between desire and principle. Even Wang Yangming (1472–1529 CE), who opposed Zhuxi on many things, was at one with him on this question. Neo-Confucianism did not espouse an ascetic retreat from all desire: the real enemy was selfish, partial desire.*

Wang Fuzhi (1619–1692 CE) was the first thinker to take a different tack, by going back once more to the original teachings. He wrote: 'Mencius continued the teaching of Confucius which is that wherever human desires are found, the Principle of Nature is found'. His influence was slight, however, and it was only with Dai Zhen (1723–1777 CE) that the Zhuxian orthodoxy came under serious question. Again, Dai Zhen was perhaps too far ahead of his time to be popular, but he had his followers even before the revival of his ideas in the early twentieth century.

Confucian, meant moral philosophy and its practice.

As a child of 10, Dai Zhen is supposed to have challenged his teachers on the authenticity of Confucian writings: 'how do we know that this is what Confucius said?' Later he came to question not what Confucius said so much as the interpretations foisted upon Confucianism by the Neo-Confucians.[80]

Dai Zhen rejected much of Neo-Confucian tradition, reinstating desire as an acceptable and natural part of life, much as did his contemporary in Scotland David Hume. He argued against the polarity of desire and principle, instead stating, 'principle consists of feelings that do not err'. This is an important restatement of Confucius' 'at seventy I followed my heart's desire and did not err'. Dai Zhen's rejection of Neo-Confucian principle is also Humean: he says that the Neo-Confucians speak of principle wrongly when they regard it as a real thing, or single essence pervading all things. Principle does not exist in a transcendent realm, but is to be found in the disciplined human heart: in other words, it is identified with *ren* or humanheartedness. He wrote perceptively, 'The ancient sages did not seek benevolence, righteousness, propriety, and wisdom outside the realm of desires, and did not consider these in isolation from blood, breath, mind and spirit.' Dai Zhen is against Daoist- or Buddhist-influenced ideas of withdrawing from the world: 'to let others live but not to live oneself is against nature'. He maintains 'all activities in the world should consist of nothing more than encouraging this fulfilment of desires and expression of feelings.' Dai Zhen is not promoting hedonism, but a sincere and disciplined way of life in which the individual plays a full part in society and lives squarely and honestly.

MAO ZEDONG (MAO TSE-TUNG)
1893–1976

Born into a poor peasant farming family in Shaoshan in the Hunan province, Mao's early childhood was hard. Gradually, the family prospered, but the formative years left an indelible impression on Mao. His primary school education included a grounding in the Confucian classics, but at the age of 13 his father took him to work on the farm. Determined to gain a full education, Mao rebelled and left the family home to study nearby. In 1905 the civil-service examinations based on Confucianism were abolished and Western learning was beginning to find its way into school curricula, marking the beginning of a period of great intellectual uncertainty for China. In 1911 Mao was involved in the rebellion against the Manchu Dynasty, his first experience of war. In 1912 the Empire that had existed more or less constantly since 220 BCE had fallen and been replaced by a republic. Mao then continued his studies, drifting from one subject to the next and learning about Western traditions, eventually graduating from school in 1918 and going on to Beijing University where he became involved with the founder members of the Chinese Communist Party. The CCP was officially formed in 1921 and Mao gradually gained prominence. He was its central figure from 1934–1935, when he led the Red Army on the Long March. Mao was instrumental in fighting the Japanese invasion from 1937 and in 1949 the civil war ended with his declaration of the People's Democratic Dictatorship (later the People's Republic of China). Mao was Chairman of the Party Secretariat and Political Bureau from 1943 but effectively he controlled the Party and China until his death in 1976. His rule did not have the grinding brutality of Stalin, but his capricious and ruthless policies often led to great destruction and suffering.

Before looking more closely at some of his policies, it is worth looking at Mao's philosophy. Mao was not a great original thinker. His ideas were derived from the Communists who preceded him: Marx, Engels, Lenin and Stalin. He did, however, think deeply about the philosophy of dialectical materialism that underlies Communism, and his practical application of its ideas is original. He was also without a doubt the most influential thinker of the twentieth century in China.

The most important concept in Mao's philosophy is that of contradiction. He

Mao (1893–1976) at a Red Guard rally in Peking (Beijing). His followers wave their 'Little Red Books' at him as he passes.

wrote, 'Contradiction is universal and absolute, it is present in the process of development of all things and permeates every process from beginning to end.' Marx's model of history is built on the principle of contradiction or conflict: the ruling class and the subject class, or capital and labour, are in perpetual conflict. One day this conflict will result in a crisis and the working class will triumph. Eventually this new situation will give rise to a further crisis, but in Marx the whole emphasis is on the logical end to the present conflict and the happy situation that will then prevail, whereas in Mao the principle of contradiction becomes 'universal and absolute'. Contradiction in Mao has something of the *yinyang* philosophy about it[81]. It seems almost an article of faith with him, as is seen in this passage from *On Contradiction:*

The sciences are differentiated precisely on the basis of the particular contra-dictions inherent in their respective objects of study. Thus the contradiction peculiar to a certain field of phenomena constitutes the object of study for a specific branch of science. For example, positive and negative numbers in mathematics; action and reaction in mechanics; positive and negative elec-tricity in physics; dissociation and combination in chemistry; forces of pro-duction and relations of production, classes and class struggle, in social science; offence and defence in military science; idealism and materialism, the metaphysical outlook and the dialectical outlook, in philosophy; and so on – all these are the objects of study of different branches of science precisely because each branch has its own particular contra-diction and particular essence.[82]

Mao's examples of contradiction in different fields are drawn from Lenin. Some are good analogies, some less so. Positive and negative numbers are a poor analogy for Marxist dialectic, because their opposition is not dynamic: the result is just another positive or negative number. Mao is on even shakier ground when he declares that these contradictions represent the 'essence' of their respective fields. Positive and negative numbers are not the 'essence' of mathematics, any more than positive and negative electricity are the essence of physics or the metaphysical and the dialectical the essence of philosophy. Mao was well educated and his misconception here can only be due to infatuation with the idea of contradiction itself. This impression was borne out in his political life, as we will see.

Mao's second important idea is his theory of knowledge, which is again derived from Marxism. Mao holds in his essay *On Practice* that knowledge proceeds from experience of the material world, and that experience equals involvement.

If you want knowledge, you must take part in the practice of changing reality. If you want to know the taste of a pear, you must change the pear by eating it yourself. If you want to know the structure and properties of the atom, you must make physical and chemical experiments to change the state of the atom. If you want to know the theory and methods of revolution, you must take part in revolution. All genuine knowledge originates in direct experience.

Only after having had the experience can one make the 'leap' to conceptualise the perceptions as knowledge. Then the knowledge is put into practice once again, and further perception takes place. Mao here has affinities not only with Marxism but also with Neo-Confucian thought going back to **Wang Yangming** (1472–1529). Wang maintained an opposite position to Mao, being an idealist: the world was entirely contained within the mind. Nevertheless, his theory of knowledge was, like Mao's, that knowledge and action were the same thing. This influenced later thinkers such as Kang Youwei (1858–1927). Kang's utopianism was an important non-Marxist influence on Mao.

We will now look at how Mao's ideas were carried into practice. His theory of contradiction distinguishes between contradictions that are 'antagonistic' and 'non-antagonistic'[83]. The antagonistic contradiction will need a struggle before it can be resolved, whereas a non-antagonistic contradiction can be dealt with through discussion. The contradictions between the proletariat and the ruling class were antagonistic, while (Mao believed) those between the Party and the people were not. In 1956 Mao announced a new policy of intellectual freedom in response to a growing desire among Chinese Communists to avoid repeating the tyranny of Stalinist USSR. He spoke of 'letting a hundred flowers blossom and a hundred schools of thought contend'. The policy was a failure, however, and resulted in a crescendo of criticism and complaint. Mao, believing that the intellectuals had failed him, then pursued a vigorous policy of suppression of their ideas. Within a year some 700,000 'rightist' intellectuals were sacked and sent to work the land.

Despite this experience, Mao used the politics of contradiction to maintain his stranglehold on power, and the principle of contradiction to pursue his vision of 'continual revolution'. Mao believed that in any revolution counter-revolutionary elements would inevitably emerge within the new power structure. He frequently declared purges against those who he saw or declared to be enemies of the revolution. The most dramatic example of this was the Cultural Revolution of 1966. All over the world students were rising up against the establishment in the 1960s. Only in China did the rulers encourage and help them.

Mao as a young man.

From the universities hundreds of thousands of students and lecturers spontaneously formed 'Red Guard' units and carried out savage attacks on the supposedly counter-revolutionary bureaucracy. Within months China was in a state of collapse and Mao was forced to call out the army to tame the Red Guards. The Cultural Revolution spiralled out of control and China descended into a civil war that involved the Red Guards, the army and other factions, only ending in 1968.

The other major disaster of Mao's career was the 'Great Leap Forward' of 1958 that involved organizing the peasantry into people's communes. This was the third major reorganization of the workers in as many years – Mao's passion for revolution being the main reason for this – and was economically disastrous. The people's communes proved cumbersome and unmanageably large units, and an estimated 19 million died from famine and disease.

It is an interesting question whether Mao represents a total break with the past or whether, despite his repudiation of Chinese philosophy, he was influenced by it. Confucianism could be seen as preparing the way for Maoism in several respects. Firstly, both philosophies have an ethical and social focus in which the needs and desires of the individual are subsumed to those of the group. Secondly, there is an emphasis on activity as opposed to reflection, which is broadly Confucian. As we saw in his essay *On Practice* Mao argues that the only way to learn anything is through practice, principally in the practice of economic activity. Thirdly, the Confucian Doctrine of the Mean was an influence on Mao's political practice: he typically followed a period of turbulent change with one of calm and peace, even at times reversing some parts of the earlier revolution, in preparation for the next convulsion. Fourthly, Confucianism does not depend on the agency of God. Overall, however, the similarities are far less than the

Mao, accompanied by his second-in-command, passing along the ranks of revolutionaries during a rally in Peking (Beijing).

differences. It would be more accurate to say that Mao recognised that the best way to make Communism work in China was to work with an awareness of the existing ideas of the culture. In this light, Confucian elements can be seen as expedient additions rather than as fundamental to Mao's philosophy.

In many ways, however, Mao has more affinities to Daoism and to the traditional philosophies of *yinyang* and the Five Agents or Elements. By identifying with the underdog and with women's rights and by opposing the establishment, the educated classes and their technical expertise, Mao aligns himself with the Daoist *yin* ethic that we saw in **Laozi**. Continual revolution, too, could be seen as an echo of the principle of revolution that characterises the Five Agents theory, with each element taking centre stage in turn. We saw in the chapter on **Hanfeizi** how the ideas of Daoism could be misused to support tyranny, when the Way

or Dao becomes identified with the Way set down by the Emperor. Mao could almost be seen as a mystical sage-king, whose perception of the Way alone defined what it was. He was certainly revered as such, particularly in his later years. In this light Mao's capriciousness becomes a virtue: only he was able to keep the sacred flame alight, while others allowed themselves to be seduced by capitalist ideology. Often this would lead to death, but in the practice of self-denunciation and re-education can be seen the twisted remnants of a mystical path, in which Mao and Communism come to replace the Way of Heaven.

A quarter of a century after Mao's death, China seems to have come through a difficult period well: far better, for example, than Russia. The lot of the average Chinese has been improved economically. Critics are undecided whether Mao should be more praised for his role in raising the peasants up, or blamed for his disastrous mistakes.

KOREAN PHILOSOPHY

*The key figures in Korean Zen are those
that attempted to show that its anti-intellectual
and anti-scholastic tendencies could be
reconciled with a highly complex system such as Huayen.*

*A little Korean girl says her prayers,
highlighted by the morning sun.*

As the smaller neighbour of China, Korea has often been in its shadow. In the history of thought and religion it has suffered from a prejudice that it was a mere bridge in the transmission of influence eastwards to Japan, and contributed nothing of its own. Korea's recent history has not helped in this. Annexed by Japan in 1910 and later divided into hermetically sealed Communist North and democratic South

Korea, the twentieth century saw Korea fall victim to external forces, leading to an inevitable neglect of its culture. In recent times a re-evaluation is beginning to give a more balanced view of Korea's contribution.

In a book such as this one, however, it is inevitable that the main stream should receive most of the attention. If it is wrong to regard Korean philosophy as negligible, its importance is principally as a contributor to the Chinese tradition of Confucianism and to Chinese-flavoured Buddhism[84]. For this reason its central figures will not be covered individually, but only sketched out here.

Buddhism should be considered first. The two most important Chinese forms of Buddhism, both in terms of their influence and in their distinctive Chinese identity, were the Chan (or as it is better-known, Zen) school and the Huayen or 'Flowery Garland' school. The latter was a refinement of orthodox Mahāyāna Buddhism and regarded itself as the pinnacle of a thousand years of Buddhist thought, subsuming and surpassing the earlier forms. It was based on the *Avatamsaka* ('Garland') *Sūtra* and almost from the very beginning Korean Buddhists were important. The central Huayen figure is **Fazang** and the influence of the

Korean thinkers, especially Wānhyo (617–686), is considered in the chapter on Fazang in the Chinese section. Wānhyo was important in other ways, however, in particular showing a talent for synthesis and unification that characterises many Korean thinkers. He hoped that Buddhism would become the state religion and proselytised tirelessly, founding the Popsong or Dharma Nature school. Wānhyo sought to understand the divisions between different Buddhist schools, such as the Yogācāra and Madhyāmika (known in China as Tiantai), by seeing them as approaching the problem from, respectively, a kind of *via positiva* and *via negativa*. Wānhyo saw the former as being an attempt to climb towards higher consciousness and the latter as an attempt to explode false thinking that gets in the way. He also promoted an esoteric Buddhism, with some doctrines revealed only to the initiate.

Zen was much more problematic for Koreans, and so the key figures in Korean Zen are those that attempted to show that its anti-intellectual and anti-scholastic tendencies could be reconciled with a highly complex system such as Huayen. Uich'on (1055–1101) was ordained as a Tiantai teacher in China and attempted to set up a monastery that brought together Tiantai (called in Korea Ch'on'tae) and Zen (in Korea, Sēn). He was in the end unsuccessful, but the Zen Buddhist Chinul (1158–1210) achieved his aim about a century later. He was the pioneer in Korea of the use of the pithy verse paradoxes known as *kungan* in Korea or *koan* in Japan. He showed that the experiential Zen approach could be combined with a more gradual, scriptural study-based Buddhism, much as the Japanese Zen master **Dōgen** would do a generation later. He was the founder of the Chogye school of Zen and did as much as anyone to ensure the dominance of Zen in Korean Buddhism since that time.

However, Confucianism steadily gained ground in this period and in the Choson dynasty of 1392–1910 was quickly established as the state religion. During this period Korea was even more strongly Confucian than China, because the competition from rival traditions was much less. The great period of Korean Confucianism was the sixteenth century. Yi T'oegye (1501–1570) and Yi Yulgok (1536–1584). The dominant thinker of Neo-Confucianism was **Zhuxi**, whose school in China received a major challenge from the idealism of **Wang Yangming**, who died in 1529. Yi T'oegye and Yi Yulgok, who are closer to Zhuxi, worked to illuminate some of the most important points in Zhuxi's thinking, in some ways more successfully than their Chinese contemporaries.

JAPANESE PHILOSOPHY

Of all the Eastern traditions considered in this book, there are very few distinctive responses to the challenge of Western modernity and of ideologies such as capitalism and communism . . . Only in Japan is the Western challenge accepted and met creatively.

Buddhist monks in the snow at the Shingon monastery of Koyasan, Japan.

Japanese, like Korean philosophy, is largely based upon the Chinese systems. The most important of these for Japan is Buddhism, followed by Confucianism. Daoism is far less significant in itself, but is an influence on the development of Zen. The native religion of Shinto will not be dealt with here.

Although there have been a great many Japanese thinkers, this book will look in detail at only a few of the most original. For this reason we pass over the early period and look first at the Buddhism of the twelfth and thirteenth centuries. It was in this period that most of the distinctively Japanese forms were developed. An important concept was the idea of the 'degenerate age' or *mappō*, the period in which it was thought that the decline in culture meant that the practice of Buddha's doctrines were almost impossible. This idea had special meaning for the Japanese. Firstly it led to the creation of various 'easy' methods of Buddhism, in particular the new Pure Land schools; secondly it eroded elitist concepts of who was an acceptable Buddhist aspirant; and thirdly it inspired a kind of Buddhism of ordinary life that fed into Zen practices such as painting, gardening and the tea-ceremony.

Among the important 'easy' methods were those of the Pure Land school. This is an ancient strand of Buddhism with its roots in early Chinese and Indian traditions, emphasising the power of the Buddha over the efforts of the individual. The Pure Land is a kind of heaven ruled over by the Amida Buddha, a transcendent being of whom the historical Buddha was said to be merely an *avatar* or incarnation. The aim of Pure Land Buddhism is to be reborn there, where the Amida Buddha will give the teaching that guarantees Enlightenment. **Honen** and **Shinran** were highly innovative in their interpretation of this teaching. In reaction to them, **Nichiren** created his own form of 'easy' Tendai Buddhism based on the *Lotus Sūtra*.

The other important development of this period, relating not so much to the 'easy way' as to the drive towards anti-intellectualism and anti-elitism, was the first successful introduction of Zen. The Rinzai Zen school of sudden Enlightenment was founded by **Eisai** and the gradualist Soto Zen school by his disciple **Dōgen**, one of the most important thinkers in any of the Eastern traditions. Notwithstanding this, Rinzai Zen is perhaps more influential today, largely through the efforts of the eighteenth-century monk Hakuin, on which a few words here are relevant. He revived Rinzai as a practical doctrine among the poor and composed many Zen *koans* including the famous 'When both hands are clapped a sound is produced; listen to the sound of one hand clapping.' He also pioneered ink-drawing and calligraphy as a Zen activity. Although Zen is originally Chinese, its modern form and name come from Japan, where it became thoroughly embedded in many aspects of art, life and culture.

Perhaps the most interesting thing about Japanese philosophy, however, are its twentieth century developments. Of all the Eastern traditions considered in this book, there are very few distinctive responses to the challenge of Western modernity and of ideologies such as capitalism and communism. By comparison, the Islamic, Hindu and modern Confucian philosophies seem like restatements of old ideas. Only in Japan is the Western challenge accepted and met creatively by figures like **Nishida** and others in his Kyoto School.

This section looks at the period of the twelfth and thirteenth centuries in which the distinctive Buddhist forms were evolved, and at the philosophy of Nishida as an example of Japanese twentieth century thought.

Japanese children practise calligraphy using a 'fude' Japanese pen.

HONEN
1113–1212 CE

In the twelfth century Japanese Buddhism was in decline. Some monasteries were said to be decadent and lax, while others hired mercenaries for protection, becoming fortresses. The first great reforming Buddhist was Honen, who believed that the decline in Japanese culture meant that a more simple, direct and easy form of Buddhism was needed. This idea was centred on the concept of *mappō*, which is a theory of history as a decline from the time of the Buddha. Honen believed that he lived in the third and last stage.

Honen is the founder of Pure Land Buddhism as a separate school – it had always featured in Japan as an aspect of Tendai and Shingon Buddhism. He was classically trained as a Tendai monk at Mount Hiei. Around 1175 he came to the conclusion that the best and most effective form of Buddhist practice was the repetition of the chant 'All praise to the Amida Buddha', known as the *nembutsu*. The Amida Buddha is the central deity of Pure Land Buddhism. This sect originated in India with the belief that if enough merit was accrued in life one could be reincarnated not on earth but in the Pure Land, a heaven in which the aspirant could continue practising until Buddhahood was achieved. This rebirth would mark the point of no return: there was no doubt of Enlightenment once the Pure Land was reached.

Honen recognised that his reduction of Buddhist practice to the *nembutsu* was extremely radical and sought to keep it a secret from all but his closest followers. He wrote down his teachings with the instruction that they only be released after his death. Nevertheless, word got out and Honen and some of his followers (including **Shinran**) were exiled for a short time. They were later pardoned but continued to have a difficult relationship with the orthodox schools[85].

The comparison has been made between Honen and his disciple Shinran and Martin Luther, the Protestant reformer of Christianity. Instead of focussing efforts on attaining merit that would then bear the aspirant to the Pure Land, Honen emphasised the agency of the Amida Buddha, who was said to have taken a vow that anyone who said his name would reach the Pure Land. Thus it was not necessary to undertake any other practice or to meditate, or even to know the meaning of the *nembutsu*: mere repetition was enough. Even the desire for enlightenment – hitherto the first essential step in Buddhism – was to be abandoned. The 'easy way' of the *nembutsu* was contrasted with the difficult way of those who tried to reach enlightenment through their own efforts. Honen's way is about faith, not works; and about grace rather than human endeavour or virtue.

SHINRAN

1173–1263 CE

Japanese Pure Land Buddhism was founded by **Honen**, who taught the 'easy way' of repetition of the *nembutsu* formula as the route to enlightenment. Honen's reticence about his teachings meant that his followers were left in some doubt as to his legacy. Shinran, the most important of these, eventually founded his own True Pure Land school, which can be regarded as the apotheosis of all Pure Land Buddhism. The Amida Buddha, the figure of worship for Pure Land Buddhists, is to be understood as the transcendent being of the historical Buddha. The Buddha Siddhārtha Gautama is known as Shākyamuni, 'the sage of the Shākya [clan]'. He is not thought to be an ordinary human being – as is claimed in the Theravāda – but an incarnation of Amida.

Shinran was among those shamed and exiled with Honen in 1207 to Echigo on the coast. There, he adopted the nickname Gutoku, meaning 'foolish' or 'stubble-haired', and married. Moving to the Kanto region, he lived among lay people for twenty years and built up a considerable following. In his sixties he returned to Kyoto, where he set down his philosophy. Like Honen, Shinran embodies a fresh approach to Buddhism; self-effacing, grounded and based on trust in the grace of Amida Buddha. Shinran took the 'easy way' still further than Honen. Amida had made a vow that anyone who repeated his name would be born in the Pure Land; Shinran asserted that even one repetition of the *nembutsu* was enough.

This did not mean that the faithful should regard their salvation as assured. Coupled with the comfort of total faith in Amida was Shinran's rejection of personal pride in all its forms. Honen had rejected the traditional Buddhist belief in the aspirant's desire for enlightenment. Shinran rejected the personal egotistical self in all its manifestations. *Ekō* or 'transferring merit' is normally understood to mean that the merit accrued by the individual is dedicated to the enlightenment of all without discrimination. Shinran's unique interpretation was that *ekō* should be regarded not as individual merit, but the merit of Amida's own practice.

The aim of Pure Land practice is normally to achieve birth there. The point about this is that the individual has then reached the point of non-retrogression and enlightenment is certain. Shinran emphasises instead the attainment of *shinjin*, or Buddha's mind. This state is to be understood as one of non-duality in which there is no difference between true reality and *samsāra* or the cycle of rebirth. Shinran taught that non-retrogression was the same as the attainment of *shinjin*. This leads on to the idea that the Pure Land is not the place to achieve enlightenment but simply the final step or aspect of the *Nirvāna* already achieved. The enlightened being then returns to earth to pursue the work of bringing every soul to Buddhahood.

True Pure Land represents one extreme of Buddhism, in which the Buddha's emphasis on good works and good intentions are almost entirely absent.

Nevertheless, Shinran's compassion, humility and practical application of Buddhist principles are yet another example of how the Buddha's real ideals could be realised by an apparently unlikely path. Like Christ, Shinran warned against the would-be holy person and taught that the sinner could be saved just as easily. His approach to Buddhism is characteristic of the Japanese love of piety. It is also a spirituality of the ordinary life, a tendency that emerges in a very different way at the opposite pole of Zen Buddhism[86].

A European family pose in front of a colossal bronze image of the Amida Buddha near Yokohama in Japan.

EISAI
1141–1215 CE

The decline in Tendai Buddhism and the sense that the last days of the world were approaching led to various reforming movements in Japan. At one extreme was the True Pure Land of **Shinran**, which emphasised the divine agency of Amida Buddha in everything. At the other was Eisai's Rinzai Zen school, which emphasised human agency and self-reliance.

Eisai was trained in the orthodox Tendai tradition and visited China at the age of 28 to gather manuscripts. Some twenty years later he made a second journey, this time meeting a Chan (Zen) master who instructed him and declared Eisai to have achieved enlightenment. Although Eisai claimed that the great Buddhist monk Saicho (764–822), founder of the Tendai school, had known of Zen and had approved of it, Eisai should certainly be regarded as its founder in Japan. Not only did he introduce its meditation and *satori* or 'sudden' enlightenment to Japan, he gave to Zen a distinctively Japanese character.

Like Pure Land, Rinzai Zen has a strong flavour of the ordinary, which led it to sacralise various secular activities such as tea-drinking. Eisai introduced tea to Japan from China and originated its ceremonial. Not only was tea useful to help monks stay awake but the activity of making and serving tea also became a form of meditation in itself. This is the origin of a number of Zen activities such as archery, gardening, flower-arranging, calligraphy and painting that have become a characteristic feature of Japanese culture.

Tea-making utensils in a Japanese home.

DŌGEN
1200–1253 CE

Born into an aristocratic family, Dōgen's father died when he was two and his mother when he was seven. He described the sight of the incense rising and disappearing at her funeral as a direct insight into the impermanence of all things. Turning away from a career at the court, Dōgen chose instead to follow Buddhism and was ordained as a monk at the age of 13. Dissatisfied with the decadence of the Japanese Tendai sect, he shortly left Mount Hiei and went to study with the aged **Eisai**, founder of Rinzai Zen in Japan. He was deeply impressed by Eisai, who died in 1214, after which the 14-year-old Dōgen travelled for three years, returning to study with Eisai's chief disciple Myozen. At the age of 23 he suggested to Myozen that they travel to China to study Zen[87]. There, Dōgen found Rinzai Zen, as it was practised in

China, ultimately unsatisfactory, but a meeting with the abbot Rujing of the Caodong (Tsao-tung) Zen sect changed his life. Rujing recognised Dōgen's qualities and at the age of 25 Dōgen was recognised as his official successor. Dōgen returned to Japan where Caodong is known as Soto Zen.

The problem that had troubled Dōgen from his earliest days as a monk was the Tendai conception of two levels of enlightenment: *hongaku* or original enlightenment and *shikaku* or acquired enlightenment. If everyone was supposed to possess *hongaku*, why was work necessary? Dōgen wondered why it should be that even already enlightened Buddhas should have to practise to achieve wisdom? Dōgen saw how Buddhism had become lax through a failure to either penetrate the theoretical side fully or to practise properly. The prevailing view was fatalistic: the truths of Buddhism were understood in an earlier age but had now become impossible to understand. One response to this was to aim for an 'easy way'. Dōgen rejected fatalism: 'If you do not seek enlightenment here and now on the pretext of the Age of Degenerate Law or wretchedness, in what birth are you to attain it?'

From Dōgen's stubborn refusal to accept mediocrity in any aspect of Buddhism came the remarkable rebirth of Soto. While Rinzai emphasised sudden enlightenment based around study of the *koan* paradoxes, Soto monks followed a gradualist path of *zazen* or constant meditation. Dōgen's distinctively Japanese form of Soto Zen nevertheless employs both *zazen* and *koan*. Dōgen applied a new methodology to the *koan*, allowing more subtle interpretations. Whereas the Rinzai use of *koan* is intended to defeat ordinary

A Buddhist shrine, Japan.

thought and so provoke a sudden realization, Dōgen held that they could be expressions of the essential emptiness (*shūnyata*) in everything.

Rinzai Zen corresponds to the Yogācāra School of 'Consciousness-Only' and seeks to defeat ordinary consciousness by the mind-bending *koan* technique. The *koan* causes the collapse of ordinary perception and gives birth to true consciousness. On the other hand, Soto Zen as practised by Dōgen corresponds to the Madhyāmika 'Middle Way' school founded by **Nāgārjuna**. The Middle Way is that of refusal to absolutely deny or affirm the reality of anything. Rinzai denies ordinary awareness; Soto puts ordinary awareness

and higher awareness on an equal footing. This explains the ancient paradox that *Nirvāna* and *samsāra* are the same. Neither is absolutely real, neither is absolutely unreal. Buddha-consciousness is not a true consciousness that invalidates a false consciousness, but the constant awareness that ultimately all states of consciousness are impermanent.

Dōgen pushes beyond even Nāgārjuna in his assertion that the Buddha-nature is itself constantly changing and subject to time. Nāgārjuna's concept of emptiness serves to create a new foundation for reality. Stripped of its Buddhist doctrinal trappings, this is not very different from Hinduism. For Nāgārjuna, emptiness itself, being the only constant, is the only resting-place. But Dōgen, like the Son of Man, has no place to rest his head. His perspective is not easy to comprehend, but it combines inner vigilance and constant practice with an unfailing attention to the things of the world. A lay-person cannot deny the need for practice, and a monk cannot deny the needs of the world. This does not mean a mediocre combination of the two. Dōgen welcomed anyone to his monasteries, regardless of talent, sex or background. His criterion for entry was sincerity. He declared the way of the Boddhisattva or 'Buddha-to-be' as 'I am Thus-ness; you are Thus-ness'. Nāgārjuna proclaimed the emptiness of all, Dōgen the fullness of all. This is what is meant when he writes:

'When the self comes forward and confirms the myriad things, it is delusion; when the myriad things come forth and confirm the self, it is enlightenment.' Our problem is not outside of us, it is our belief that there is an outside, our desire to ring-fence a part of reality as 'me' rather than aiming at a total perception of one reality.

The Soto Zen emphasis on meditation is reminiscent of the ancient Buddhist teachings of the Theravāda, but without the turning-away from the world. Dōgen is also

Dōgen

a profound poet, his insights into the natural world reminiscent of Daoism. In his insistence on practice Dōgen went against the flow of the time and this made it difficult for Soto to thrive against the easier paths offered elsewhere, that seemed less elitist. Nevertheless, Dōgen is regarded as perhaps Japan's greatest philosopher as well as a great Buddhist teacher. His penetrating insights are still debated today and fuelled the remarkable modern revival of Zen as perhaps the only Eastern philosophy to engage fully with the West on its own terms.

NICHIREN
1222–1282 CE

The great reforms of Pure Land and Zen Buddhism in twelfth century Japan were inspired by the idea of the *mappō*, the third and final era of Buddhism in which it would decline. Their response was to look for an 'easy way', a simplification that would help those living in a time of anarchy and worldliness to find salvation. The third great movement to come out this was that of Nichiren, a combative and strident monk who railed against the political rulers of his time.

Educated in the dominant Tendai tradition, Nichiren was taught that the essence of Buddhism was contained in the *Lotus Sūtra*. Untypically for a Buddhist, he attacked all the other sects of his time as heretical and petitioned to have them outlawed. In particular Pure Land and Zen were singled out as innovations. He pointed to natural disasters and the threat of invasion by Kublai Khan's Mongols as indications that Japan was under threat because of its failure to follow the true path of the *Lotus Sūtra*. He was exiled twice for his pains and on being rebuffed a third time retired with his followers late in life to Mount Minobu. Nichiren's political involvement was unusual to say the least, however unsuccessful. He was an influential figure in later times with his heartfelt nationalism and his desire to be 'the pillar of Japan, the eyes of Japan, the great ship of Japan'. Several new movements and religions were to be inspired by Nichiren's unusual Buddhism, which still thrives today.

Like the Pure Land Buddhists **Honen** and **Shinran**, Nichiren reduced the essentials of his Buddhism to the bare minimum. To him, a single recitation of the sacred formula, *Namu Myōhōrengekyō* ('Adoration to the Lotus of the True Law') was enough to guarantee salvation. Like his predecessors he claimed that it was not necessary to understand the *Lotus Sūtra*: the mere words were enough. Even if someone paused while reciting the heretical Pure Land formula, the *nembutsu*, it would be enough to reach enlightenment. Nichiren was the only major figure of his time who taught that women could reach enlightenment – a point of some debate at the time – without first being reincarnated as men.

Nichiren's statue standing on top of the hill of Asahi-ga-Mori on Mt. Kiyosumi, Chiba.

NISHIDA KITARO

1870–1945

The two most important figures in modern Japanese philosophy are D.T. Suzuki and Nishida Kitaro. Both are influenced by Zen Buddhism but have a profound engagement with Western philosophy. Suzuki and Nishida were friends from their high school days and remained in close contact throughout their lives. The former was one of the representatives at the World Parliament of Religions in 1893[88] and was influential in the comparative study of Western and Eastern modes of thought. Nishida, on the other hand, created a genuine synthesis of the two that is neither forced nor artificial. He and others, in what came to be known as the Kyoto School, represent the most interesting modern Eastern response to Western challenges.

Nishida spent his whole life in study and teaching, a life as apparently bland as Kant, who influenced him greatly. He once characterised his life as being in two halves: the first half was spent looking at a blackboard, the second half was spent in front of a blackboard, teaching. 'With regard to a blackboard I have made only one complete turn – with this my biography is exhausted.'

Nishida's philosophy follows logic indefatigably, but he admitted in the preface of a work of 1917: 'After a long struggle with the Unknowable my logic itself bade me surrender to the camp of mysticism.' Nishida practised Zen meditation in his early years and most of his work can be seen as an attempt to explore that experience. Ultimately, in Nishida's view, intellectualism will only take the thinker so far; logic, as

Gödel was to prove in 1925, shows the inadequacy of logic. Mysticism, or direct perception of the transcendent, has always been a part of Eastern thought, whether as meditation, yoga, *zazen*, Zen *koan* or Bhakti devotionalism.

One of the fundamental questions considered by Nishida is that of the relationship between subject and object. His solution to the polarities of mind-body, self-world, me-other is to posit an original ground of existence that is beyond such distinctions. In his first work, *Zen No Kenkyo* (A Study of Good) he writes variously on this topic:

> *When one experiences directly one's conscious state there is as yet neither subject nor object, and knowledge and its object are completely united. This is the purest form of experience.*
>
> *Why is love the union of subject and object? To love something is to cast away the self and unite with that other.*
>
> *As emphasised in basic Buddhist thought, the self and the universe share the same foundation; or rather, they are the same thing.*

This is a traditional Eastern monism based upon mystic experience. Language apart, these insights could be found not just in Buddhism, but also in Advaita Vedānta, Sufism or Daoism. However, because of Nishida's awareness of Western philosophy the concepts underlying millennia of Eastern speculation and practice are allowed to play in a different context.

Nishida recognised that this scheme was problematic when applied to individual psychology. The appeal to mystic experience was unsatisfactory and Nishida next worked with the ideas of the German philosopher Fichte, an idealist and monist in the Western tradition. Nishida worked with Fichte's concept of self-consciousness as total free will, but this too proved inadequate.

In the late twenties, Nishida put forward a new thesis, that the ultimate reality is the *mu no basho*, the 'place of absolute

*As a Buddhist,
the ultimate good for
Nishida is the realisation
of the true self,
the Buddha-nature.*

nothingness'. 'Nothingness' here corresponds closely to the **Nāgārjuna's** *shūnyata* or emptiness. This nothingness is not an absence of God or self, but an absence of quality or division or concept – of all of the things we need in order to define the separate existence of the ego-self. Nishida also calls it the 'self without self'. By not being anything in particular, we are everything. Nishida here eliminates the psychological terminology that had characterised his earlier work. By moving 'From the acting to the seeing self' we become the eternal, transcendent and indefinable witness.

Again, the influence of the past is obvious, but Nishida's *basho* is a radically new

concept. It seems to function as an antidote to the Western philosophical preoccupation with the individual subjective self. By imagining the self as *basho* or 'place' rather than as a point, consciousness or presence, we get away from all ideas of individuality. Nishida sees in the extinguishing of the ego-self in the *basho* the birth of the 'self as basho'.

Another important influence for Nishida's philosophy of *basho* is that of Hegelian dialectic. The *basho* has the power to unify the contradictions that underlie all existence, to effect the 'continuity of the discontinuity'. In terms of Western logic, the *basho* violates the principles of contradiction (a thing cannot be both *p* and *not-p*) and identity (a thing is itself and not something else). These selective violations prove extremely fertile for Nishida's late-period philosophy. Nishida claimed that the contradictions at the heart of everything were what caused the constant change and motion we observe in the universe. Only in the *mu no basho* are these dynamic oppositions reconciled.

Although Nishida led a life of academic quiet (and was castigated by Japanese Nationalists before WWII), his philosophy has a strong ethical tendency. As a Buddhist, the ultimate good for Nishida is the realisation of the true self, the Buddha-nature. As a Zen Buddhist, Nishida argues that this realisation should take place in the active world. His concept of 'acting intuition' illustrates this – the physical world of actions is expressive of the inner creativity of the *basho*. Only by living fully as historical individuals will the power of the self as *basho* be manifest. Nishida is reminiscent here of the Zen of **Dōgen,** who emphasised the need for full engagement in both the ethical world and meditation.

SELECTED BIBLIOGRAPHY

INDIA

Cenkner, William, *A Tradition of Teachers: Shankara and the Jagadgurus of Today*, Delhi: Motilal Banarsidass, 1983.

Conze, Edward (trans.), *Buddhist Scriptures*, Harmondsworth: Penguin 1957.

Gambhīrānanda (trans.), *Eight Upanishads*, Calcutta: Advaita Ashrama, 1957.

Isherwood, Christopher, *Ramakrishna and his Disciples*, Hollywood: Vedanta Press, 1965.

Mādhavānananda, *The Brihadāranyaka Upanishad*, Calcutta: Advaita Ashrama, 1934.

Nāgārjuna, *The Fundamental Wisdom of the Middle Way: Nagarjuna's 'Mulamadhyamakakarika', with a Philosophical Commentary*, trans. Jay L. Garfield, New York and Oxford: Oxford University Press, 1992.

Radhakrishnan, Sarvepalli, *Indian Philosophy*, 2 vols, London: George Allen & Unwin, 1923.

Rahula, Walpola, *What the Buddha Taught*, London: Wisdom Books, 1990.

Raju, P.T., *The Philosophical Traditions of India*, London: George Allen & Unwin, 1971.

Sargeant, Winthrop (trans.), *The Bhagavad Gītā*, Albany: State University of New York, 1994.

Sen, K.M., *Hinduism,* Harmondsworth: Penguin, 1987.

Thera, Nārada (trans.), *Dhammapada*, London: Butler & Tanner, 1954.

Vivekānanda, *The Complete Works,* 8 vols, Calcutta: Advaita Ashrama, 1948–55.

SELECTED BIBLIOGRAPHY

THE MIDDLE EAST

Afnan, Soheil M., *Avicenna: His Life and Works,* London: George Allen & Unwin, 1958.

Al-Fārābi, *Philosophy of Plato and Aristotle,* trans. Muhsin Mahdi, Glencoe Free Press, 1962.

Al-Ghazālī, *Tahafut al-Falasifah (The Incoherence of the Philosophers)*, trans. Sabih Ahmad Kamali, Lahore: Pakistan Philosophical Congress, 1963.

Al-Kindī, *On First Philosophy,* trans. Alfred L. Ivry, Albany: State University of New York, 1974.

Armstrong, Karen, *Islam: A Short History*, London: Phoenix, 2000.

Averroës, *Tahafut al-Tahafut (The Incoherence of 'The Incoherence'),* trans. Simon van den Bergh, E-text conversion Mohammad Hozien, London: Luzac, 1969.

Enan, Mohammad Abdullah, *Ibn Khaldun: His Life and Works,* New Delhi: Kitab Bhavan, 1979.

Fakhry, Majid, *A History of Islamic Philosophy,* New York: Columbia University Press, 1983.

Sharif, M.M. (ed.), *A History of Muslim Philosophy*, 2 vols, Wiesbaden: Harrassowitz, 1963–65.

Zaehner, R.C., *Hindu & Muslim Mysticism,* Oxford: One World, 1994.

SELECTED BIBLIOGRAPHY

THE FAR EAST

Chan, Wing-Tsit, *A Source Book in Chinese Philosophy*, Princeton: Princeton University Press, 1963.

Confucius, *The Analects*, trans. D.C. Lau, Harmondsworth: Penguin, 1979.

Cotterell, Arthur, *China: A Concise Cultural History*, London: John Murray, 1988.

Fung Yu-Lan, *A History of Chinese Philosophy*, trans. Derk Bodde, 2 vols, Princeton: Princeton University Press, 1952–53.

Kitaro, N., *A Study of Good,* trans. Masao Abe and Christopher Ives, Newhaven CN, 1990.

Mao Zedong, *Selected Works,* Peking: Peking Foreign Press, 1967.

Mencius, *Mencius*, trans. D.C. Lau, Harmondsworth: Penguin, 1970.

SELECTED BIBLIOGRAPHY

OTHER

Collinson, Diané et al., *Fifty Eastern Thinkers*, London and New York: Routledge, 2000.

Dante, *Divine Comedy*, trans. Rev. Francis Cary, London: Bibliophile Books, 1988.

Grenville, J.A.S., *The Collins History of the World in the Twentieth Century*, London: HarperCollins, 1994.

McGreal, Ian (ed.), *Great Thinkers of the Eastern World*, New York: HarperCollins, 1995.

Russell, Bertrand, *A History of Western Philosophy*, London: George Allen & Unwin, 1946.

Smart, Ninian, *World Philosophies*, London: Routledge, 1999.

WEB RESOURCES

Chad Hansen's Chinese Philosophy Pages
http://www.hku.hk/philodep/ch/

The Diamond Sutra
http://community.palouse.net/lotus/diamondsutra.htm

Dvaita Vedanta
www.dvaita.org

Hindu Studies
www.swaveda.com

The Internet Indian History Sourcebook
www.fordham.edu/halsall/india/indiasbook.html

Islamic Philosophy
www.muslimphilosophy.com

Ramanuja
www.ramanuja.org

The Stanford Encyclopedia of Philosophy (Online) on Laozi, article by Alan KL Chan
http://plato.stanford.edu/archives/win2001/entries/laozi/

The Stanford Encyclopedia of Philosophy (Online) on Zhuangzi, article by Harold Roth
http://plato.stanford.edu/archives/win2001/entries/zhuangzi/

Zhuangzi translated by Burton Watson
http://users.compaqnet.be/cn111132/chuang-tzu/

NOTES

1 This book uses 'BCE' (Before the Common/Christian Era) and 'CE' (Common/Christian Era) in preference to 'BC' (Before Christ) and 'AD' (Anno Domini, 'Year of Our Lord').

2 Brahmin is not grammatically correct, but is the usual Western spelling and helps to distinguish the priestly caste from Brahman, the Absolute, and Brahma, the Creator.

3 An attitude not unlike that of Confucius in his own culture.

4 The *Chandogya* and *Mandukya Upanishads* are early and late examples of this argument.

5 Madhva translates this as 'that self, you are not that', an interpretation that is exceptionally strained.

6 See Jaimini.

7 Other Machiavellis of the East in this book include Hanfeizi in China and Ibn Khaldūn in Islam.

8 See the chapter on the Buddha.

9 See chapter on Vasubandhu.

10 For an account of the Veda, see the Introduction to this section.

11 Jaimini's view is not entirely upheld by the Vedas, which do depict others participating in sacrifices. Bādari is also criticised for his willingness to let *shudras* participate, so the strict Mīmāmsāka teaching
that developed from Jaimini was not inevitable. Later Mīmāmsākas also developed more reasonable doctrines.

12 According to some authorities he is as early as fourth century BCE.

13 Translations of the *Gītā* are generally from Sargeant, Winthrop (trans.) *The Bhagavad Gītā*, Albany: State University of New York, 1994.

14 The only significant change Yoga makes to the categories of Sānkhya is to add God.

15 The three qualities are an aspect of nature in Sānkhya-Yoga and therefore alien to the *purusha* or spirit. For more details see the chapter on Kapila.

16 For a discussion of this important concept, see the chapter on Buddha.

17 Trans. by Jay L Garfield.

18 For example, *Mundaka* Up. I. i. 4: 'there are two

kinds of knowledge to be acquired—the higher and the lower'.

19 See chapter on Kapila

20 See also the Chinese philosophers Cheng-I and Cheng-Hao, in the chapter on Zhuxi.

21 The *Prajnāpāramitā*, on which Nāgārjuna based his Mādhyamika teachings.

22 The Garland or *Avatamsaka Sutra* was greatly influential in Chinese Buddhism. See chapter on Fazang.

23 Idealism is used in the sense of a philosophy that believes in the primacy of the mind over matter, not in the more common sense of 'believing in ideals'.

24 See chapters on Bādarāyana, Gaudapāda, Shankara, etc.

25 See chapters on al-Fārābi and Avicenna.

26 See chapter on Fazang.

27 Quoted in Zaehner *Hindu & Muslim Mysticism*.

28 See the chapters on Rabi'āh, al-Hallaj, al-Ghazālī and Rūmī in the Islamic section.

29 See the Introduction to this section.

30 *Mundaka Upanishad*, III, i, 6.

31 17:6

32 23:1

33 See chapters on Shankara et al. elsewhere in this book.

34 The term 'fundamentalist' is not really appropriate as all Muslims regard themselves as fundamentalist. The Western sense of the word implies the extremist, unreflective and aggressive element in modern Islam.

35 Quoted in *Islam, a Short History*, by Karen Armstrong p. 9.

36 5:59

37 The kind of threat that hung over many Islamic philosophers, even if it did not always happen.

38 Ibrahim Madkour, *A History of Muslim Philosophy*, ed. Sharif, p 463.

39 For a discussion of this see the chapter on Ramanuja.

40 MacDonald, *Development of Muslim Theology, Jurisprudence and Constitutional Theory*, pp. 200–201, quoted in Sharif, *A History of MuslimPhilosophy*.

41 *Encyclopaedia Britannica*

42 Quoted by Sharif, M. M., *A History of Muslim Philosophy* [Wiesbaden: Harrassowitz, 1966], p 588.

NOTES

43 The Islamic calendar has a different starting point dating from the *hijrah* or flight of the Prophet from Mecca. The dates do not correspond to solar years, being based on the lunar calendar. The Christian calendar is used throughout this book for simplicity.

44 See the chapter on al-Hallaj.

45 See al-Fārābi and Avicenna.

46 Tahafut al-Tahafut, quoted in *A History of Muslim Philosophy*, ed. Sharif p. 559.

47 Quoted in Sharif, M.M. (ed.), *A History of Muslim Philosophy*, 2 vols, Wiesbaden: Harrassowitz, 1963–65.

48 All quotations are from *The Analects*, trans. D.C. Lau, Penguin, 1979.

49 See chapter on Zhang Zai for an exploration of this concept.

50 Wing-Tsit Chan, *A Source Book in Chinese Philosophy*, Princeton, 1963, p. 218.

51 Quoted in the chapter on Confucius.

52 Contrast Zhuangzi's discussion of the 'happiness of fishes' about 150 years later.

53 All translations of Daode Jing from Wing-Tsit Chan, *A Source Book in Chinese Philosophy*.

54 An account of 'the rectification of names' is on page 130.

55 All Zhuangzi translations by Burton Watson unless otherwise indicated.

56 Translated by Harold Roth, 'Zhuangzi', *The Stanford Encyclopedia of Philosophy*.

57 *Kena Upanishad*, I. 5.

58 Translated by Lin Yutang.

59 Here, as elsewhere, we use the Westernised version of the name where it is better known.

60 A philosopher who apparently refused to sacrifice a hair of his head to benefit the state.

61 Mencius translated *ren* as 'the human heart'.

62 *Mencius*, trans. D.C. Lau, Penguin, 1970. IV.B.19.

63 Quotations unless otherwise stated are from Wing Tsit Chan, *A Source Book in Chinese Philosophy*, Princeton, 1963. pp. 49–83.

64 *Mencius*, trans by D.C. Lau, Penguin 1970. II.A.2.

65 See the chapter on Hanfeizi.

66 All quotations from Xunzi are from Wing-Tsit Chan, *A Source Book in Chinese Philosophy*, Princeton 1963, pp 115 – 135.

67 Quotations from Wing-Tsit Chan, *A Source Book of Chinese Philosophy*, Princeton, 1963.

68 To make a chariot wheel.

69 Ibid. p 254.

70 Quoted in Cotterell, *China: A Concise Cultural History*, John Murray, 1988, p.87.

71 See the chapter on Nāgārjuna for a discussion of this and related issues.

72 See the chapter on Huineng.

73 See the chapter on Buddha.

74 See the chapter on Vasubandhu.

75 The sixth century Buddhist thinker Vasubandhu and his brother Asanga are perhaps the only other example, but their case is less well documented. See the chapter on Vasubandhu.

76 Not to be confused with *li* meaning ritual or propriety, as discussed in the chapter on Confucius.

77 See chapter in this book on Fazang.

78 See the chapter on Zhuxi.

79 See box on page 127.

80 A brief account of the Neo-Confucian movement is in the chapter on Zhuxi.

81 See box on page 165.

82 *On Contradiction*, from Mao Zedong *Selected Works of Mao Tse-Tung*, vol. I, Peking: Foreign Language Press 1967, pp. 311–346.

83 Another idea he derived from Lenin.

84 Daoism, the third aspect of Chinese thought, was of minor importance in Korea.

85 The chapter on Shinran has more details on his experiences in this period.

86 See Dōgen.

87 An account of Chinese Zen is in the chapter on Huineng.

88 Vivekānanda was the Hindu representative.

INDEX

INDEX

INDEX

INDEX

INDEX

INDEX

INDEX

INDEX